ON BEING A JEWISH FEMINIST

A Reader

Edited and with Introductions by
SUSANNAH HESCHEL

SCHOCKEN BOOKS • NEW YORK

First published by Schocken Books 1983
10 9 8 7 6 5 86

LIBRARY OF CONGRESS CATALOGING IN PUBLICATION DATA
Main entry under title:
On being a Jewish feminist
Includes bibliographical references.
1. Women in Judaism—Addresses, essays, lectures.
2. Feminism—Addresses, essays, lectures. I. Heschel, Susannah.
BM729.W6J83 296.3′878344 81–16543 AACR2

Designed by Nancy Dale Muldoon
Manufactured in the United States of America
ISBN 0–8052–3837–9 (hardcover)
0–8052–0745–7 (paperback)

PERMISSIONS

Rachel Adler, "The Jew Who Wasn't There: *Halakhah* and the Jewish Woman," reprinted from *Response,* vol. 7, no. 22 (Summer 1973), pp. 77–82. Reprinted by permission of *Response.*

Alice Bloch, "Scenes from the Life of a Jewish Lesbian," reprinted from *Dyke Magazine,* 1977. Reprinted by permission of the author.

Aviva Cantor, "The Lilith Question," reprinted from *Lilith Magazine,* no. 1, Fall, 1976. Reprinted by permission of the author.

Erika Duncan, "The Hungry Jewish Mother," reprinted from *The Lost Tradition: Mothers and Daughters in Literature,* ed. Cathy N. Davidson and E. M. Broner (New York: Ungar, 1980). Reprinted by permission of Frederick Ungar Publishing Co., Inc.

Lynn Gottlieb, "The Secret Jew: An Oral Tradition of Women," reprinted from *Conservative Judaism,* vol. 30, no. 3 (Spring 1976), pp. 59–62. Reprinted by permission of the Rabbinical Assembly.

Lynn Gottlieb, "Spring Cleaning Ritual on the Eve of Full Moon Nisan," reprinted from *Response,* no. 41–42 (Winter/Fall 1982), pp. 29–31. Reprinted by permission of *Response.*

Rita M. Gross, "Steps toward Feminine Imagery of Deity in Jewish Theology," reprinted from *Judaism,* vol. 30, no. 2 (Spring 1981), pp. 183–193. Reprinted by permission of *Judaism.*

Lesley Hazleton, "Israeli Women: Three Myths," reprinted from *Israeli Women: The Reality Behind the Myths,* by Lesley Hazleton, pp. 15–37. Reprinted by permission of Simon & Schuster, a Division of Gulf & Western Corp.

Paula Hyman, "The Jewish Family: Looking for a Usable Past" reprinted from *Congress Monthly,* vol. 42, no. 8 (October 1975), pp. 10–15. Reprinted by permission of *Congress Monthly.*

Rosa Felsenburg Kaplan, "The Noah Syndrome," reprinted from *Davka,* Winter, 1975. Reprinted by permission of the author.

Cynthia Ozick, "Notes toward Finding the Right Question," reprinted from *Lilith Magazine,* no. 6, 1979. Reprinted by permission of the author.

Arleen Stern, "Learning to Chant the Torah: A First Step," reprinted from the *Long Island Jewish World,* July 31–August 6, 1981. Reprinted by permission of the *Long Island Jewish World.*

To my parents, Abraham and Sylvia Heschel

I Kings 8:27

Contents

Acknowledgments

THIS book evolved out of my long-standing concern with the problem of being a Jew and a woman in the modern world. I have not attempted to offer an exhaustive account of the encounter between Judaism and feminism. Rather, I have brought together essays that focus on those issues I consider of greatest relevance to further social and theological development.

I am indebted in the preparation of this book to far more women and men than I can ever acknowledge. I thank the many talented contributors to this volume for their stimulating and thoughtful essays and for their gracious cooperation. I appreciate the generosity of my colleagues, Diane Levenberg, Ellen Golub and Peggy Sanner, for reading and offering helpful comments on sections of the manuscript. My teacher, Professor Samuel Kassow, of the Department of History, Trinity College, has for some years been an intellectual guide as well as a close friend, his advice in the preparation of this book being but one instance of his continuing support. Professor Barbara Reed, of the Department of Journalism, California State University, Los Angeles, offered many useful suggestions concerning style.

Arthur Samuelson, then editor at Schocken Books, guided this project with expertise and enthusiasm during its initial stages. Subsequently, Bonny Fetterman, with insight and acuteness, helped me refine the manuscript and steered me as I completed the work. Laurie Kalb handled many details with care and concern. Harvey Horowitz and Michael Gruenberger, of Hebrew

Union College Library, Los Angeles, and Gratz College Library, Philadelphia, graciously helped me to locate important sources.

Professor Todd Hanlin, then of the Department of German, University of Pennsylvania, is rare among teachers in the extent of warmth and advice that he gave me at trying moments during the composition of this volume. Henry Furst, a friend of many years, was unstinting in his personal and practical day-to-day support in the preparation of the manuscript. I will always be grateful to Marilyn Silberberg for the insightful conversations we have had over the years. My oldest and closest friend, Hilary Huttner Fylstra, has shared with me the maturation of our own feminist and Jewish values and lent her talents as a writer to early drafts of the manuscript. To have such fine, sensitive human beings as friends is a rare and precious blessing.

Introduction

A LEARNED, observant, and committed young woman applied in 1903 for permission to study in the rabbinical school of the Jewish Theological Seminary. Daughter of a rabbi, she had long been involved in Jewish education and was employed as an editor and translator at the Jewish Publication Society. She was clearly an applicant of considerable distinction. The faculty of this renowned center for advanced Jewish studies voted to allow her to attend all the classes, with one condition: that she not use her knowledge to seek rabbinical ordination.

Henrietta Szold attended classes, assisted Talmud professor Louis Ginzberg in editing his monumental, six-volume study of Jewish legends, translated and edited articles for other scholars in the field of Judaica, and then went on, some years later, to found Hadassah, the women's Zionist organization, the largest Jewish organization in America today.[1]

Much remains the same since Szold's lifetime—the Jewish Theological Seminary still does not ordain women rabbis—but a fundamental change has taken place: a modern-day Henrietta Szold would not stand alone. Increasing numbers of women are demanding entry into rabbinical schools, into the quorum for communal prayer (the *minyan*), and into leadership echelons of community organizations, forming a movement of Jewish feminism that is continually gathering momentum.

The history of Jewish women is just beginning to be written,[2] but it is clear that many issues raised today under the banner of feminism represent the strivings of past generations. Legal responsa literature from the Middle Ages, in discussing marriage and divorce, property ownership and inheritance, frequently reveals the frustration felt by many women over their restricted lives in families and communities. Occasional, minor changes were made, but the first major shift in women's status came with the ban on polygamy in medieval France and Germany—a ban recognized only by the Ashkenazic community.[3]

The advent of modern secularism and movements of religious reform did not bring many actual changes in Jewish laws pertaining to women, but did bring the possibility of escaping their control. By the nineteenth century, some women were able to elude rabbinic strictures over their lives and seek educations and professions as well as changes in the expectations of their husbands and families. In poetry, fiction, essays, and through organizations, the position of women in Judaism was challenged. Leaders of the Reform movement in Central Europe and the *Haskalah* movement [Enlightenment] in Eastern Europe rejected women's position in the synagogue and the traditional roles of women and men in the home.[4] The movement was often felt to be for the benefit of men no less than women; Sholem Aleichem once remarked that Jews don't write novels about love because relations between Jewish men and women are so primitive.

The early writers of secular Hebrew and Yiddish described traditional religious life in their fiction, depicting the unhappiness of women in their arranged marriages, in their limited educations, and in their lack of control over their own lives. Organizations such as the Jüdische Frauenbund in Germany, directed by Bertha Pappenheim, strove to alleviate discriminatory conditions of European Jewish women, demanding full voting rights in Jewish communal affairs and fighting against Jewish participation in the white slavery market.[5]

The concerns for equality within the Jewish community continued to be articulated as national organizations of Jewish women were formed in the United States at the turn of the century. They were also given passionate voice in the short stories and novels of women such as Anzia Yezierska and Mary Antin writing before and after World War I. The heroines of these stories usually take their shattered lives and repair them through education, careers, or financial independence, but invariably without assistance from family or community. Liberation was achieved only by breaking off and struggling alone.

The most recent wave of Jewish feminism, beginning during the 1960s, is assuming the opposite posture: not breaking away from the community, but struggling to become full members of it. Feminists are calling today for changes within *halakhah* to end discrimination in areas from divorce laws to synagogue separation; for inclusion in secular leadership; for concrete changes in the structure of the community to accommodate changing lifestyles of women, from day-care centers to greater community acceptance of single mothers. At the same time, new studies concerning various aspects of women and Judaism are being published: women in the Bible, women resistance fighters during World War II; images of women in aggadic literature.[6]

The first group of articles on Jewish feminism, somewhat tentative and querying in tone, appeared in a special issue of *Davka* magazine in 1971. The articles ranged from personal testimonies of women to general discussions of the place of women in Jewish law, community life, history, and the Bible. That same year a group of women came together to form Ezrat Nashim, a group which continues to function today for study and consciousness-raising. By 1972 *Response,* a new journal directed to an emerging Jewish counterculture, published a special issue on "The Jewish Woman," containing what became the classic expressions of Jewish feminism that set the tone for the following decade.

Institutional changes took on rapid momentum during the same year, 1972. Sally Priesand was ordained rabbi by Hebrew Union College, the seminary of the Reform movement; Ezrat Nashim issued a "Call for Change" at the annual convention of Conservative rabbis; task forces on the status of women in the community were established by various Jewish organizations; groups of women formed throughout the country to celebrate Rosh Hodesh, the new moon, which is referred to in early Jewish sources as a woman's holiday; and feminism became a hotly debated topic in the community.

As the general feminist movement made great strides and earned wide acceptance within the United States, the Jewish feminist movement also won greater legitimacy and respect. By mid-decade more publications had appeared, conferences of Jewish women were being held, steps were being taken to increase women's participation in religious and secular Jewish life, and new women's rituals were being created and practiced. Nineteen seventy-six saw the publication of several books, including *The Jewish Woman: New Perspectives,* based on the *Response* anthology;[7] *The Jewish Woman in America,* tracing women's experiences from the immigrant generations to the present; *Siddur Nashim,* a prayer book of nonsexist language and new, women's prayers; *Blessing the Birth of a Jewish Daughter,* a collection of baby-naming ceremonies for girls; and the first issue of *Lilith* magazine, the first Jewish feminist periodical. Educational opportunities for women have grown dramatically during the decade, from traditional *yeshivah*-style schools in the United States and Israel to doctoral programs in Jewish studies at major universities. Courses on women and Judaism are beginning to be offered at colleges throughout the country, and nonsexist educational materials are being developed for day and afternoon school programs. Sessions on women and Judaism are scheduled at academic conferences, reflecting the burgeoning scholarship in the field.

Equality of women in synagogue services was a major issue from the beginning. By the mid-1970s the Orthodox community began debating the use and height of the *mehitzah,* the curtain separating women and men during prayers; the Conservative movement's Committee on Law and Standards voted to count women in the *minyan,* a decision which was ratified by many, but not all, Conservative synagogues; the Reconstructionist Fellowship granted full equality of women with men "in all matters of ritual," ordaining its first woman rabbi in 1974; and the Reform movement initiated a review of sexism in its liturgy, organizations, and community life. Both Reform and Reconstructionist movements have now ordained over seventy women rabbis. The burgeoning *Havurah* movement has been strengthened by women who prefer traditional services but reject the inequality of women within Orthodoxy. Informal prayer groups of women, some including men, are beginning to flourish, as are groups for study of the traditional texts, particularly the Talmud, inaccessible to women still excluded from male-only *yeshivot.*

The attitudinal changes of the past ten years can be illustrated by comparing editorial comments from two issues of *Keeping Posted,* a Reform movement youth magazine. In 1972 a series of rhetorical questions introduced a special issue on women: "Does Judaism 'debase' woman, as some Women's Libbers charge? Does the Bible itself keep alive the myth of female 'inferiority' by depicting—among other things—Eve as a disobedient, irresponsible dimwit?"[8] In 1980, the same magazine declared: "We are in the midst of a social revolution that has changed the course of Jewish life in America. It started about ten years ago when Jewish women began to reexamine and to challenge religious laws and communal practices that relegated them to second-class status."[9]

While their issues have clearly gained legitimacy, the mood among feminists is not entirely optimistic. Many women rabbis encounter prejudice, even discrimination, when they search for a job. Women who find greater equality in the synagogue often see more and more meaningful traditions eliminated. Others feel frustrated that further efforts are not being made to radically rewrite the traditional liturgy in order to rid it of sexism. Defeat of the Equal Rights Amendment may presage declining support for feminism in the Jewish community as well. Many feminists feel the movement is in a quiet period of retrenchment, recapitulating the gains of the past decade, articulating a program for the future, and responding to the challenges of their opponents.

Even while feminists were making important progress in the Jewish community, a strong counterresponse began to emerge. Opponents accuse feminists of destroying Jewish principles and practices, threatening the stability of the Jewish family, undermining the masculinity of Jewish men, and bringing about a general deterioration of Judaism at a time when "nothing but its own present and future is at stake."[10]

There are those—both men and women—who oppose feminism on the basis of Jewish law; others do so for social and psychological reasons. Feminism is blamed for the high divorce rate and low birth rate and for the dissolution of traditional Jewish values regarding the home. "The creative survival of the Jewish community rests first and foremost in the creative survival of the singular Jewish mother," writes Conservative Rabbi Richard Yellin.[11] Concerning women who pursue careers, he adds: "Let her pursue her human interests, but Judaism as a religious system is not going to raise the level of these women, or careerist men for that matter, as models for the Jewish community, for that image would not add to the creative propagation of the Jewish species."[12] Reform Rabbi Sylvan Schwartzman writes: "Women with *seichel* [intelligence] recognize that couples do have a responsibility to advance the careers of one another, and there is nothing wrong with expecting one's wife to support the goals and ambitions of her husband."[13] Her role as mother is designed by God, writes Orthodox Rabbi Moshe Meiselman: "It is not easy to form children in the Jewish mold and prepare them to become Jewish adults, and such a task would not have been primarily assigned to women had they not been especially prepared for it, physically, psychologically, intellectually, and spiritually, by Almighty God Himself."[14]

Secular leaders, too, condemn feminism as a form of narcissism for placing personal needs above community and the present above the future of Jewry. What feminists want, writes Midge Decter, "is a freedom demanded by children and enjoyed by no one: the freedom from all difficulty."[15] Others, such as Chana Poupko and Devora Wohlgelernter, who are themselves Orthodox, worry that feminism results in "a gnawing feeling among many Orthodox Jewish women that there is something more important about the man's role."[16] To overcome such feelings, they suggest that "something can be done within the framework of *halakhah* to create a strong sense of pride in women coupled with the conviction that what they do is religiously significant. Thus it would be quite simple for a rabbi to announce the name of a bat mitzvah girl, praise her for her attendance at a synagogue or Hebrew school, and congratulate her parents."[17] But there are limits, warns halakhic authority

Rabbi J. David Bleich, in considering whether women might serve on synagogue boards: "It is precisely in the public arena, in the holding of public office and thereby commanding constant public attention, that the Torah saw the greatest possible violation of feminine *tzni'ut* [modesty]."[18]

Suggestions that women be ordained rabbis or simply be counted in a prayer quorum arouse protest on even more blatantly obvious psychological—and sexual—grounds. Writing in opposition to the ordination of women as rabbis in the Conservative movement, Ruth Wisse fears that feminism will emasculate Jewish men: "Judaism's ability to create an alternative model of virility, which depended on intellectual and spiritual prowess rather than political and physical might, helped to compensate for the great social dependency of the Jews without undue sacrifice of masculine self-confidence and biological zest."[19] Her argument implies that to protect some degree of self-esteem during the long centuries of persecution and ghetto life, Jewish men were justified in subjugating Jewish women.

Wisse's concern for the mental health of Jewish men is echoed by psychiatrist Mortimer Ostow and by historian Lucy Dawidowicz. Ostow, considering proposals that women receive *aliyot,* lead services, and officiate as rabbis, warns that "there is the problem of sexual arousal, consciously or unconsciously, by women performing [*sic*] on the *bimah.* In our society it is generally true that men are far more readily aroused by an attractive woman than women are by an attractive man. That being the case, a woman appearing as a central figure in a religious service is likely to distract some of the male worshippers from a reverent attitude and encourage erotic fantasies."[20] According to Ostow, the synagogue traditionally serves as a "refuge from the struggles of the marketplace, struggles for self-worth as well as for economic survival."[21] But as women enter the marketplace alongside men, it is imperative, Ostow insists, that the synagogue remain a stronghold of men: "One would not wish to sponsor a program that will convert the synagogue from a refuge to an arena where a man will feel that he must struggle again to defend his self-esteem; this, I suspect, is the psychologic truth behind the dictum: '*ishah lo tikra batorah mipnei kavod ha'tsibur*' (*Megillah* 23a): 'a woman should not read the Torah, out of respect for the congregation.' "[22]

Dawidowicz fears the effect of women's participation on the community as well as the psyche:

> Women, when passive, can turn the synagogue into something like a provincial Italian Catholic church. The rabbi assumes all sacerdotal functions, the women become his dutiful parishioners whose religion is part devotion, part ignorance, and part superstition. Religion, then, becomes a womanish thing. Men stay away out of contempt. But even more forbidding—to me at least—is the threat of female power, female usurpation of the synagogue. Women are efficient; they can organize, raise funds, bring order out of chaos. They can turn the shul into a Hadassah chapter. Not that I disapprove of Hadassah, its activities, or its ladies. But I do not like the idea of their taking over the synagogue. To my mind, the assumption by a woman of rabbinic or priestly function in the synagogue undermines the very essence of Jewish tradition.[23]

By focusing on these kinds of concerns, opponents skirt the more serious theological issues that feminism is raising—issues also missed by some Jewish feminists who are endeavoring to answer them. Talmud professor Judith Hauptman, in her article "Rabbinic Images of Women," sharply criticizes the position of women in classical Jewish law and calls for the revision or elimination of those laws.[24] Yet she raises no challenges to the halakhic system as such; on the contrary, she calls for change according to the procedures laid down by the Talmudic rabbis. Hauptman even defends the ancient rabbis, claiming they showed greater sensitivity to women's legal status than did leaders of neighboring, non-Jewish societies.

Blu Greenberg, in her recent book, *On Women and Judaism: A View from Tradition,* defines feminism as a call for the equality (though not identity) of men and women.[25] She sees feminism as an ethical movement worthy of attention by Jews who value Judaism's historic sensitivity to ethical dilemmas. Greenberg also criticizes aspects of the position of women in certain classical Jewish laws as maintained today by Orthodoxy, and calls for changing those laws. Like Hauptman, Greenberg claims it is possible to contrive to operate within the halakhic system, since she views what she dislikes in Judaism's treatment of women as the outgrowth of an earlier period and environment.

This approach may make certain Orthodox opponents more sympathetic to feminism, but it does not stem from a coherent theological position. The historical method cannot be applied only in some areas and not in others. Once we acknowledge the laws regarding women as products of a particular historical period and outlook, what is to keep us from considering other Jewish practices—such as the synagogue service—as a comparable historical outgrowth that has outlived its meaning and relevance? In fact, the entire system of *halakhah* might be similarly regarded as the religious expression of a particular community, living in Palestine and Babylonia nearly two thousand years ago. If the Talmud is the product of a particular time and particular individuals, what religious authority does it hold, and why should we return to it after discovering teachings and rulings within it that limit and oppress us?

Opponents who protest feminism's social and psychological ramifications, as well as many feminists proposing change through halakhic procedures, are not confronting the core arguments and insights of the feminist critique. Feminism is not calling for a renunciation of womanhood, as Wisse and Ostow would have us believe, nor for simple equality between women and men, as Greenberg presents it. Rather, feminism's central insight contends that not only do women not shape and control their own lives, but that our most basic understandings of human nature are drawn primarily from men's experiences. A patriarchal outlook begins by making men's experiences normative, equating the human with the male. Not only are women excluded from the process of shaping the outlook, but women's experiences are projected as something external, "other" to that norm. As Virginia Woolf long ago pointed out, the vast literature that attempts to define "woman's nature" clearly reveals the assumption that women lie outside the general definitions of humanity and constitute a separate category in need of explication.[26] No comparable literature exists to define "men's nature," since that is equated with all intellectual endeavors generally. Simone de Beauvoir writes, "Thus humanity is male and man defines woman not in herself but as relative to him; she is not regarded as an autonomous being. . . . She is defined and differentiated with reference to man and not he with reference to her; she is the incidental, the inessential as opposed to the essential. He is the Subject, he is the Absolute—she is the Other."[27]

This insight, applied to Judaism, exposes the magnitude of the conflict. Both the most traditional Jew and the most radical feminist would agree that thorough and rigid sex-role differentiation is deeply imbedded in Judaism. Judith Plaskow, writing in this volume, puts the matter bluntly: "Our legal disabilities are a symptom of a pattern of projection that lies deep in Jewish thinking, one that must be addressed and rooted out at its core." She concludes that women cannot be fully part of Judaism without a complete transformation of the bases of Jewish life. The Jewish feminist writers represented in this volume have moved beyond criticizing specific traditions and institutions to recognize the marginality of Jewish women extending beyond the synagogue, Orthodoxy, tradition, and *halakhah.* The problem, as today's writers see it, runs throughout the course of Jewish history, penetrating the basic theological suppositions of Judaism: its imagery of women and men, its liturgy, its conceptions of the Jewish people and community, its understanding of God as Father and King. Woman as Other is expressed, for instance, by Judaism's "purity" laws, in which women convey impurity not to themselves or to other women, but only to the men with whom they come into contact. Similarly, women enter into discussions in Judaism's law codes only as they affect men's lives; there exists no Talmudic tractate discussing the experiences of women's lives, how they are to be guided halakhically and interpreted religiously. In another example, women are placed behind a curtain in some synagogues, or denied *aliyot* and positions of leadership, not for any reasons concerning them, but because their visible presence might affect the concentration of men at prayer.

These issues, all concerning the authority and relevance of key aspects of Judaism, lie at the root of the feminist challenge. Here the question arises: if feminists do indeed bring about all the changes their critique implies, what will remain as recognizably Judaism? What criteria, what grounds of authority, will be used to retain some aspects of Judaism while rejecting or radically modifying others?

The implications of the feminist inquiry clearly involve more than the repair of particular laws or traditions, as suggested by Wohlgelernter and Poupko, or by Greenberg and Hauptman. The very bases of Judaism are being challenged—from *halakhah* to the prayer book to the very ways we conceive of God. The challenge emerging today demands a Copernican revolution: a new theology of Judaism, requiring new understandings of God, revelation, *halakhah,* and the Jewish people in order to support and encourage change.

To an extent, the conflict emerging between feminism and Judaism today parallels the conflict between Jews and Western culture that began to take shape with the Emancipation of Jews in Europe two hundred years ago. Just as none of the great ideological movements of the modern period—from liberalism to Marxism to nationalism—seemed able, ultimately, to incorporate and accept Jews and Judaism, so, too, none of the religious movements of modern Judaism seems capable of coming to terms with women and feminism. And just as Jews became the crucible of modern political thought, so, too, feminism is the crucible for modern Judaism. Today's confrontation with feminism exposes the failure of Jewish religious movements to cope with modernity's challenges to theology and to respond effectively to them.

Questions arose with the beginnings of modern Judaism, over two hundred years ago, regarding the place of *halakhah* in an age of individualism and decline in regard for rabbinic authority; the implications of history to an oral and written tradition held as timeless and immutable; the real nature of God in an era when our images and language are understood to be human projections. Feminism's challenge to *halakhah,* for example, is at bottom an extension of these earlier challenges to theology. If we view a tradition as having developed in a far different period and setting than ours, and as proclaiming values inimicable to ours, what authority can it claim over us? On the other hand, if we become the authority over the tradition, what relevance does it retain as God's commandment?

While theoretical questions still await resolution, the practical implications of modernity already display their impact. Before the modern era, when Jewish law and tradition encompassed all of life, even the most threatening of issues were taken on by the leadership, often with dramatic concessions resulting. Yet since the advent of modernity Jewish law has become increasingly rigid, ignoring the exigencies of life as it ceases to govern that life. One example is the dilemma of the *agunah,* the woman whose husband has deserted her without granting her a divorce—a problem more pressing when modern times bring increased mobility, freedom from rabbinic power, and the option of civil marriage. Yet despite the worsening situation, no solution has gained acceptance. A living legal system never has the luxury to ignore a serious conflict; it must respond in one way or another. Only when a legal system dies can problems be ignored or passed over.

The issue is not that feminism poses insoluble problems to Jewish law, but that Judaism has long ago died in the way it had existed for nearly two thousand years. The crisis has not been brought on by feminism, but feminism clearly discloses the morbid condition of Judaism that has continued, untreated, throughout the modern period.

Thus, from Judaism's perspective, the conflict emerges not so much from the particular agenda of feminism, but from the weakness of Jewish theological responses to modernity, which are thrown into relief by the challenge of feminism. In reality, a large part of the opposition to feminism arises from displaced concern over the impact of secularism. Attacks on feminist demands for changes in *halakhah* simply reveal the absense of a coherent position regarding the authority of Jewish law in an age of relativism. Claims that feminism violates Jewish principles and values reveal general confusion over what constitutes Judaism in today's context of pluralism and free choice.

Feminists, often unaware of the magnitude of the problem, have attempted to seek accommodation within one of the religious denominations of American Judaism—Orthodoxy, Conservatism, Reform, or Reconstructionism. In raising issues ranging from rabbinical ordination to divorce proceedings feminists have achieved greater or lesser degrees of success. Indeed, during the past decade, these denominations seem to have been occupied more with questions raised by the women's movement than with any other single issue.

Yet feminists may be misdirecting their efforts by attempting to remain within the frameworks of the denominations, whose confrontations with feminism raise the question whether these branches of Judaism have succeeded in their ostensible goal of meeting modernity's challenges. Modernity strikes not so much at the specifics of traditional theology, but at the general concept of theological absolutism. Yet these Jewish denominations have responded to modernity by substituting new dogmas for the older traditional ones. For Orthodoxy, the absolute core is *halakhah,* while Reform lays claim to a spirit or idea, and Conservatism and Reconstructionism adhere to an historical consciousness or civilization of the Jewish people.

Yet none of these approaches provides clear, normative criteria for implementing the changes called for by feminism. In fact, the changes made by these denominations in response to particular feminist demands were made not by applying the central principles of each movement. Whatever progress made during the past decade by feminists was not because of, but in spite of, the core ideas of each of the movements.

Orthodoxy, for example, responds to modernity by insulating itself from modernity's challenges. Historical method is accepted only warily, and in any case never applied to the key texts, the Bible and the Talmud, which are held to be the literally revealed word of God from Sinai. Any challenge to that revelation is not recognized. To Orthodoxy, the historical method suggests that the Talmudic rabbis were not transmitting the revealed word of God, but were actually creating something new. Moreover, it implies that what was created by one generation of Jews may be changed by another generation—which clearly violates the integrity of divine revelation at Sinai.

Orthodoxy cannot permit itself to tolerate religious pluralism: There can be either one truth or no truth, and hence other modern forms of Jewish religious expression are heretical. All Jewish laws hold equal value, it proclaims: laws regarding women's ritual impurity are interwoven with prohibitions against murder and commandments to observe the Sabbath. To challenge one commandment means to challenge all; remove one brick, and the entire edifice collapses. This train of thought leads to the conclusion that women who want to use the traditional liturgy, but without the separating synagogue curtain, can be considered as heretical as those who deny God's existence and refuse to pray altogether.

Reconciliations between feminism and Orthodoxy can succeed only by not touching upon the absoluteness of *halakhah*. Lowering the *mehitzah* a few inches or permitting a woman to say the blessing over bread in her home on the Sabbath are acceptable changes as long as they can be justified according to the rules and methods of *halakhah* and so avoid any challenge to its inviolability. Yet that approach hardly represents a feminist perspective, inasmuch as it perpetuates women's dependence on a legal system conceived and operated entirely by men. Regardless of how many laws can be "legally" changed, there remains the very real probability of hitting a stumbling block, such as the very existence of the *mehitzah* altogether.

Reform Judaism seeks to preserve a spirit or idea as historically transcendent, constituting the essence of Judaism. Abraham Geiger, the nineteenth-century formulator of the Reform position, himself was at pains to define exactly what that spirit is or should be, and the movement suggests at various times religiosity, morality, or personal elevation. Changes in Judaism are permitted, even welcomed, within Reform as expressions of the further development of this eternal Jewish spirit. Yet when it comes down to practical questions of how this spirit is to be applied, or just what constitutes Jewish values, there is no clear basis for resolving conflicts. Thus Geiger considers Judaism to be endowed with the highest moral sense: "Judaism . . . establishes itself as a religion that adores God as the Holy One, as the ideal of moral purity, by the fact that it invariably emphasizes moral worth also in its human relations, that it does not recognize the mightier one as possessing exclusive rights, but grants them power only as far as they are justly entitled thereto. Justice, the pure moral relation between man and man [*sic*], is its highest consideration, the gauge wherewith to measure the conditions."[28] At the same time, Geiger can state that "the very views concerning slavery and the treatment of the weaker sex [*sic*] is a true gauge for the high or low plane of their religious ideas. . . . And what noble pictures of women we find throughout the Jewish literature!"[29] Yet to most women, there seems little morality in Judaism's laws of Sotah (the suspected adulteress) or divorce or inheritance, a distinct lack of personal elevation in the image of woman as the "weaker sex," and an oppressive spirit that permits women to hold positions as self-sacrificing nurturers, but rarely as leaders, in Reform synagogues and communities. As one contemporary congregant writes, "We're tired of being tea-and-cookie servers. . . . We permit our women to sit on the *bimah,* read from the Torah, open the ark doors . . . yet we still respond in Orthodox fashion towards the feminine leadership role."[30]

Despite Geiger's rallying words, Reform has not applied its own principles as a basis for changing women's status. Reform called over a hundred years ago for complete equality of men and women within Judaism, not out of a commitment to women, but in order to modernize Judaism by removing embarrassing vestiges of "orientalism" from its public religious services. At their 1846 conference in Breslau, Reform rabbis declared: "It is our sacred duty to declare with all emphasis the complete religious equality of women with man in view of the religious standpoint that we represent, according to which an equal degree of natural holiness inheres in all people, the distinctions in Sacred Writ having therefore only relative and momentary significance. . . . It is therefore our mission to make legal declaration of the equal religious obligation and justification of woman in as far as this is possible; we have the same right to do this as had the synod under Rabbenu Gershom eight hundred years ago, which passed new religious decrees in favor of the female sex."[31]

These rabbis expressed their commitment to women's equality within Judaism in terms of Jewish law. By being obligated to perform the same religious commandments as men, women became eligible for the same privileges. Yet by rejecting Jewish law as central and binding over Jewish practice, Reform eliminated the basis upon which it had reconstituted women's position without substituting a new basis. Left without internal Jewish teachings to motivate specific alterations, Reform failed to translate its declarations into practice. Mixed seating did not originate in the synagogues of the German rabbis who formulated the original declarations of equality, but only later, in the United States. Similarly, the practice of ordaining women rabbis was accepted only in the early 1970s. Essentially, Reform equalized women with men in just that area—*halakhah*—that lay outside its own sphere of Jewish concerns and activities. Thus, equality did not grow out of Reform Judaism's stated commitment to justice and to God as a "moral ideal."

Like its counterparts, the Conservative movement—the largest of the Jewish movements in America—also lacks a basis for changing women's position, due to its inability to balance its various commitments. Conservative Judaism attempts to hold before it at all times several different and conflicting tenets: sensitivity to the findings of historical research on biblical and rabbinic texts; respect for the customs and mores of traditional Jewish observance; responsiveness to changing circumstances of different generations. Unable to mediate among these values and unclear regarding its position on each, Conservative Judaism remains theologically confused. Some changes that clearly flout rabbinic law as well as most of Jewish history, such as allowing men and women to sit together in the synagogue, have readily found acceptance. Others, rooted more in ethos than law, such as the suggestion to ordain women rabbis, arouse dissent and even the threat of schism. "Yes, the Conservative rabbinate had liberated women from the women's gallery, but then kept us sitting passively in our mixed pews, perennial observers, watchers, listeners," writes congregant Ruth Seldin.[32]

These responses vary because the movement remains in flux; it has yet to ally a clear approach to Judaism with its procedures and organizational structure. Fearful of criticism from Orthodoxy and wishing to distinguish itself from Reform, the Conservative movement acts without clear direction. Each decision announced by the Rabbinical Assembly's Committee on Law and Standards may be ratified or rejected by each congregration. As a result, women may count in the *minyan* in some congregations, but not others, or be called for an *aliyah* at Sabbath morning services but not at the daily *minyan* at the same synagogue.

Conservatism claims to employ a perennial historical consciousness of the Jewish people as the guide to religious observance and belief. Jewish law, while held to be divinely inspired, may be reinterpreted in accordance with that consciousness. Historical consciousness can serve at best as a motivating force, binding a community or inspiring individuals to follow the dictates prescribed by the leadership. But historical consciousness in itself carries no normative power, no guide or principle by which the concrete decisions regarding belief and observance can be determined. More problematic is the fact that this historical consciousness has yet to be clearly defined. Does it refer to the experiences of Jewish leaders or of the populace? Can it claim to include the vastly differing histories of Sephardim and Ashkenazim? How far back in Jewish history does it reach? How can it be authentically captured and expressed in the rapidly changing terms of modernity? Ultimately, since the Jewish history we know is the history of Jewish men, it is precisely that historical consciousness that is invoked by Conservative leaders when they want to oppose any changes in the status of women.

Conservative leaders, unable to employ the idea of historical consciousness as the basis for their decisions, return to the halakhic framework, asking less what Jewish law permits than what it can be used to justify. Rabbi Phillip Sigal, a member of the Law Committee, acknowledges that "a particular mind-set, unfavorable to women, predominated in classical thinking and determined the ensuing halakhic disabilities which prevailed throughout the Middle Ages," but then proceeds to determine whether women may participate in the synagogue services by examining just those halakhic sources.[33] Rabbi Aaron Blumenthal, another member of the Law Committee, concurs with Sigal's view: "Jewish men must recognize the fact that the *halakhah* often has been unfair, ungracious and discriminatory towards our women. We cannot undo the past, but we can measure up to the needs of the present by granting full equality to Jewish women under the *halakhah*."[34] Feminists agree with Sigal's and Blumenthal's evaluation of Jewish law, but question why the Law Committee then proceeds to search for halakhic justifications for their decisions. Clearly, whatever principles Conservatism has developed to distinguish itself as a movement are now not functioning constructively as bases for their decisions regarding feminist demands.

Reconstructionism, the smallest of the denominations, is willing to make notable changes in its interpretation of the position of women in Jewish law. Revolving around a notion of Judaism as a civilization, Reconstructionism gives *halakhah* only "a vote and not a veto," in the words of its founder, Mordecai Kaplan. His concept of Jewish civilization, encompassing a wide variety of expressions and folk customs as well as Torah, includes nearly all aspects of Jewish life, except traditional belief in a supernatural deity. Kaplan rejects this belief because it seems incompatible with modern science and philosophy. However, Jewish women are coming to feminism not from the rather narrow aspects of modern secularism which gave birth to Reconstructionism, but instead from a recognition of the importance of spirituality and the desire to express belief and pray to God—or Goddess. Within Reconstructionism, there is no more room for Goddess than there is for the God of Abraham, Isaac, and Jacob.

Some feminists question the scope of the Jewish civilization as it is proclaimed by Reconstructionism. Whose civilization is it, they ask. To what extent does it include the new role of women and feminist insights? What if they conflict with those of the tradition composed and transmitted by men? Actually, Kaplan writes, "since Judaism is more than a religion or religious philosophy, it cannot even begin to function in the individual as such. The family is the smallest social unit through which it can articulate itself."[35] There is little room for those who reject that life-style or who have lost it through death or divorce.

All the denominations are struggling to meet the challenges of the modern world and to determine just what constitutes Judaism. They fear that the changes feminists call for will be the final blow of modernity, shattering whatever links to tradition and history the denominations preserve to guarantee a Jewish future.

But this book argues the contrary. It is not feminism which poses the threat to Judaism, but the denominations' own inability to come to terms with the challenges posed by modernity; the threat lies in their own inability to develop constructive theological positions which can respond to modernity's challenges—including feminism. It is the weaknesses inherent in modern Jewish theology, and not feminism, that are bringing about the impasse of today.

Also clear is that feminists cannot turn to one or more of the denominations in hope of developing a positive, constructive reconciliation with Judaism. Not only are such efforts naively optimistic about the ability of the movements to cope with the changes demanded, but they also function discretely, lacking their own coherent theological positions.

Until now, feminists have concentrated on individual, isolated issues within Judaism, such as changing divorce laws or attaining leadership positions within Federation. Gradually a fuller picture is emerging that shows the connections among these various issues. The essays in this volume begin by examining images of women in various facets of contemporary Jewish life. Taken together, they reveal that older, biblical, rabbinic, and medieval images continue to thrive even in secularized contexts. These images reveal not who women really are, but how women are made to appear and function from a male-dominated perspective. When opponents describe the sexual danger of ordaining women as rabbis, for example, they cannot point to statistics of women assaulting men in the synagogue. Rather, they unconsciously draw on ancient Jewish legends such as those describing the mysterious, threatening power of Lilith, the mythical female demon. In their struggle with contemporary discrimination, feminists are actually wrestling with these unspoken, hidden images which often keep the community from making changes even when no rules forbid them.

Such inherited, intangible images and attitudes affect the personal lives of both men and women, particularly in their relations with one another. The traditional roles assigned to women within Judaism are the representations of those images. If women are presented in legends as possessing a power threatening to men, they must in reality be kept from roles of independence and equality. Similarly, if woman is Other in the synagogue, *halakhah,* liturgy, and theology, she is bound to be treated as Other in the home, the family, and the community. Questions of role and identity cannot be raised outside the larger context of the images which give rise to them and the theological positions which legitimate them. The essays in the second section of this volume discuss the effects of traditional Jewish images on women's identity and establish perspectives from which new roles and new self-understandings of women and men may emerge.

Clearly, there is a need for theological reinterpretations to transform women in Judaism from object to subject. For only theology can offer the solution to the present problem, determining the role of rabbinic tradition in contemporary Judaism and its application to the lives we lead. Theology must apply feminism's concern for women's dignity and humanity in examining the meaning of religious symbols, traditions, and beliefs, and strive to give answers to humankind's ultimate questions.

Religious beliefs and observances have life cycles of their own. They may take different shapes, flourish, or wane. Some die because of their incredibility or irrelevance; others receive new life through reinterpretation. This process proves the vitality of a religious tradition, not its instability or impending demise. Theology establishes a relationship to Judaism as a whole, guiding this process of growth not simply by changing one or another particular points of *halakhah,* but by creating a framework for understanding larger questions of revelation, tradition, authority, and change. A feminist theology of Judaism must resonate with women's experience, must ground women's lives in a Jewish dimension. The outcome may be new or revised traditions, observances, and prayers. But above all, in the future when a woman looks to Judaism, she should not see only a reflection of the experiences of Jewish men.

In helping to create a new theology, women will become receivers and transmitters of Judaism, not onlookers. That shift can be illustrated through a parable by Franz Kafka, "Before the Law."[36] In Kafka's parable, a man from the country arrives at a door, seeking entry into the law, but the doorkeeper tells him that entry is impossible; a guard sits before each of many doors, and each guard is larger and fiercer than the one before. The man from the country sits down before the open door and remains there for years, until his death, begging and bribing the doorkeeper for permission to enter. Finally, as the man faces death, he asks why no one else has ever sought admission during the many years. The doorkeeper informs him that this door was intended solely for him—and then shuts it.

Although the doorkeeper forbids entry into the law to the man from the country, in reality he cannot prevent it. The man from the country fails to gain entry when he passively assumes that authorities are obstacles to the law, instead of taking the initiative and walking through the door himself. His error becomes twofold: first, he believes he can achieve his aim only through the guard and only if he begs and bribes him correctly, and, second, he blames his failure to gain entry on the doorkeeper, whose refusal to give help is seen as unfeeling and evil.

Many women in recent years have come seeking entry into Judaism. Some give up and eventually leave. Others plead and argue for admission, and are offered counterarguments, warnings, barriers, and a few ameliorating changes.

By assuming a posture like that of the man from the country, women continue their relation to Judaism as outsider or Other—even if they walk past the guards and through the doors. A profound error underlies this approach. Kafka's parable applies well to the situation of modern Judaism, which has built the doors of denominations, guarded by rabbis, institutions, and ideologies. But Judaism is not an edifice lying behind doors and guards and we should not have to go through a denomination to reach it. Rather, our relations should be with the diversity and totality of Jewish tradition, unmediated by one of its modern forms. There are no doors, there are no guards. Through theological exploration Judaism can belong to all who desire it.

NOTES

1. Several biographies of Henrietta Szold have been published; not one explores her decision to attend the seminary or her academic interests. See Elma Ehrlich Levinger, *Fighting Angel: The Story of Henrietta Szold* (New York: Behrman House, 1946); Rose Zeitlin, *Henrietta Szold* (New York: Dial Press, 1952); Alexandra Lee Levin, *The Szolds of*

Lombard Street (Philadelphia: Jewish Publication Society, 1960); Irving Fineman, *Woman of Valor: The Story of Henrietta Szold* (New York: Simon and Schuster, 1961); Joan Dash, *Summoned to Jerusalem: The Life of Henrietta Szold* (New York: Harper and Row, 1979).

2. Sondra Henry and Emily Taitz, *Written Out of History* (New York: Bloch Publishing Co., 1978) is a good general introduction, although it is based on secondary sources and so contains some inaccuracies.

3. The ban on polygamy is generally attributed to Rabbi Gershom ben Judah of Mainz, Germany (c.960–1028). But Ze'ev Falk, in his study *Jewish Matrimonial Law in the Middle Ages* (London: Oxford University Press, 1966), pp. 14 and 18, argues that "Gershom did not himself proclaim the ban. . . . An examination of sources dating from the eleventh and twelfth centuries thus apprises us that monogamy found its way into French/German Jewry by slow degrees, and not as a result of a single legislative act."

4. Changes in the Jewish family in nineteenth-century Germany are discussed by Julius Carlebach, "Family Structure and the Position of Jewish Women," in *Revolution and Evolution: 1848 in German-Jewish History,* ed. Werner Mosse, Arnold Pauker, and Reinhard Rurup (Tubingen: J. C. B. Mohr, 1981). For discussion of the Jewish family in America during the late nineteenth and early twentieth centuries, see Charlotte Baum, Paula Hyman, and Sonya Michel, *The Jewish Woman in America* (New York: Dial Press, 1976).

5. Marion A. Kaplan, *The Jewish Feminist Movement in Germany: The Campaigns of the Jüdischer Frauenbund, 1904–1938* (Westport, Conn.: Greenwood Press, 1979).

6. Aviva Cantor, ed., *On the Jewish Woman: A Comparative and Annotated Listing of Works Published 1900–1979* (Fresh Meadows, N.Y.: Biblio Press, 1979); Ora Hamelsdorf and Sandra Adelsberg, *Jewish Woman and Jewish Law: Bibliography* (Fresh Meadows, N.Y.: Biblio Press, 1980).

7. Elizabeth Koltun, ed., *The Jewish Woman: New Perspectives* (New York: Schocken Books, 1976).

8. *Keeping Posted,* vol. 27, no. 7 (April, 1972), p. 2.

9. *Keeping Posted,* vol. 25, no. 5 (February, 1980), p. 2.

10. Ruth Wisse, "Women as Conservative Rabbis?" *Commentary,* vol. 68, no. 4 (October 1979), p. 59.

11. Richard Yellin, "A Philosophy of Jewish Masculinity: One Interpretation," *Conservative Judaism,* vol. 32, no. 2 (Winter 1979), p. 93.

12. Yellin, p. 90.

13. Sylvan Schwartzman, "Is There Still Room for the Rebbetzin Today?" *Journal of Reform Judaism,* vol. 28, no. 4 (Fall 1981), p. 64.

14. Moshe Meiselman, *Jewish Woman in Jewish Law* (New York: Ktav Publishing House and Yeshiva University Press, 1978), p. 16.

15. Midge Decter, "The Liberated Woman," *Commentary,* vol. 50, no. 4 (October, 1970), p. 44.

16. Chana K. Poupko and Devorah Wohlgelernter, "Women's Liberation—An Orthodox Response," *Tradition,* vol. 15, no. 4 (Spring 1976), p. 45.

17. Poupko and Wohlgelernter, p. 51.

18. J. David Bleich, "Women on Synagogue Boards," *Tradition,* vol. 15, no. 4 (Spring 1976), p. 66.

19. Wisse, "Women as Conservative Rabbis?" pp. 63–64.

20. Mortimer Ostow, "Women and Change in Jewish Law," *Conservative Judaism,* vol. 29, no. 1 (Fall 1974), p. 6.

21. Ostow, p. 11.

22. Ostow, p. 11.

23. Lucy Dawidowicz, *The Jewish Presence: Essays in Identity and History* (New York: Holt, Rinehart, and Winston, 1977), pp. 52–53.

24. Judith Hauptman, "Images of Women in the Talmud," in: *Religion and Sexism,* ed. Rosemary Ruether (New York: Simon and Schuster, 1974), pp. 184–212.

25. Blu Greenberg, *Women and Judaism: A View from Tradition* (Philadelphia: Jewish Publication Society, 1982).

26. Virginia Woolf, *A Room of One's Own* (New York: Harcourt, Brace and World, 1957; first published in 1929).

27. Simone de Beauvoir, *The Second Sex,* trans. and ed. H. M. Parshley (New York: Knopf, 1953, 1972; first published in 1949 as *Le Deuxième sexe*), p. 16.

28. Abraham Geiger, *Judaism and its History,* trans. Charles Newburgh (New York: Bloch Publishing Co., 1911; first published in 1864 as *Das Judenthum und seine Geschichte*), pp. 61–62.

29. *Ibid.,* pp. 61 and 56.

30. Cited in *Keeping Posted,* April 1972, p. 19.

31. Quoted in David Philipson, *The Reform Movement in Judaism* (New York: Macmillan Company, 1907), pp. 309–310.

32. Ruth Seldin, "Women in the Synagogue: A Congregant's View," *Conservative Judaism,* vol. 32, no. 2 (Winter 1979), p. 81.

33. Phillip Sigal, "Elements of Male Chauvinism in Classical Halakhah," *Judaism,* vol. 24, no. 1 (Winter 1975), p. 226.

34. Aaron H. Blumenthal, "The Status of Women in Jewish Law," *Conservative Judaism,* vol. 31, no. 3 (Spring 1977), p. 40.

35. Mordecai M. Kaplan, *Judaism as a Civilization* (Philadelphia and New York: Jewish Publication Society, 1981; first published, 1934), p. 416.

36. Franz Kafka, "Before the Law," *Parables and Paradoxes,* trans. Willa and Edwin Muir (New York: Schocken Books, 1946), pp. 61–80.

Part One

OLD MYTHS AND IMAGES

Introduction

THE first step in the feminist critique of Judaism is exploring the religion's implicit view of women. Judaism's teachings and commandments never convey only what they state, but suggest and perpetuate hidden images and beliefs. Because of their sensory nature, images have great potential power to influence and manipulate, generally without our realizing it; their messages are often conveyed and received unconsciously. As women carefully explore the history and traditions of Judaism, they become aware of subtle negative or limiting messages about women's nature that underlie the more visible evidences of legal inequality. Most of these images originate in Judaism's classical sources, composed centuries ago—sources often unknown to modern-day, secularized Jews. Yet feminists are discovering that these images often persist, even in nonreligious contexts, and so form an unexpected link between Orthodox believers and radical assimilationists.

Such links are found by the authors of the essays in this section, who have examined aspects of Judaism ranging from halakhic texts to the modern family to contemporary fiction. Rachel Adler's essay, "The Jew Who Wasn't There," has been basic reading for feminists since it was first published in 1973. Adler compares the many positive teachings and legends about women in Jewish tradition with the legal restrictions imposed upon their religious, marital, and social status. She concludes that teachings which explicitly extol women's virtues do not accord with the much stronger, negative attitudes toward women implied by Jewish law. Accepting only the explicit teachings and ignoring the implicit messages of the laws is self-deceiving. "Ultimately our problem stems from the fact that we are viewed in Jewish law and practice as peripheral Jews," she contends.

Excluded from the central religious obligations of Judaism and from knowledge of its sources, little else is left to women under *halakhah* other than to act as facilitators for husbands and sons. The result is an identification of women with physical work—childbearing, cooking, cleaning—while men are identified with spiritual activities—prayer, study, rituals. Here, cause is confused with effect: are women excluded from most time-bound positive commandments because they are busy with physical concerns, or are they occupied with caring for the physical needs of others because they are excluded from the spiritual dimension? Identifying women with the physical encourages them to be seen as a danger to male spirituality. Whether women are regarded as sexual temptresses or as light-minded and ignorant beings, they are essentially threats to men's pursuit of their religious goals.

Despite her strong critique, Adler chooses to find solutions within the structures she criticizes: "The problem is how to attain some justice and some growing room for the Jewish woman if one is committed to remaining within *halakhah.*" Yet Adler's moderate position has been denounced as too radical by Orthodox opponents, and too modest by feminists. To other feminists, Adler's suggestion of changing *halakhah* according to the methods and limits of the rabbinic system may alter particular rules, but will only perpetuate the traditional message: women remain outside, petitioning a system of life regulated by men, rather than eliminating a situation in which women must request such changes of men.

The crystallization of feminism occurred simultaneously with major changes in the Jewish community. From its strong interest in social problems during the 1960s, the Jewish community turned inward during the 1970s, struggling to maintain ethnicity, to remember its own history, and to assure its future strength. The central vision shifted from social justice to survival under the impact of various factors, including rising assimilation and intermarriage, declining population growth, decreasing immigration to Israel, and growing awareness of the Holocaust. Feminism, emerging in full strength during this period of retrenchment, was not viewed as a movement for equal rights, like the Civil Rights Movement or the Free Soviet Jewry Movement of the 1960s. Rather, feminism was perceived as a threat to Jewish survival, a danger to be opposed rather than a cause to be supported. Reaction to this threat comes not only from religious leaders, but from the larger, secular community as well. Jewish leaders oppose feminism by popularizing the false notion that the family and particularly the traditional, self-sacrificing mother, were predominantly responsible for preserving the Jewish people through the centuries. Feminist calls for day-care centers to support working mothers and for greater acceptance of single women were portrayed as antithetical to the interests of contemporary Judaism.

The question of the family and women's role within it is a key issue to feminists and the issue most often targeted by their opponents for attack. In fact, most feminists seek not to abolish the family but to redefine it, to make roles more flexible, to accommodate women with careers and to share domestic and child-care responsibilities with men. Equally important, they seek community support for the growing numbers of single women and men. Yet many opponents claim that any change in the traditional family threatens the heart of Judaism. They draw teachings from classical Jewish sources to argue that the woman's role is to be provider and care-giver to her family, enabling her husband and sons to fulfill their religious obligations. But Paula Hyman, in her essay, sees a great discrepancy between the traditional Jewish teachings regarding the family and its actual functioning during the course of Jewish history.

While Adler argues that women's role within Judaism should be changed within the parameters of the halakhic system, Hyman uses history to uncover the reality of Jewish life, debunking false images that are used today to justify antifeminist positions. What we need today, Hyman concludes, "is not myths but a 'usable past' . . . which will provide us with meaningful role models for the present." Drawing such models from Jewish history will not only be faithful to the reality of the Jewish experience, but will also serve to balance the picture of women and men that is presented by traditional religious literature. According to Hyman, while religious teachings may have fostered one set of images of men and women, the reality beyond those images was far different. Traditional images may have presented women as light-minded, confined to housework and child-rearing; but history reveals that women were busy earning money to support their families, as well as cooking, cleaning, bearing and raising children. These women were strong, capable, and shrewd. It was their husbands, occupied with prayer and study, who more often demonstrated the traditionally feminine qualities of gentleness and emotional expressivity. Hyman's historical survey points to conclusions important to contemporary debate: "Sex-role differentiation was strict in many areas of Jewish life, but not in the sphere of personality characteristics. Here . . . is a part of our usable past which should find its way into our educational curriculum and into our thinking."

The theme of family dominates Jewish prose and poetry, whether written in Hebrew, Yiddish, or English. Literature of all languages has long been a significant barometer of social change, and women often appear as central characters to illustrate the breakdown of social structures and values. Women in Jewish fiction most frequently assume the role of mother, and, particularly in American fiction, these mothers are presented either as warm nurturers who transmit a love of *Yiddishkeit* to their children; or as overbearing smotherers who render their sons unable to form lasting relationships with other women; or (particularly in feminist fiction) as women starved for affection and understanding.

The contradictions among these images only confuse a community already unclear about the role its women wish to assume. Are Jewish women the bearers and transmitters of tradition, bulwarks in their families against the perils of assimilation? Or are they stifling whatever identity their children seek as individuals and Jews? Since most of this literature was created by men, we know little of the heroine's feelings apart from her relationship to the male characters. Erika Duncan's essay "Hungry Jewish Mothers" explores the character of the Jewish mother who, despite all her varieties, leaves us knowing little of her own inner life.

The image of hunger unites the mothers in Jewish fiction, Duncan finds, as she explores both the hunger these women strive to satisfy in others through their constant self-sacrificing, and the hunger they themselves experience as their sensitivities are neglected and their emotions starved. "Too well we know the Jewish mother our male writers have given us, the all-engulfing nurturer who devours the very soul with every spoonful of hot chicken soup she gives, whose every shakerful of salt contains a curse. . . . Yet we do not know enough of the other hungry one who feeds others because it is the only access she knows to a little bit of love." Only gradually, with the growth of feminism and the autonomy it brings, has the hunger diminished, Duncan writes; only gradually "through learning to suckle herself and other women has the hungry Jewish mother been transformed."

The women Duncan locates in Jewish fiction are shadows, not real figures. They exist in relation to their environment—to children, husbands, parents. But even when they explore their own emotions, they express reactions to their treatment by others, and rarely a sense of autonomous selfhood. The people in this literature are still filled with pain, not joy; they are only beginning to move from anonymous reflections of broad and dominant Jewish images to unique individuals.

The polar images of mother as nourisher and smotherer in contemporary fiction parallel the twin female figures of the *Shekhinah* and Lilith found in ancient and medieval Jewish sources. Appearing in legends, mystical speculations, and amulets, Lilith is the demon woman, the source of evil, temptation, and sin, who haunts the world, seducing pious men and murdering innocent babies. The *Shekhinah,* in contrast, is the gentle, loving presence of God, the daughter, queen, bride, and lover figured in prayer and prominent in Sabbath liturgy. Yet Aviva Cantor, in searching for a positive image for Jewish women today, turns not to the *Shekhinah,* but to the legends surrounding Lilith.

According to the legends, God created Lilith long before Eve as Adam's equal partner, but after she thwarted Adam's efforts to make her subservient to him, Lilith was banished from the Garden of Eden and Eve was created to take her place as Adam's submissive helpmeet and mother of the world. Later

Jewish traditions embroidered the story, claiming that Lilith, angered by her exile, became a vengeful demon, tempting pious men to sexual sin and murdering newborn babies. But feminists, according to Cantor, should identify with Lilith as a figure of independence and power, in sharp contrast to Eve and the matriarchs, who are presented in the Bible and in later tradition as their husbands' enablers, rather than as equal agents of history. The demonic element in Lilith's career was created later by rabbis who wanted to warn women of the consequences of independence and rebellion, Cantor argues. Some women may sympathize with Lilith's demonic activities, feeling a similar rage toward their banishment from Judaism. Cantor acknowledges the legitimacy of the rage, but points out that God created Lilith to be equal with Adam. It was Adam who insisted she be subservient to him. Judaism, she concludes, has followed Adam's example, not God's, and feminists should choose to identify as women were originally created, in the image of Lilith, as full equal partners with men.

Until traditional images are changed or given new meaning, their impact persists. The idealization of the family lingers even among secular Jews, sometimes with insidious results. Mimi Scarf, studying wife-beating in the Los Angeles Jewish community, found that idealized images of the Jewish family exacerbate the incidence of family violence. Scarf discovered that women who have been beaten feel they are personally to blame; after all, Jewish men don't beat their wives—or so they were raised to believe. "This shame renders them so helpless and so afraid of disclosure that many prefer being battered than run the risk of admitting it," she writes. Jewish communal leaders, from rabbis to social workers, fearing a growing divorce rate and reluctant to admit the image of the Jewish family is tarnished, deny the existence of any problem, and so provide little or no social, psychological, or legal services to these families.

The battered women Scarf interviewed experienced such an extreme clash between the kinds of marriages they were raised to expect and the reality they encounter that at first they simply could not believe they were actually being beaten. The exalted image of the Jewish family that has always been the central focus of their lives "prevents them from being prepared to defend themselves against their husbands and from believing it has happened, but makes them feel guilty and responsible for their husbands' actions." Not only images of the family, but the traditional image of Jewish men as gentle and nonviolent compounds the situation of battered wives, according to Scarf. "When they had been warned against dating and marrying non-Jewish men, the real warning was that if they married non-Jewish men, they would run into rough treatment. Ironically, the opposite now seemed to be true, and the corollary was that when they ran into rough treatment from a Jew, it must be their fault."

Another example of the effect of internalized images on a community is the case of Israeli women. According to Lesley Hazleton, the myth of equality of women and men in Israel is false, yet few Israeli women are willing to acknowledge the reality of their social position. Israeli women have long been touted as a new breed in the history of the Jews. The kibbutz worker, the soldier, even the former prime minister, Golda Meir, are held as models for Jewish women, implying that Judaism—as interpreted by Zionism—does not hinder equality of women. But Hazleton argues that Israeli society "resolved the conflict between ideology and emotion by denying the existence of conflict. . . . For despite an intellectual commitment to women's liberation, the emotional commitment was to the traditional role of women." Israel has neither a constitution guaranteeing equality nor a law prohibiting sex discrimination, and rabbinic law controls marriage and divorce proceedings. Despite the examples of Golda Meir, women soldiers, and kibbutz members, the status of women in Israel is highly limited in all areas of life, and the limitations are worsened by false myths of equality: "Their attitude is one of suspended disbelief, making them willing victims of an empty but soothing ideology. Surrendering their real identity to the 'cover identity' ascribed them by ideology, they move in a male world of reality in the false guise of equals."

Patriarchy, the assumption by men of supremacy and control over women, is the basic defining characteristic of Judaism, according to Batya Bauman. Women's inferiority is guaranteed under patriarchy and reforms are "simply a method of co-opting women into the patriarchy in order to perpetuate it," she writes. The hierarchy extends even to men's treatment of other men; homosexuality, for example, is prohibited in the Bible because "the dominant male treats the subordinate male as men treat women: as inferior." Yet the dilemma is double: while Bauman argues that Judaism can never be divorced from patriarchy and the subordination of women, she also acknowledges her own strong ties to women in Jewish history: "We feel that we are a link in Jewish history, a history in which so many women as well as men have suffered and died just because they were Jews and in order to remain Jews. . . . How can we, after all that has come before us, break this chain?"

Thena Kendall, raised in an Orthodox home, writes that she could not find meaning in the religious expression permitted her as a woman. Her exclusion as a woman led Kendall to question Orthodoxy as a whole: "It was the static nature of the observances that worried me. I could not accept the immutability of the many rules and regulations that ruled our daily lives. . . . Somehow holy days seemed to involve drudgery and restrictions but none of the compensating joyousness with which our Hasidic ancestors had celebrated their faith." A turning point for Kendall was her frustrated attempt to say Kaddish for her parents in the face of Orthodox opposition: "My experiences within the Orthodox community left me feeling for some years that my religious needs were better met away from religious institutions." Ultimately, Kendall turned to Reform Judaism: "It was partly the personality of a particular Reform rabbi, and partly the atmosphere of real worship that I experienced in his congregation that led us to align ourselves with this less traditional approach to Judaism."

Similar feelings are expressed by Gail Shulman, who describes a childhood filled with Jewish observance and celebration. But growing up became a process of loss for her, as she was excluded more and more from communal participation. For Shulman, Judaism's concern with justice and compassion led her to feminism. That realization brought her, as a feminist estranged from religion, to return to Judaism. Yet upon her return, she found "I affirm my Jewishness in a way that Judaism seems unable and unwilling to accept or return . . . for it fails to support and affirm the woman that I and many other feminists have become."

Overcoming images is far more difficult than changing institutions. Undesirable images cannot simply be removed; they must be changed or replaced. Analyzing the subtle messages conveyed by the images is the first step toward understanding their impact on individuals and the community. As women reject a range of images offered of them by Judaism, they must simultaneously create new images that lend credence to the roles they are shaping.

The Jew Who Wasn't There

HALAKHAH AND THE JEWISH WOMAN

Rachel Adler

IT is not unusual for committed Jewish women to be uneasy about their position as Jews. It was to cry down our doubts that rabbis developed their prepackaged orations on the nobility of motherhood; the glory of childbirth; and modesty, the crown of Jewish womanhood. I have heard them all. I could not accept those answers for two reasons. First of all, the answers did not accept *me* as a person. They only set rigid stereotypes which defined me by limiting the directions in which I might grow. Second, the answers were not really honest ones. Traditional scholars agree that all philosophies of Judaism must begin with an examination of Jewish law, *halakhah,* since in the *halakhah* are set down the ways in which we are expected to behave, and incontestably our most deeply engrained attitudes are those which we reinforce by habitual action.

Yet scholars do not discuss female status in terms of *halakhah*—at least not with females. Instead, they make lyrical exegeses on selected *midrashim* and *aggadot* which, however complimentary they may be, do not really reflect the way in which men are expected to behave toward women by Jewish law. I think we are going to have to discuss it, if we are to build for ourselves a faith which is not based on ignorance and self-deception. That is why I would like to offer some hypotheses on the history and nature of the "woman problem" in *halakhah.*

Ultimately our problem stems from the fact that we are viewed in Jewish law and practice as peripheral Jews. The category in which we are generally placed includes women, children, and Canaanite slaves. Members of this category are exempt from all positive commandments which occur within time limits.[1] These commandments would include hearing the shofar on Rosh Hashanah, eating in the Sukkah, praying with the *lulav,* praying the three daily services, wearing *tallit* and *tefillin,* and saying *Shema.*[2] In other words, members of this category have been "excused" from most of the positive symbols which, for the male Jew, hallow time, hallow his physical being, and inform both his myth and his philosophy.

Since most of the *mitzvot* not restricted by time are negative, and since women, children, and slaves are responsible to fulfill all negative *mitzvot,* including the negative time-bound *mitzvot,* it follows that for members of this category, the characteristic posture of their Judaism is negation rather than affirmation.[3] They must not, for example, eat nonkosher food, violate the Shabbat, eat *hametz* on Pesach, fail to fast on fast days, steal, murder, or commit adultery. That women, children, and slaves have limited credibility in Jewish law is demonstrated by the fact that their testimony is inadmissible in a Jewish court.[4] The *minyan*—the basic unit of the Jewish community—excludes them, implying that the community is presumed to be the Jewish males to whom they are adjuncts. Torah study is incumbent upon them only insofar as it relates to "their" *mitzvot.* Whether women are even permitted to study further is debated.[5]

All of the individuals in this tripartite category I have termed peripheral Jews. Children, if male, are full Jews *in potentio.* Male Canaanite slaves, if freed, become full Jews, responsible for all the *mitzvot* and able to count in a *minyan.*[6] Even as slaves, they have the *brit milah,* the covenant of circumsion, that central Jewish symbol, from which women are anatomically excluded. It is true that in Jewish law women are slightly more respected than slaves, but that advantage is outweighed by the fact that only women can never grow up, or be freed, or otherwise leave the category. The peripheral Jew is excused and sometimes barred from the acts and symbols which are the lifeblood of the believing community, but this compliance with the negative *mitzvot* is essential, since, while he cannot be permitted to participate fully in the life of the Jewish people, he cannot be permitted to undermine it either.

To be a peripheral Jew is to be educated and socialized toward a peripheral commitment. This, I think, is what happened to the Jewish woman. Her major *mitzvot* aid and reinforce the life-style of the community and the family, but they do not cultivate the relationship between the individual and God. A woman keeps kosher because both she and her family must have kosher food. She lights the Shabbat candles so that there will be light, and hence, peace, in the household. She goes to the *mikvah* so that her husband can have intercourse with her and she bears children so that, through her, he can fulfill the exclusively male *mitzvah* of increasing and multiplying.[7]

Within these narrow confines, there have been great and virtuous women, but in several respects the *tzidkaniot* [saintly women] have been unlike the *tzaddikim.* Beruria, the scholarly wife of Rabbi Meir, the Talmudic sage, and a few exceptional women like her stepped outside the limits of the feminine role, but legend relates how Beruria came to a bad end, implying that her sin was the direct result of her "abnormal" scholarship.[8] There is no continuous tradition of learned women in Jewish history. Instead there are many *tzidkaniot,* some named, some unnamed, all of whom were pious and chaste, outstandingly charitable, and, in many cases, who supported their husbands. In contrast, there are innumerable accounts of *tzaddikim,* some rationalists, some mystics, some joyous, some ascetic, singers, dancers, poets, halakhists, all bringing to God the service of a singular, inimitable self.

How is it that the *tzaddikim* seem so individualized and the *tzidkaniot* so generalized? I would advance two reasons. First of all, the *mitzvot* of the *tzadeket* are mainly directed toward serving others. She is a *tzadeket* to the extent that she sacrifices herself in order that others may actualize themselves spiritually. One has no sense of an attempt to cultivate a religious self built out of the raw materials of a unique personality. The model for the *tzadeket* is Rachel, the wife of Rabbi Akiva, who sold her hair and sent her husband away to study for twenty-four years, leaving herself beggared and without means of support; or the wife of Rabbi Menachem Mendel of Rymanov (her name, incidentally, goes unremembered) who sold her share in the next world to buy her husband bread.

Frequently there is a kind of masochism manifest in the accounts of the acts of *tzidkaniot.* I recall the stories held up to me as models to emulate, of women who chopped holes in icy streams to perform their monthly immersions. A lady in the community I came from, who went into labor on Shabbat and walked to the hospital rather than ride in a taxi, was acting in accordance with this model. Implicit is the assumption that virtue is to be achieved by rejecting and punishing the hated body which men every morning thank God is not theirs.[9]

Second, as Hillel says, "an ignoramus cannot be a saint."[10] He may have the best of intentions, but he lacks the disciplined creativity, the sense of continuity with his people's history and thought, and the forms in which to give Jewish expression to his religious impulses. Since it was traditional to give women cursory religious educations, they were severely limited in their ways of expressing religious commitment. Teaching, the fundamental method of the Jewish people for transmitting religious insights, was closed to women—those who do not learn, do not teach.[11] Moreover, expressions of spiritual creativity by women seem to have been severely limited. Religious music written by women is virtually nonexistent. There are no prayers written by women in the liturgy, although there were prayers written in Yiddish by women for women who were unable to pray in Hebrew.

It was, perhaps, most damaging that the woman's meager *mitzvot* are, for the most part, closely connected to some physical goal or object. A woman's whole life revolved around physical objects and physical experiences—cooking, cleaning, childbearing, meeting the physical needs of children. Without any independent spiritual life to counterbalance the materialism of her existence, the mind of the average woman was devoted to physical considerations; marriages, deaths, dinners, clothes and money. It was, thus, natural that Jewish men should have come to identify women with *gashmiut* [physicality] and men with *ruhniut* [spirituality].

The Talmudic sages viewed the female mind as frivolous and the female sexual appetite as insatiable.[12] Unless strictly guarded and given plenty of busywork, all women were potential adulteresses.[13] In the Jewish view, all physical objects and experiences are capable of being infused with spiritual purpose; yet it is equally true that the physical, unredeemed by spiritual use, is a threat. It is therefore easy to see how women came to be regarded as semidemonic in both Talmud and Kabbalah. Her sexuality presented a temptation, or perhaps a threat which came to be hedged ever more thickly by law and custom.[14] Conversing with women was likely to result in gossip or lewdness.[15] Women are classed as inadmissible witnesses in the same category with gamblers, pigeon-racers and other individuals of unsavory repute.[16]

Make no mistake; for centuries, the lot of the Jewish woman was infinitely better than that of her non-Jewish counterpart. She had rights which other women lacked until a century ago. A Jewish woman could not be married without her consent. Her *ketubah* [marriage document] was a legally binding contract which assured that her husband was responsible for her support (a necessity in a world in which it was difficult for a woman to support herself), and that if divorced, she was entitled to a monetary settlement. Her husband was not permitted to abstain from sex for long periods of time without regard to her needs and her feelings.[17] In its time, the Talmud's was a very progressive view. The last truly revolutionary ruling for women, however, was the Edict of Rabbenu Gershom forbidding polygamy to the Jews of the Western world. That was in 1000 C.E. The problem is that very little has been done since then to ameliorate the position of Jewish women in observant Jewish society.

All of this can quickly be rectified if one steps outside of Jewish tradition and *halakhah*. The problem is how to attain some justice and some growing room for the Jewish woman if one is committed to remaining *within halakhah*. Some of these problems are more easily solved than others. For example, there is ample precedent for decisions permitting women to study Talmud, and it should become the policy of Jewish day schools to teach their girls Talmud. It would not be difficult to find a basis for giving women *aliyot* to the Torah. Moreover, it is both feasible and desirable for the community to begin educating women to take on the positive time-bound *mitzvot* from which they are now excused; in which case, those *mitzvot* would eventually become incumbent upon women. The more difficult questions are those involving *minyan* and *mehitzah* [segregation at prayers]. There are problems concerning the right of women to be rabbis, witness in Jewish courts, judges and leaders of religious services. We need decisions on these problems which will permit Jewish women to develop roles and role models in which righteousness springs from self-actualization, in contrast to the masochistic, self-annihilating model of the postbiblical *tzadeket*. The halakhic scholars must examine our problem anew, right now, with open minds and with empathy. They must make it possible for women to claim their share in the Torah and begin to do the things a Jew was created to do. If necessary we must agitate until the scholars are willing to see us as Jewish souls in distress rather than as tools with which men do *mitzvot*. If they continue to turn a deaf ear to us, the most learned and halakhically committed among us must make halakhic decisions for the rest. That is a move to be saved for desperate straits, for even the most learned of us have been barred from acquiring the systematic halakhic knowledge which a rabbi has. But, to paraphrase Hillel, in a place where there are no *menschen*, we may have to generate our own *menschlichkeit*. There is no time to waste. For too many centuries, the Jewish woman has been a golem, created by Jewish society. She cooked and bore and did her master's will, and when her tasks were done, the Divine Name was removed from her mouth. It is time for the golem to demand a soul.[18]

Postscript: "The sort of *piskei halakhah* requested in the text of this article are *genuine* decisions based on sources and understanding of the halakhic process made by people who understand and observe the Torah. Rationalizations will not do." [R.A.]

NOTES

1. *Kiddushin* 29a.
2. *Kiddushin* 29a; but see also *Mishnah Sukkah* 2:9 and *Mishnah Brachot* 3:3.

3. *Kiddushin* 29a.

4. *Sh'vuot* 30a. See also *Rosh Hashanah* 22a.

5. *Sotah* 20a.

6. It must be admitted that Canaanite slaves were only to be freed if some overriding *mitzvah* would be accomplished thereby. The classic case in which Rabbi Eliezer frees his slave in order to complete a *minyan* is given in *Gittin* 38b.

7. *Mikvah* is not itself a *mitzvah.* It is a prerequisite to a permitted activity, just as *shehitah* is prerequisite to the permitted activity of eating meat. See *Sefer Hahinukh, Mitzvah* 175.

8. *Avoda Zara* 18b. See Rashi.

9. In the Traditional Prayer book see the morning blessing, "Blessed are You, Lord our God, King of the universe, who has not created me as woman."

10. *Avot* 2:6.

11. Exactly this expression is used in *Kiddushin* 29b, where it is asserted that the *mitzvah* of teaching one's own offspring the Torah applies to men and not to women.

12. *Kiddushin* 80b contains the famous statement, "The rational faculty of women weighs lightly upon them." Interestingly enough, the *Tosafot* illustrate this with an ancient misogynistic fabliau whose written source is the *Satyricon* of Petronius Arbiter. See also *Sotah* 20a.

13. *Mishnah Ketubot* 5:5.

14. This is the context in which one may understand the statement of the Kitzur Shulchan Aruch, "A man should be careful not to walk between two women, two dogs, or two swine." Ganzfried, Rabbi Solomon, Code of Jewish Law I, trans. Hyman E. Goldin, 2nd ed. (New York: 1961), p. 7.

15. *Avot* 1:5. See also the commentaries of Rashi, Rambam, and Rabbenu Yonah.

16. *Rosh Hashanah* 22a.

17. *Mishnah Ketubot* 5:6.

18. There is a famous folk tale that the scholar Rabbi Loewe of Prague created a golem or robot, using the Kabbalah. The robot, formed from earth, came to life and worked as a servant when a tablet engraved with the Divine Name was placed in its mouth. When the tablet was removed, the golem reverted to mindless clay.

The Jewish Family
LOOKING FOR A USABLE PAST

Paula Hyman

MYTH-MAKING about the Jewish family, and particularly about the role of women in that family, has become virtually a preoccupation of the contemporary Jewish community. And understandably so. The last century has witnessed tremendous upheavals in Jewish life as a result of mass emigration, assimilation, and the Holocaust. Concern for continued Jewish group survival has led scholars and communal leaders alike to look for those social factors which accounted for Jewish survival in the past, even in the face of centuries of persecution. Often the Jewish family has been held up as the source of past stability in Jewish life; and a restored Jewish family has been proposed as a bulwark against further erosion of Jewish solidarity and consciousness. Some Jewish leaders doubtless would go so far as to echo Heinrich Heine at his most romantic when he described the Jewish home as "a haven of rest from the storms that raged round the very gates of the ghetto."

A conference sponsored in 1973 by the American Jewish Committee and B'nai B'rith on "The Role of Jewish Women in Strengthening the Jewish Family" illustrates certain commonly held assumptions about Jewish family life. Participants in the conference assured the audience that it was the Jewish family which had preserved Judaism. And they asserted, as well, that it was the Jewish woman who was central to the proper functioning of the family and to the perpetuation of Jewish values. One speaker declared that "it was the mother who taught the children the way to be Jewish," while another, in the same vein, described the mother as "the educator of both boys and girls." To combat the problems of low fertility and rising rates of intermarriage, it was suggested that Jewish women consider retiring from their careers and returning to the home. "The woman committed to a career is not likely to have more than 1.2 children," it was pointed out. "Perhaps we have to urge the Jewish woman to withdraw from other activities." Thus, the Jewish woman presumably is to stay home and "be Jewish," thereby resolving the major social problems confronting American Jewry.

It seems to me that such advice flies in the face of both history and common sense. It perpetuates a myth, when what we need is not myths but a "usable past." A usable past is one which will provide us with meaningful role models for the present, one with which we can feel a link. But building that past on myths is destructive; myths translate poorly into patterns for living.

The first myth is that the Jewish famly preserved the Jews and Judaism. A glance at the history of the Jewish family, at least since early modern times, and at the position of the woman in that family, casts doubt upon the accepted wisdom. While it is true that even critics of the Jews pointed to their exemplary family life, it is simplistic to suggest that the Jewish family therefore preserved the Jews in the Diaspora.

A variety of factors—socioeconomic, cultural, and ultimately religious—are responsible for Jewish survival. Persecution combined with governmental tolerance of an autonomous Jewish community which had coercive authority over its members were central to Jewish existence. The medieval Jewish community was small and intimate and fulfilled the social as well as religious needs of its members. And every Jew had to live up to the norms of his community or leave Jewry completely.

The family was but the smallest link in the chain of communal institutions. In the premodern period, when religious faith was secure and Judaism and Jewishness were inextricably bound, there was no way for a Jew to be Jewish except within the confines of his immediate family and his larger family, the community. To separate the historic influence of the two is virtually impossible. It can be argued, then, that religious commitment, the external situation, and the nature of the Jewish community served to preserve the traditional Jewish family, rather than that the Jewish family preserved Judaism.

The world in which Jews live has changed, and the Jewish family along with it. We cannot go back—nor would most of us want to—to a situation where rational skepticism had not challenged religious faith and where contact with the surrounding environment was limited primarily to economic exchanges. That is, we cannot return to a pre-emancipation situation. To solve our contemporary problems not only must we find a style of family living suited to our own age, but, more importantly, we must also develop Jewish communal institutions which will meet the changed needs of modern Jews. For, in contrast to our ancestors, Jews in a post-emancipation world have social and cultural alternatives to Jewish institutions, alternatives which do not explicitly require them to abandon their Jewishness. Only if they are successfully socialized by the Jewish community will contemporary Jews create families which are actively Jewish.

The absence of Jewishness in the home is a symptom, not a cause, of the breakdown of traditional Jewish life. It is one of the prices we have paid for emancipation. It is important to restore the family as a center of religious observance and worthwhile to strive to revitalize the Jewishness of the Jewish home in any way possible. But we should not place the primary burden upon the family. Changed conditions suggest that many functions formerly performed by the Jewish family will now have to become communal concerns.

The second myth is the suggestion that the Jewish woman always played the central role in transmitting Judaism to her children. The theory that women are culture bearers is one which many women are inclined to accept without challenge, despite its inaccuracy, because it is flattering. It connotes power and a recognition of the value of the mothering role, which certainly includes teaching by example and by daily reminders. True, the Jewish mother wielded enormous moral influence over her children, and provided the proper atmosphere for Jewish celebration. However, the transmission of Jewish culture does not really lie in cleaning the house, baking *hallah,* lighting candles, or even urging children to be good Jews.

Religious celebrations within the home were presided over by the husband and father. Moreover, learning and teaching were central to cultural transmission within the Jewish community, and both were the preserves of men—the father and the *melamed.* From the age of three or four, the Eastern European Jewish boy was removed from his mother's care for virtually the entire day to study in the *heder.* So little regarded was a mother's influence on the older child that in Islamic lands after a divorce all children of the marriage, once they had reached the age of six, were given automatically into the custody of their father.

The notion that the Jewish woman has been the culture bearer may thus appear attractive at first sight to those of us who would like to expand the role of women in the Jewish community, but if it is to serve as part of our usable past it must be infused with new (and greater) content. Moreover, the Jewish father's role as culture bearer is equally deserving of revitalization to meet present needs. What we must avoid is the use of the "Jewish mother as teacher" argument as a means to suggest that the only good Jewish mother is one who stays home and spends her time teaching her children in some indefinable way how to be Jews. The argument won't work—no woman will quit her job as a result of it—but it may produce a group of angry and guilty Jewish working mothers who feel that their community is not supportive of them.

That would be regrettable, because the Jewish working mother has a long and noble history which we should make our own. The image of the *yiddishe mamma* spending all her time and energy *tsittering* over her children, cooking, scrubbing her home, and mothering her husband as well as her children, is only part of her historical role. The very incompleteness of the image, then, has made it a myth—and one that is hard to live up to.

Ashkenazic women in Central and Eastern Europe, at least, were far different from the stereotypical *yiddishe mamma.* They were traditionally responsible for much of what we would now describe as masculine roles. It was not uncommon, for example, for the Jewish wife to be the primary breadwinner of the family, particularly if her husband was talented enough to be able to devote himself to study. The halakhic tradition even accommodated itself to the expanding economic role of women. While halakhic prescriptions had traditionally prohibited a Jewish woman from being alone with any man other than her husband, that tradition was relaxed in those areas where women peddlers had to take business trips alone and enter Gentile homes to peddle their wares. In western Germany in the eighteenth century, for example, religious authorities issued a dispensation to allow women to peddle, thus legalizing what was already accepted in practice. Yet the economic aspect of the Jewish mother's role has tended to be omitted from the popular image.

As Solomon Maimon, an eighteenth century Polish Jew who became a philosopher, relates in his memoirs, the much-sought-after scholar, after his years of study supported by his father-in-law, is "either promoted to some learned office or he spends his whole life in learned leisure. In either case," continues Maimon, "the wife undertakes the management of the household and the conduct of business; and she is content if, only in return for all her toils, she becomes in some measure a partaker of her husband's fame and future blessedness."

His comment reflects a general pattern, which was not confined solely to the wives of scholars. Particularly in the Eastern European *shtetl,* from which the vast majority of American Jews derive, economic responsibility for the family was at least partly the woman's obligation. Isaac Bashevis Singer's grandmother is not atypical. He describes her in his memoir *Of A World That Is No More* as

> a saintly woman who never assumed that it was her husband's duty to support her. She left him to his beloved Torah and Cabbala and herself traveled to Warsaw to buy goods and earn a living for her family, since her husband's wages [as a rabbi] could not keep a bird alive. . . . It never occurred to her that one day her precious son would be expected to earn a living. She always considered this a wife's responsibility.

The *yiddishe mamma* found various ways to earn "the living." Many were peddlers who stood in the marketplace, baskets over their arms, selling roots or bagels they had baked themselves, or tea, beans and other foodstuffs. Others, like Singer's grandmother, bought small lots of manufactured articles in the cities to barter with peasants who brought their produce to market. The more fortunate women had shops were they sold food, staples, linens, piece goods, crockery, glassware and fancy goods, and other items. Both girls and women also sewed clothing to sell, either independently or through small-scale contractors.

Economic need, and not self-fulfillment, was the primary motive for women's participation in economic activities. But it was not the only motive. Even Glückel of Hameln, that seventeenth-century pious and wealthy German Jewish woman, whose children married into the families of prominent court Jews, helped her husband in his trade in precious jewels and metals and ran the business for years after his death. In the nineteenth and twentieth centuries, it is true, women tended to retire from business activities as their families rose in wealth and status.

However, the working Jewish wife and mother was a common phenomenon in the immigrant generation in this country. While most married women did not work in factories, they did continue to share in the financial support of the family—by doing piecework at home for garment industry subcontractors, taking in boarders, selling from pushcarts, or helping their husbands in "mom and pop" stores. The Jewish working woman should be recognized, and encouraged, as heir to a valid Jewish life-style rather than blamed for contemporary Jewish problems and urged back into the home.

For it is to our credit that the Jewish community fostered a variety of life-styles for women. Despite the secondary role that the Jewish halakhic tradition assigned women in the spheres of ritual and study, life did not allow itself to be confined by law. Within the Jewish family the wife and mother developed a strength and sense of self-confidence and authority that mocks stereotyped notions of female fragility.

Moreover, the Jewish husband and father was no remote tyrant, his role as patriarch notwithstanding. How fortunate for both Jewish women and men that the "macho mystique" was not a Jewish cultural value. Deprived of political independence and, in most places, of the right to bear arms, Jewish men denigrated physical prowess as a cultural ideal. Instead, they cultivated intellectual and spiritual pursuits. They expressed their masculinity in the synagogue and in the house of study, not on the battlefield and not through the physical oppression of their women.

This absence of the "macho mystique" freed Jewish men and women from the sharpest differentiation of gender characteristics: the strong, emotionally controlled, yet potentially violent male vs. the weak, emotional, and tender female. Jewish culture "permitted" men to be gentle and emotionally expressive and women to be strong, capable, and shrewd. Sex-role differentiation was strict in many areas of Jewish life, but not in the sphere of human personality characteristics. Here, it seems to me, is a part of our usable past which should find its way into our educational curriculum and into our thinking.

There is much in the traditional Eastern European Jewish family that we lack and for which we should seek substitutes. For most of us, distance, economic independence and work schedules have consigned the extended family to the past of our childhoods. That is a historical trend which the Jewish community should seek to reverse, if individual families cannot, for the extended family offered a kind of flexibility to its members that communes often seek in vain. I am not suggesting a return to the three-generation family living in three rooms. But I am suggesting that the extended family serve as a model for types of communal associations that transcend the nuclear family—a voluntary extended family. At its best, for example, a *havurah* whose members live within walking distance fulfills many of the functions of the extended family of the past.

The Jewish community should also recognize the need to assume some of the responsibility for child care which was previously divided among the members of the extended family. Given present work patterns and aspirations, the modern nuclear family needs, and will continue to need, good day care institutions. The Jewish community will be missing a great opportunity to participate in the early socialization of its own young if it fails to provide day care under Jewish auspices. A Jewish day care center, by employing Jewish senior citizens as aides, could also recreate, in a new setting, the intergenerational contact which was integral to traditional Jewish family life. Only if the community takes a share in child rearing can its leaders presume to urge Jewish women—for no one would deny that child care duties remain primarily theirs—to have larger families.

Sacrifice for the good of the community is a traditional Jewish value. However, it appears unlikely to prevail over the legitimate desire for self-realization which many women today harbor, particularly since the self-sacrifice called for seems to be so unevenly distributed. Many women will find self-fulfillment in the traditional roles of wife and mother; but many will not. And the latter also deserve communal support and a sense that their life-style has its place within the Jewish historical experience. Looking for a usable past is one way to meet the needs of the two-career Jewish family.

The Hungry Jewish Mother

Erika Duncan

NOW they put a baby in her lap. Do not ask me, she would have liked to beg. . . . Unnatural grandmother, not able to make herself embrace a baby . . .

It was not that she had not loved her babies, her children. But when the need was done—oh the power that was lost in the painful damming back and drying up of what still surged, but had nowhere to go . . .

And they put a baby in her lap . . . warm flesh like this had claims and nuzzled away all else and with lovely mouths devoured. . . . the long drunkenness; the drowning into needing and being needed . . .

And all that visit, she could not touch the baby.[1]

Thus Tillie Olsen wrote of the old grandmother in *Tell Me a Riddle,* "Mrs. Unpleasant," typical yenta and nag, who in her dying turns away from all those she was forced to nurture in her life. Her husband calls her every mean, degrading name he can because she refuses to move to "The Haven," a rest home where everything will be done and arranged for her. But she will not cooperate in taking the late-offered comfort he has stolen from her all her life. Throughout the story, the husband's hunger mounts in rhythms with the stomach cancer that is eating his wife alive. His own bitter salt tears are all that stay upon the midnight tray he is forced to fetch himself. Dying in bed, she makes up soliloquies that leave him out.

Too well we know the Jewish mother our male writers have given us, the all-engulfing nurturer who devours the very soul with every spoonful of hot chicken soup she gives, whose every shakerful of salt contains a curse. Too well we know the feeder whose hard-wrung offerings are imbibed as poisons. Yet we do not know enough of the other hungry one who feeds others because it is the only access she knows to a little bit of love. In Jewish literature by women, mothers are the "bread givers" who try to make feeding into a replenishing, ecstatic act. But the mothers are themselves starved in every way, sucked dry and withered from being asked almost from birth to give a nurturance they never receive. They are starved not only for the actual food they are forced to turn over to others, but for the stuff of self and soul, for love and song. The oldest daughter in *Tell Me a Riddle* cries, "Pay me back, Mother, pay me back for all you took from me. Those others you crowded into your heart. The hands I needed to be for you, the heaviness, the responsibility." But the dying grandmother, her mother, can only chant:

> "One pound soup meat . . . one soup bone. . . . Bread, day-old. . . . Please, in a wooden box . . . for kindling.
> I ask for stone; she gives me bread—day-old. . . .
> How can I give it, Clara, how can I give it if I don't have?"[2]

The mother's starvation is, needless to say, scary for the child, who has no choice but to take. For underlying all the taking is the fear of being eaten up alive and the guilt of stealing from the empty one. This, I imagine, is why so many male writers have turned the one who endlessly spoons out the chicken soup into a mad devourer from whom they have to flee lest their identities be eaten up. Thus our Portnoys, knowing on some level that they have been thieves, eliminate their debt by making their tormented mothers into cardboard demons, distancing them by robbing them of their pains and hunger and humanity, so some day they in turn can steal the nurturance they have always counted on from other women. Thus is the demon Jewish mother shrunk and manhood reached.

But for our Jewish women writers the journey is far more complicated, for they are both the takers of the food their mothers do not really have to give, and the future providers. They are at once devourers and the devoured, and it is this extra layering in their experience which allows them to enter the pain of their mothers all the men are fleeing from:

from the beginning
she was always dry though
she'd press me close
prying open my lips:
the water warm
the fruit sour brown
apples bruised and soft.
hungry for dark i'd sit
and wait devour dreams
of plain sun and sky
large leaves trunks dark
and wet with sweet thick sap.
but mornings
brought back the space
and cement her weakened
body my head against her
breast: my mouth empty.
yet she was all
my comfort.[3]

This is the beginning of Irena Klepfisz's poem from "The Monkey House and Other Cages." Below the title is a heading in parentheses that says, "The voice is that of a female monkey born and raised in a zoo." Irena Klepfisz was born a girl child in Warsaw, Poland where "during the war / germans were known / to pick up infants / by their feet / swing them through the air / and smash their heads / against plaster walls. / somehow / i managed to escape that fate."[4] She was born in 1941. But the images of violence and incarceration never leave her work. Her monkey poem continues with the daughter's hunger for a warmth and softness that her mother monkey does not have, to the daughter's first rape before the watching mother's eyes.

Mothers turning over their daughters to the hunger of men while they sit by weakly and watch: this occurs over and over in the literature of our Jewish women writers, from Anzia Yezierska's *Bread Givers,* where each of four daughters in turn is sacrificed so that the Talmud scholar father can be free of toil to focus on the holy light: to E. M. Broner's repeated images of women being sacrificed on altars of men's sexual religious ecstasies in *A Weave of Women,* set in Jerusalem. Though a female baby born in ecstasy can be hammered to death through one man's rage during a ritual Purim rite, the women of "the Land" in *A Weave of Women* are expected to be ever-ready and replenishing. Gerda says:

> "My body can walk miles. My feet never get bunions, calluses or plantar warts. My thighs do not rub. . . . I climb Masada up and back down and do it again. I have climbed down Mount Sinai without losing breath, four hours each way. I came down hungry and ready to cook a meal for a crowd."

Another woman asks, "What can't your body do?" Gerda replies:

> "It doesn't know how to say, 'I'm sorry. I apologize. Did I hurt you?' . . . It doesn't know how to feel what other people are feeling. Since the camps I have been careful not to know too much about my surroundings."[5]

The Holocaust in all its horror has become the ultimate expression of the violence done to us; the concentration camp, the black barred cage which locks us all from our own nurturance and warmth; the hunger.

Yezierska's *Bread Givers* is the story of a woman growing up in a Lower East Side ghetto. The book deals with the same hungers passed on from mothers down to daughters, and their helpless rage. The book begins with the narrator in the kitchen trying to peel potatoes and clumsily cutting too much away: "I was about ten years old then. But from always it was heavy on my heart the worries for the house as if I was mother."[6] In this book, it is the mother who must pay all the bills and somehow find the fat to put into her husband's soup so his attention will be free to concentrate upon the Torah. When the mother enters and sees her two oldest daughters unable to find work, the third only wanting to tie ribbons upon her hat and go hear the free music, she lets her market basket fall from her arm in despair. Her rage at her responsibility, having no better place to go, turns on the youngest and most helpless daughter, the narrator, the teller of the tale:

> "*Gazlin! Bandit!*" her cry broke through the house. She picked up the peelings and shook them free before my eyes. "You'd think potatoes grow free in the street. I eat out my heart, running from pushcart to pushcart, only to bargain down a penny on five pounds, and you cut away my flesh like a murderer."[7]

Out of utter repentance the child goes out to gather bits of unburned coal from ashcans, even though it makes her "feel like a beggar and a thief."[8] Far better to rob dregs from strangers than to suck the emptiness of one's own source of life.

But the narrator's childish efforts cannot sustain the women in her family. One by one, the narrator watches her mother and sisters weaken as they feed the father and his work:

> We sat down to the table. With watering mouths and glistening eyes we watched Mother skimming off every bit of fat from the top soup into Father's big plate, leaving for us only the thin, watery part. We watched Father bite into the sour pickle which was special for him only; and waited, trembling, with hunger, for our portion.[9]

The father thanks God for the food and tells his assembled family not to worry about feeling starved, for " 'the real food is God's Holy Torah. . . .' At Father's touch, Mother's sad face turned into smiles. His kind look was like the sun shining on her."[10]

Each of the three older daughters as they go out to seek men will try to find that touch of magic radiance that deadens direst need. Bessie, the oldest, finds it in the "cutter" from her sweat shop for whom she makes a spread of snow-white oil cloth to cover the greasy table in the single room where they all eat and sleep and live. But though she has no dowry and is already considered old, her father will not let her go, for she is the best worker, the best wage earner, and the "burden bearer" of the family. Later, after she has lost the man she really loves, her father sells her to an old ugly fishmonger who wants her to raise his five unmanageable grieving children whose mother has just died. She almost rebels, the fishmonger repels her so, but the needs of the bereaved little ones soon draw her in.

Masha, the beautiful one, falls in love with a musician, but her father will not let him in because he is not holy enough. The man her father picks for her, because he makes believe he is a diamond merchant, keeps her half-starved in a hovel.

And the mother, grown old before her time, stands by and watches this, and watches the third daughter, who loved a poet once ("False gods," the father said), sold to a gambler who takes her to empty riches far away on the west coast.

The mother, even as she dies from a gangrenous foot that could have been cut off had anybody cared, had she herself cared, is remembered by the neighbors only by how well she starved herself:

> "Such a good mother, such a virtuous wife," wailed a shawled woman with a nursing baby in her arms and two little tots hanging to her skirts. "Never did she allow herself a bit to eat but left-overs, never a dress but the rags her daughters had thrown away."
> ". . . Only two days ago she told me how they cook the fish in her village sweet and sour—and now, she is dead."
> At this, all the women began rocking and swaying in a wailing chorus.[11]

This is one level of the tale, the hungry mother giving all. But in its very unfolding we find a major turning. For the fourth daughter, who has seen her mother and sisters slain by the age-old patterns, rebels. She leaves her father's house amidst his curses and his blows to find an education and a life that she can call her own. She learns to gather strength from all she suffered through, and will not bend her will under the whips of the husbands who enslave her sisters, her teachers in the college she forces her way into, or the soup server in the corner restaurant who only dishes stew with meat in it to men. Using what she has learned in hunger in the ghetto, she rises in school and in the world. And, interestingly, in her self-made rise, she becomes the only daughter who can take their mother's shyly offered new support. Her mother travels miles to bring her bread and herring when she is starving, studying alone and outcast. The others berate her for going to college, leaving her mother alone to die. But her mother, on her deathbed, greets with a radiant joy this last daughter who has turned into a "teacherin." It is a high moment of the book when, at her mother's funeral, this daughter watches the others let the undertaker slice their clothes to tatters, rending them according to the old biblical law, and refuses to be a part of it: "I don't believe in this. It's my only suit, and I need it for work. Tearing it wouldn't bring Mother back to life again."

Anzia Yezierska, in her work and in her facing of the hungers that have crippled all women, all mothers in the old tradition, has given us all a chance to carry on the lives our mothers never gave themselves or us.

"Mother, I'm pregnant with a baby girl." This is the ever-varying refrain that lilts and sobs and sings through E. M. Broner's book, *Her Mothers:*

> *"Mother, I'm giving birth to a baby girl."*
> *"What does she want to do with her life?"*
> *"Be a mother."*
> *"And then what?"*
> *"A grandmother."*
> *"No more?"*
> *"A great-grandmother."*
> *"And what else?"*
> *"Nothing else."*[12]

This novel interweaves tales of mothers and daughters in modern times to our most ancient foremothers, through the reclamation of literary "mentor-mothers" who, more often than not, gave their life blood away to men. It is the story of a Jewish mother's search for her own biological daughter, conceived at a time in her life when she could not accept or give. The daughter has now grown into her own nerve-wracking adolescence and runs away. It is the tale of how only through finding the strong mothers of the past, the female power-figures, and the powers in the self, can any mother truly have her daughter back. It is a long and complicated journey, through sob stories, kitsch, and utmost ecstasies, through petty suburban confusions, and the horrors of the Holocaust.

Here is the story of Sarah and Abraham retold in the section entitled "Foremothers" beginning, "Looking for Past Mothers, Way Past Mothers":

Four are the Matriarchs: The First Matriarch

"Mother, I'm pregnant with a baby girl."

"May she be the mother of heroes."

She journeyed to the South for there was a famine in the land. . . .

Avram suffered from thirst, from fear. She like a camel did not seem to have his hunger or his need for water. . . . So he offered her strong body to the passing soldiers to obtain what he could not do without.

They took their pleasure with her while Avram sat outside of the tent, drinking their water, eating their provisions. Then the soldiers brought her to the Great House. They pulled aside her garments from her body. Despite famine, the flesh curved. Despite thirst, the shoulder and buttocks meat was juicy. She was given to Pharaoh, who had her while Avram sat outside of the Great House counting his newly gained sheep, oxen, asses, camels. . . .

The nomadic years passed. Maybe because of the great journey in the desert, or the early famine, or the time she was had by shepherds and soldiers, by princes and pharaoh, Sarai in no way thickened, never bore fruit. All life around her fattened—the camel, the oxen, the she-goat. Trees bore fruit—the date, the fig—but she remained boney.[13]

The great journey in the desert, the early famine, the dryness of the breasts Irena Klepfisz's daughter-monkey first sucked, don't we all know them all? In the larger-than-life biblical stories the women who were emptied too much became quite literally barren. Later on it was only the feelings of giving and receiving that were sucked dry. But recently our women writers, in retracing those old hungry journeys and those thefts, are teaching us how to take in, to suckle and to grow again.

Beatrix, the mother, starts to cook and feed herself. She reads:

"*Embryein* (gr.) to swell inside. Compare to *sauerkraut*. . . . Each leaf is added, each thick, veined sheet. . . ." If an "unhatched young vertebrate," an "embryo," soaks in that female brine, . . . and all of life is pickled and floating and will be sucked by that originator, that fruitful, happy, lucky originator, no wonder that men, not feminine, must hate us. We are the inception, the water jar, the nourishment, the expelling from the Garden of Eden.

How could they not hate us? . . . They grow too big to slip back in through the slits of nipple, the eye of the navel, the mouth of the womb.

So they punish us at birth and give us pain and punish us in life and give us pain.[14]

It is only through the disconnection with the life-denying forces that women will be able to have back their lives, their long-lost mothers, and give birth to daughters breathing and alive and strong. This is the theme of *A Lament for Three Women,* a play by Karen Malpede in which women of three generations wait in a special cancer research center for their respective father, son, and husband to complete their dying. They have all lived only for these men. Naomi, the oldest, remembers how when her son was young she used to rise with him.

"to light the fire and make the breakfast, pack his lunch, and get him off to school. What a flurry we would make in the kitchen. He would pull on his trousers standing by the stove, hopping from one foot to the other. I would stir the oatmeal over his jumping head. Sweeten it with jam or honey, pour in rich milk. And bread, big slices of black bread with cheese between them. . . .

The last weekend they let me take him home I made honey cake for him and lentil soup . . . we drank wine together. . . . I would have lit the candles but I was so busy in the kitchen, I missed the sunset. . . . When I sit with him I pretend he has another fever. I sing to him. A grown man. I sing to him and stroke his forehead. Sitting by his bed I half forget and half expect the fever to break suddenly and his eyes to open clear and out of pain."[15]

Naomi's memories of mothering her son first come out only in a sensual ecstasy. We feel the fullness of each piece of food she handles to pass on to him. But as the younger women tell their stories, Naomi lets her voice rise in fury that the son she fed so well now moans and only feels that he has been betrayed by her:

"I've prayed to God to end my life instead of his. But with every pain he suffers I am stronger. Every time he cries my determination grows. The joke of motherhood. When her child needs her, she endures. Joke again. The child never feels more abandoned, never turns against her with more bitter rage than he does now, watching his own mother watch him die."[16]

Ruth too has always mothered men. She tells of how her father who loved her as he had never loved her mother turned from her in violent rage at having been aroused. But it is Rachel, whose father cried in her arms when he found out that he was dying, kissed her neck, her ear lobes and her lips and made her cry, who felt betrayed when in his pain he turned back to her mother. It is Rachel who asks the other two women for the mothering she never got from men. She says:

> "Naomi, as much as your son needed you when he was young, I need you now. Or more than that. When he was a baby sucking at your breast. No. More. When he was a fetus breathing your blood, taking his form from your flesh. I need you that much. I give up my father as I have to. Come with me now. Give up your son since you must. . . . Fear of death keeps him living. Fear of life keeps you clinging to him. It's not unnatural to be frightened, living is a frightening occupation. But remember, you made children from the center of you where eating, feeling, loving are united. Find the healthy breath inside you that allows you to still his heavy breathing. Take life for yourself from the one who is dying."[17]

Lament ends with a mourning, a keening and wailing which is the only way the hurt and hungry women can come close to one another. *Rebeccah,* Karen Malpede's second play, starts with a mother smothering an infant son who cries while they hide during a pogrom. It chronicles the mother's struggle to salvage her life with her surviving daughter, after the men turn her out because of what she's done.

Malpede was very young when she started to write her plays. Her early work goes deep into the roots of human tragedy, the horrors done to women by the world of men. But gradually we see how with the strengthening of feminist philosophy, the themes of love and hope and healing are beginning to supplant the hungers and the pain. Her newest play, *Making Peace,* is about the use of the most primal forms of nurture to undo those barren hungers that have made us hate. It is a play affirming all of human possibility through letting in the wild ecstatic loves the world has not allowed. Upon a heavenly mound three spirits of Utopians who have been hungry in their lives meet and undo the sorrows of their personal pasts, then go back down to earth to help the living ones erase denial. The spirit of Mary Wollstonecraft takes Shaker Mother Ann into her arms and says:

"Mother, take my breast, pretend you gave me birth and that I grew without resentment, without fear, strong enough to share that blessed gift with you. Suck, mother, suck. I suckled both my daughters thus. It was only then I understood the wild release that comes from giving love boundless as the ocean's own throbbing underneath the suckling moon."[18]

Thus, through learning to suckle herself and other women has the hungry Jewish mother been transformed. From E. M. Broner's reinvention of sacred ceremonies of birthing and feeding among a community of women in the old stone house in *A Weave of Women* to Irena Klepfisz's final poem in *periods of stress,* written to a woman she loves, women are finding new ways of giving birth to life within each other and themselves, of being reborn:

last night i dreamt i was
a gaunt and lifeless tree
and you climbed into me to nest . . .
wherever your human skin
touched my rough bark i
sprouted branches till
lush with leaves i grew
all green and silver frail
like tinsel holding you
asleep in my wooden arms.[19]

Women are beginning to learn their own softness and their songs. Thus it is a young woman, Jeannie, the granddaughter in *Tell Me a Riddle,* who puts to words the music the dying woman heard but never spoke. She looks so beautiful as she tends her grandmother that her grandfather wonders if she is in love. And, in a way, of course she is, with all the songs of all the generations of women, long buried, maimed and trapped. But through the ardor of her listening, we feel that she might have the strength to set it free.

It is the voice of Tillie Olsen singing hope, through Jeannie, in the last passage of the book:

"Grandaddy, Grandaddy, don't cry. She is not there, she promised me. On the last day, she said she would go back to when she first heard music, a little girl on the road of the village where she was born . . . . Leave her there, Grandaddy, it is all right. She promised me. Come back, come back and help her poor body to die."[20]

Thus shall we all go back to where the music in us is and find the music in our mothers that will help us live. As *Her Mother* ends:

"Mother, I'm pregnant with a baby girl."
"What is she doing?"
"She is singing."
"Why is she singing?"
"Because she is unafraid."[21]

NOTES

1. Tillie Olsen, *Tell Me a Riddle* (New York: Dell, 1956), pp. 92–93.
2. Olsen, p. 123.
3. Irena Klepfisz, poem from "The Monkey House and Other Cages," *Frontiers* 3, No. 2 (1978), 12.
4. Irena Klepfisz, *periods of stress* (Brooklyn: self-published, 1975), p. 7.
5. E. M. Broner, *A Weave of Women* (New York: Holt, Rinehart, and Winston, 1978), pp. 258–59.
6. Anzia Yezierska, *Bread Givers* (1925; reprint ed., New York: Persea Books, 1975), p. 1.
7. Yezierska, p. 7.
8. Yezierska, p. 7.
9. Yezierska, p. 10.
10. Yezierska, p. 11.
11. Yezierska, p. 254.
12. E. M. Broner, *Her Mothers* (New York: Holt, Rinehart, and Winston, 1975), pp. 93–94.
13. Broner, *Her Mothers,* pp. 149–51.
14. Broner, *Her Mothers,* p. 217.
15. Karen Malpede, "A Lament for Three Women," in *A Century of Plays by American Women,* ed. Rachel France (New York: Richard Rosen Press, 1979), p. 206.
16. Malpede, pp. 204–5.
17. Malpede, p. 207.

18. Malpede, "Making Peace: A Fantasy" (unpublished play, performed by the New Cycle Theatre, Brooklyn, New York, 21 February 1979), Scene 7.
19. Klepfisz, *periods of stress,* p. 61.
20. Olsen, p. 125.
21. Broner, *Her Mothers,* p. 241.

The Lilith Question

Aviva Cantor

After the Holy One created the first human being, Adam, He said: "It is not good for Adam to be alone." He created a woman, also from the earth, and called her Lilith.

They quarreled immediately. She said: "I will not lie below you." He said, "I will not lie below you, but above you. For you are fit to be below me and I above you."

She responded: "We are both equal because we both come from the earth."

Neither listened to the other. When Lilith realized what was happening, she pronounced the Ineffable Name of God and flew off into the air.

Adam rose in prayer before the Creator, saying, "The woman you gave me has fled from me." Immediately the Holy One sent three angels after her.

The Holy One said to Adam: "If she wants to return, all the better. If not, she will have to accept that one hundred of her children will die every day."

The angels went after her, finally locating her in the sea, in the powerful waters in which the Egyptians were destined to perish. They told her what God had said, and she did not want to return. (ALPHABET OF BEN SIRA 23A-B)

And God created the human species in His own image . . . male and female created He them. (GENESIS: 1:27)

THE most ancient biblical account of the Creation relates that God created the first man and the first woman at the same time. Jewish legends tell us that the first woman was Lilith.

Lilith, we learn, felt herself to be Adam's equal ("We are both from the earth") but Adam refused to accept her equality. Lilith, determined to retain her independence and dignity, and choosing loneliness over subservience, flew away from Adam and the Garden of Eden.

Jewish tradition characterized Lilith after her escape from Adam as a demon and embellished this reputation with legend upon legend of her vengeful activities to harm children and women who give birth in rooms without industrial-strength amulets to ward her off. The *Alphabet of Ben Sira* provides us with the most coherent account of the Lilith myth, embodying features of past legends and providing the basis for future additions. The *Alphabet* tells of Lilith's struggle for equality and her escape, Adam's complaint to God, and the dispatching of three angels to bring his recalcitrant mate back. She refused to return and accepted the punishment of 100 of her "demon children" dying daily, for which she takes revenge. The demonic Lilith overshadowed the original independent Lilith in all subsequent legends to the point where the name Lilith engendered only the association of demon/witch. It is this demonic image which has both reflected and shaped men's thoughts and feelings about women for generations. But the time for reassessment of the Lilith myth has arrived.

Who is Lilith? Or, more to the point, which is the true, the real Lilith—the rebel against tyranny or the wild-haired vengeful witch? Is Lilith a myth without historical basis, and, if so, why was it necessary to invent her? Or does she embody a clue to our past and if so, what?

Is Lilith a model for Jewish women and if so, can only part of her history constitute the model? Should we forget her revolt because of her later (alleged!) crimes and thus reject her; or should we forget her later crimes and focus only on her revolt because only this is significant; or do both parts have value for us?

All these are aspects of the The Lilith Question.

Let's begin by taking a close look at Lilith as she appears in the *Alphabet of Ben Sira.* We immediately see how significant it is that she perceived herself as an equal to Adam, to man; her consciousness of equality was not only high, but it was a given, a natural thought process. Anything less than equality was unthought of and unthinkable, unnatural.

Not only does Lilith immediately recognize tyranny for what it is, but she immediately resists it, too. Nowhere do we see her complain (as Adam does); she states her case and takes risks for her dignity. She is courageous and decisive, willing to accept the consequences of her action.

Her strength of character and commitment of self is inspiring. For independence and freedom from tyranny she is prepared to forsake the economic security of the Garden of Eden and to accept loneliness and exclusion from society. Her strength of character also comes through in her taking total responsibility for her life. Note that she does not appeal to God to straighten out her relationship with Adam. She draws on her own strength; she is self-nurturing, self-sustaining.

Lilith is a *powerful* female. She radiates strength, assertiveness; she refuses to cooperate in her own victimization. By acknowledging Lilith's revolt and even in telling of her vengeful activities, myth-makers also acknowledge Lilith's power. Even if we accept Lilith's vengeful activities (and whether or not to accept them is a subject we will deal with later), we can regard them as having originated in self-defense against male domination and as a consequence of having to fight on alone, century after century, for her independence. What men are saying, really, is that Lilith "fights dirty." But this is a meaningless concept designed to keep women from developing and utilizing their strength to fight, period. Lilith, it must be emphasized, is a fighter and a fighter in a good cause.

Finally, besides having physical power, she has spiritual power and knowledge. She utters God's secret name and flies off to the Red Sea (significantly, the scene of the Jews' transition from the security of bondage in Egypt to the insecurity of freedom in the desert). Adam did not know or utter the Ineffable Name. But Lilith is a knower of secret wisdom.

We must bear in mind here that the Lilith stories, like the rest of our tradition, were written by men. We know that most of whatever women have invented or created has been destroyed or discounted, and very little has come down to us, certainly nothing in its pure, original form. We must consider the possibility that the story of Lilith's revolt may be one of women's creations which was told by mother to daughter over many generations before surfacing in the *Alphabet* and then being contaminated with male bias.

The Lilith story may be a clue to our own history, reflecting some assertive, rebellious behavior of women in the past. Lilith may represent a whole group, a whole generation; or she may reflect the existence of a type of woman who appeared in generation after generation, a woman who would not be dominated, a woman who demanded equality with man. Or she may embody the thoughts and feelings of women about their equality, even if they could not act on them in their generation. With so few materials about women, particularly of this nature, it would be unthinkable for us to let Lilith be forgotten simply because of the male biases grafted onto the story of her revolt.

These legends of Lilith-as-demon, the vengeful female witch, are, of course, not unique to Jewish culture and tradition. Many scholars theorize that vengeful female deities or demons, like the Greek *hecatae,* represent the vestiges of the dying Matriarchy or are an attempt by men to discredit the Matriarchy.

What we have to explore are the uniquely Jewish aspects of the Lilith story, and how they relate to the Jewish experience, to Jewish history. After all, Jews lived among many different peoples and were subject to a bombardment of cultural and religious concepts and myths from all sides. What they accepted is important because it shows us what Jews perceived as necessary and appropriate to Jewish life and its continuity. How they transmuted what they accepted is also significant for this reason.

The account of Lilith's revolt in the *Alphabet* is, to the best of my knowledge, intrinsically Jewish; no non-Jewish source tells of a female struggle for equality or gives it as a reason for the vengeful behavior of a female demon. This is especially important to us in exploring how the Lilith myth connects with our unique history.

What is particularly intriguing about the Lilith myth is that most of the legends about her developed in Exile, either after the Babylonian Exile (586 B.C.E.) and certainly after the Roman deportations of Jews into captivity (70 C.E.). Lilith appears in the Babylonian Talmud in rudimentary form; her character is developed in the *Zohar* and other medieval mystical works. No scholar has dated the *Alphabet of Ben Sira* but all agree it was written in the Gaonic period, before 1000 C.E. The Babylonian Talmud, *Zohar, Alphabet* are all texts written or compiled outside Eretz Israel presumably after 70 C.E., although they may draw on earlier legends, oral or written.

The destruction of the First Jewish Commonwealth in Eretz Israel and the deportation of most of the population to Babylonia was a shock; the destruction of the Second Jewish Commonwealth was a traumatic watershed in Jewish history. It marked the Jews' break from life in their own homeland, to existence as an international minority with no control over their own destiny. For the next 2,000 years (until 1948), Jews would live at the fringes of societies, marginal to their socioeconomic structures, their history, culture, religion, politics and passions; subject to the whim of the ruling class; to summary expulsion; to persecution by the law and the lawless; to humiliation; and to murder.

Exile was understood and perceived by Jews as a threat to Jewish survival that had to be endured and overcome.

When the Jews went into Exile, they decided that the only way to survive without a land was through study (create one, two, three Yavnehs). *Halakhah*—Jewish law—became the constitution of a Jewish "government in exile" under which scholars made basic decisions. The model role for Jewish men was to be scholars (this model, begun earlier, reached its apotheosis during the Exile).

Even before the Exile, Jewish society was patriarchal. The role of woman under patriarchy is that of enabler. The woman is programmed to submit to and please men, doing whatever it is that men of a particular time or place demand in order to enable them to do their thing and to ensure their "manhood" and power. Part of being an enabler involves withdrawing from the areas of activity that men have marked off as their domain and which, thus, in the absence of women, come to define "manhood." Enabling also means altruism: doing what is in the man's interest, the family's interests or society's interests, not one's own.

The Bible portrays women in various positive model enabler roles. In the Exile, it became even more important that Jewish women continue to function as enablers because of the threat to Jewish survival. The enabler role expanded to include doing everything to make possible men's study of the Torah. Lilith is the embodiment of the woman who refuses to be an enabler.

Elizabeth Janeway, in her pioneering study *Man's World, Woman's Place,* points out that every positive role has a negative flip side, a "shadow role." The shrew, she writes, is the shadow role of the public pleasing woman; the bitch, of the private loving woman; the witch, of the all-giving mother. Negative roles support the patriarchal order just as positive ones do; the positive ones are promises, the negative ones, threats.

Lilith is a negative, shadow role, the flip side of Eve. Eve is the enabler ("helpmeet"), Lilith, the disabler; Eve, the "mother of all life," Lilith, a destroyer of life. In creating the Lilith shadow role, men are telling a woman that if she is independent, assertive, free, as Lilith was, she'll end up a frigid nymphomaniac childless witch.

It is especially significant that Lilith, the only important negative female role model invented by Jews, was primarily an Exile invention. Why was her creation as a negative role model so important at this particular juncture in history?

Let's look at the unifying theme behind the three "crimes" of the postrebellion Lilith. She allegedly: kills child-bearing (pregnant and birthing) women; injures newborn babes (boys until the bris, girls until twenty days of age); excites men in their sleep and takes their sperm to manufacture demon children to replace her own. Of all the indeterminate number of qualities a negative role could embody it was precisely these three that were incorporated in Lilith. All three of these embody several crucial male fears: loss of potency and "manhood," loss of a woman's companionship and emotional support, and threat to survival. While all these male fears have been embodied separately in various non-Jewish myths, their coalescence into one Jewish mythical character at this point in history is not hard to understand. The Exile was a stress situation in which Jewish men feared the loss of manhood, the destruction of their morale, and the extinction of the Jewish people.

In patriarchal societies where a man's manhood is defined in whole or part by his ability to father children, the fear that Lilith (woman) can prevent men from having children in one way or another means that she robs them of their manhood. In their powerless condition in Exile, Jewish men needed to prove their maleness to differentiate themselves from women, the group whose condition of ultimate powerlessness they feared being reduced to.

Fathering children also guaranteed survival of the Jewish people, something that was threatened in the Exile and that Jews were anxious about. Another fear was woman's power to withhold herself from man, either by refusing comfort or even her very presence (Lilith actually left Adam). In the stress situation of the Exile, Jewish men may have been especially anxious that women would not fulfill their role of providers of emotional support. All these fears of Jewish men were projected onto woman as if she held the power to make them into reality by refusing to stay in the subservient enabler role.

When the Exile reduced Jews to subservience, it was a discontinuity for Jewish men, a condition they were unfamiliar with, a situation in which they felt they had lost all their bearings—in which the whole order of the universe was turned upside down.

For Jewish women, like all women, it was not different in kind, only in degree—more stress, more problems, but not a discontinuity: the real ruler was still at home. Perhaps they were therefore better able to cope with the practical realities than were the men.

As the men needed them more and perceived their strength, they may have feared that the women would use their strength in their own self-interest and stop being enablers. It had to be made forcefully clear to the women that their strength was tolerable—even desirable—*as long as it did not connect with power.*

We can ask here, could it be that there was also some rebellion in the women's ranks at this time that also contributed to the men's need to threaten them with a negative role myth? Janeway writes that negative roles often appear in times when there is social change and when power is no longer bound by customary limits. New roles are called for but at the same time, people feel nervous because they do not know what the new role player expects of them. They want to "separate themselves from the troublemaker and hold him at a distance. *The means they find at hand is to call up the negative shadow role.*"

Perhaps women did become more assertive at this time because their situation demanded it. Men must have realized that this assertiveness could be harnessed to altruism, thus creating an even better enabler than before. Thus began the role model of the altruistic-assertive woman, personified in Esther, also an Exile creation. Actually it is Esther, not Eve, who is the flip side of Lilith, the nonaltruistic-assertive woman.

Megillat (Scroll of) *Esther,* which tells the story of Purim, is an excellent source for the substantiation of some of the assumptions we have been dealing with here: the threat to Jewish survival in the Exile, and the role of the Jewish woman as an altruistic-assertive enabler.

The *megillah* tells how Jews in Persia were apparently leading a good life but actually lived at the edge of a volcano. When the king, persuaded by his premier that the Jews were bad for his Empire, put his approval on a pogrom, there was nothing the Jews could really do. What saved the Jews? Mostly Esther's action, first in becoming Queen, which necessitated her living apart from her own people and being a closet Jew, all because her cousin, Mordechai, thought it best (altruism, self-sacrifice); and then, taking her life in her hands by asking the king to save her people (assertiveness). Esther's altruistic assertiveness, which is obviously "good for the Jews," is sharply contrasted in the *megillah* with the nonaltruistic assertiveness of her predecessor, Vashti, who lost her crown (some even say her head, too) for refusing to obey the king. The punishment of both Vashti and Lilith states, in effect: Jewish women, be enablers . . . or else.

One final word about Lilith as an Exile creation. The real

threat to the Jews, as we know, was not that women would rebel, but the Exile *itself.* For it is the Exile that made Jews powerless and put them at the mercy of the rulers, on the fringes of society and into roles that turned the masses against them. Exile is a threat, but the Exile cultures—or more accurately, the adoption of Exile cultures (assimilation)—is a seductive solution that in most periods was held out by non-Jews as an inducement to fame, fortune and sometimes even life itself. Many Jews were seduced by assimilation, only to find it sterile and unsatisfying.

Lilith is seductive but unsatisfying. She saps a man's "life fluid," a metaphor for strength; she destroys his possibility for achieving immortality. She attacks Jews when they're most vulnerable or unaware. She robs them of their power and of their future. Lilith is thus in some ways a metaphor for the Exile itself.

We have seen how the creation of Lilith as a negative role model served to coalesce the fears of the men and project them onto the woman, thus reflecting a fear of woman's power to refuse to be the enabler; and to warn all women of the fate awaiting a woman who refuses to be an enabler.

Is there anything we can learn from all the negative portrayals of Lilith? Are they of any use to us? Should we reject them outright?

Ahad Ha'am, founder of "spiritual Zionism," once wrote an essay called "Half-Consolation." He asked: how can Jews know if what the non-Jews say about Jewish inferiority isn't really true? Ahad Ha'am cited the blood libel. Look at it, he said. If non-Jews can believe this dangerous nonsense, they're wrong about Jews' "inferiority," too.

Similarly, as we struggle for our liberation, we hear men insult and vilify feminists as man-haters and child-haters, destroyers of the family in particular and Jewish life in general. Is this, we might ask tremblingly, *could* this be true? So it's not at all bad to have in front of us the Lilith story with all its ugly smears. How candid it is about why Lilith is punished! If men could have invented these hateful smears—like non-Jews invented the blood libel—if there is so much hostility toward women inside their addled brains, then there is no need to think there is any truth in the latest pseudo-sociological smears of feminists. Women need not fear that if they become assertive and independent, they will no longer be "women" but monstrosities, as men say Lilith became. Such smears and lies are, of course, something we should expect. Lilith is a role-breaker and, as Janeway points out, role-breakers should be prepared to find themselves "attacked, regarded as unattractive and frightening [and running] into all kinds of hostility."

Knowing all this now we have the choice of how to look at Lilith, or rather, at what aspect of her character to focus on when we look at her. In doing so, we can bear in mind that mythological characters have never remained constant or immutable; they are always changing in response to human need. The character of Lilith changed—but so did that of Elijah—from the fire-eating prophet of First Commonwealth times to the latter-day jolly beggar who wandered from *shtetl* to *shtetl,* pack on back. There is nothing in tradition which dictates the acceptance of either the later Elijah or of the earlier Elijah as the "real" Elijah.

Furthermore, Jewish tradition has been very flexible in what it seeks to emphasize in role models. King David is a much-beloved character in Jewish lore. But tradition could easily have emphasized his immoral personal behavior and cavalier political maneuverings instead of his love of God and the Jewish people. Had this been done. David could have become a negative role-model of adulterer and Machiavellian politician. Jewish tradition, however, chose to forget and forgive those reprehensible aspects of his character because it did not regard them as intrinsic to his soul.

It is both necessary and within our tradition to use the same approach with Lilith, bearing in mind the aspect of human needs as a factor in focusing on specific aspects of a historical or mythological character. What is intrinsic to Lilith, what is the most central aspect of her character is her struggle for independence, her courage in taking risks, her commitment to the equality of woman and man based on their creation as equals by God. It is this Lilith who is faithful to her innermost self, her nature and her principles.

The other aspects of the Lilith character can in no way be considered central to her very essence, because they do not flow out of a commitment to self but are a reaction to an outside event: Adam's refusal to accept her as an equal. Had Adam accepted her equality, these negative traits would be absent; in fact, there would be no war between the sexes at all, a war based on men's unwillingness to accept women's equality.

The traits attributed to Lilith after she lost her struggle for equality are tainted with male bias and fear. Moreover, Lilith's postrevolt "character" cannot be accepted because it is not a character at all but a hodge-podge of negative traits that contradict each other (seductive / frigid; mother of demons / sterile) and thus cancel each other out. We can relegate all these contradictory traits to the realm of differing speculations as opposed to a definite image that all agreed upon. We can thus do what Jewish tradition does with King David: accept the essence, glorify the essence, and reject the later additions as contradictory, contaminated by fear and distrust, and not central to the intrinsic nature of the character of Lilith.

Finally, we must ask ourselves: which Lilith is closer to the spirit of the first account in Genesis, the account that tells us how God first created human beings—the female who accepts the idea of equality and fights for it, or the female who has lost sight of the original struggle and persists in seeking revenge? There is no doubt that the Lilith who claimed her equal birthright with Adam is closer in spirit to both the original biblical account and to Jewish women of today.

Jews have periodically created movements to "return to the source" of Judaism, and Jewish history is replete with such efforts. When we struggle for equality of woman and man and see Lilith as the personification of that struggle, we are part of this tradition of returning to the source and building from its pure, uncontaminated foundation. This pure beauty is contained in the words "And God created the human species . . . man and woman created He them." The equality of man and woman is embodied in that sentence. This equality must be embodied in our lives if humankind and all the values we hold dear are to survive.

Marriages Made in Heaven?[1]
BATTERED JEWISH WIVES

Mimi Scarf

JEWS living in the Diaspora have frequently spread much propaganda about themselves in order to keep a low profile, and as a consequence, have tended to downplay social problems of their own. Thus, Jews are not alcoholics, Jewish fathers do not desert their children, Jewish mothers do not batter their children, Jewish men do not beat their wives. Many Jews have come to believe these myths and have convinced themselves that wife beating in Jewish homes is aberrant. Although efforts of the feminist movement have brought to public attention the scope of violence committed against women in general in the United States, until now we did not know that wife beating is alive and well in Jewish families.[2]

Traditionally, Jewish women have been taught, sometimes in very subtle ways, to believe in the stereotypical Jewish husband—that he is smart, successful, of sound mental health, generous with his family, and very little given to violence. They were also taught to believe that a Jewish family is sacrosanct, and that the Jewish home is a bulwark against the "outside" world. Because they have been socialized according to these traditional beliefs, Jewish women who are beaten by their husbands are almost always convinced that it is their fault. *Jewish men do not beat their wives. It does not happen in Jewish families.*

This centrality of the image of the family in Jewish life, indeed, this idealized concept of the Jewish family itself, while not causing wife beating, does prevent women from seeking help, and prevents those who are in a position to give help from giving it. Rabbis and other Jews in the helping professions, in their zeal to promote the Jewish home and family, frequently prevent themselves from recognizing that problems that afflict other cultural, ethnic, or religious groups exist in their own. Thus a situation has been created in which a very strong image contradicts reality; this in turn leads to a cognitive dissonance, for those involved deny what is happening to them by clinging to what they believe ought to be the reality.

Portrait of a Battered Jewish Wife

Premarital Experiences

The battered Jewish wife lived with parents who did not hit each other, and she would not have approved if they had. Her mother may have spanked her but she was rarely hit by her father, and she describes her childhood home as warm and loving. She would not consider using corporal punishment to control her own children (except for a "potch" [slap] in extreme situations), because she believes no one should ever hit anyone. She does not include arguing or loud voices in her definition of domestic violence, because she thinks typical Jewish families are vocal about everything. She definitely identified with her father, whom she thinks of as being kind and sweet and gentle and patient, though not as strong as her mother, and she wanted to be like him.

Although her parents operated under strict male-female roles with the mother responsible for the home and the father for the business, she was treated as an equal with her brothers in almost every way except, perhaps, if her brother went to *heder* [afternoon Hebrew school] to study for bar mitzvah and she did not, which she still resents. There were Jewish books around her home, Shabbat candles were lit, Jewish holidays were celebrated, and the home and family were considered an inviolable sanctuary because it was Jewish. She had no reason to believe that her future would not be as her past, and she daydreamed that she would marry a Jewish boy and she would spend her life surrounded by a loving husband and children.

Most likely, the battered Jewish wife dated only Jewish boys, and unless she lived in a dormitory (or had comparable living arrangements) she lived with her parents until she married. She and her husband knew each other for many months before they married, and they had a formal engagement and an elaborate wedding in a synagogue. Both sets of parents were delighted with the marriage and talked of it as if it were a match "made in heaven." Everyone had great hopes for their future.

Rough treatment started during the courtship, but the Jewish wife did not identify it as a precursor to violence. Only much later did she recall practical jokes that had hurt her—being hugged so hard that it brought tears to her eyes, or her arm being twisted by her fiancé when he helped her with her coat.

She also remembers other violent outbursts, though not necessarily against her, such as slamming doors, throwing objects for her to catch (such as a telephone or a book), but which missed and hit her in the face or head. All done in good humor, of course, or so she thought. If she wanted to back out of the marriage before the wedding, her mother assured her that her feelings were normal, that all brides are nervous and have second thoughts at the last minute, or that the momentum of the wedding plans was too great and presents were already arriving. She was told to pull herself together, that everything would be all right.

The Honeymoon

The battered Jewish woman, typically married in her early 20's, was greatly disappointed by her honeymoon. Even though her husband may have shown great promise as a lover during courtship, he was ineffectual or displayed no interest in sex on their honeymoon. She returned very upset and fearful that that was how things were going to be, and she began to have grave doubts about spending the rest of her life with her husband. Some women reported that their new husbands had either ignored them altogether or had initiated their controlling tactics during this first time alone together. One husband refused to allow his new wife to buy necessities even though she had brought her own money along, and some husbands cut the honeymoon short.

When they returned from their honeymoon, the soon-to-be battered Jewish wife often went to her parents, saying she was afraid she had made a terrible mistake and wanted to end the marriage. She was told by her mother that the first year is hard, that things would get better, to stick it out—or that she must be mistaken, because this marriage had been made in heaven.

The First Beating

But things do not get better, and before long, the horror starts and she takes her first beating. If the attacks do not begin immediately, they surely do during the first pregnancy, when the husband directs punches and kicks to his wife's abdomen. The Jewish wife-beater's attacks do not increase in intensity over the years: they are severe from the first.

A Jewish husband attacks with fists and feet, rarely with belts (though some Jewish women report being beaten with belts on their buttocks). He never uses whips or chains, and very rarely knives (though threats with knives are not unusual). He throws heavy objects at his wife's head and face, beats her on her back, chest, stomach, arms, legs, breasts, buttocks, and face. The wife is slapped on the face more than punched there—possibly because her husband does not want any bruises to show. Rape is usually not a consequence of the beating, and it is unusual if sex follows.

After a beating, a Jewish wife is bruised and bleeds, and sustains broken bones. It is difficult to think of a part of her body which has not been hit, and she is demoralized and appalled by the beatings. Contrary to the beliefs of the uninitiated, she does not "like it or she would leave," nor does she "ask for it" in any way.

Subsequent Beatings

The reasons for the beatings vary with the personality of the husband and his mood of the moment. One woman was beaten because she cried; her husband said she was behaving like a spoiled brat. Another was beaten because she had "hogged" the covers when they were sleeping, one because she initiated sex and her husband was not interested, still another because he initiated sex and she was not interested. One woman reported having been beaten because she would not let a newspaper rest on her lap for fear that the newsprint would ruin a new dress. Whatever the reasons, whatever she does, the beatings continue. They take place at any time of night or day except never when the children are in sight of the house, or awake. She is astonished and overwhelmed each time she is beaten.

The battered Jewish wife does not scream, not once, through all the beatings, throughout all the years. Nor does she try to run away or defend herself. To her, there is a quality of unreality about it all. She cannot believe it is happening to her because *Jewish men do not do this sort of thing. This does not happen to Jewish women.* During all her beatings, the Jewish wife just lies there apologizing for what she has done, for what she is making her husband do to her, promising never to do "it" again, whatever "it" was. Her husband repeats over and over again, "Look what you are making me do to you. I hate you for what you make me do." He may even cry and beg her forgiveness—the first time.

When the beating is over, and the husband loses his strength, he may go to a movie, visit friends, go to work, or just go into another room. Often, his wife does not know where he has gone, just that he has left and she is alone. When he is gone, the wife takes a shower and straightens up the room where the battle took place (usually the living room or the kitchen, unless the children are home, and then it is the bedroom). She cleans up food which he has thrown at her or on the floor, or mops up the whiskey that he threw in her face from the sparkling floor she has so often waxed. Or she picks up the broken dishes.

While cleaning up, she tries to figure out what went wrong. She thought she was a good Jewish wife and mother. She took care of her husband, put his well-being before her own, cooked his favorite meals (she takes pride in being a gourmet cook), did his laundry, listened to him carefully when he talked about his job or classes if he were still a student, and encouraged him. She has tried to be kind and supportive and loving, and she does not know where she has failed.

The Jewish wife is determined not to do "it" again, determined to repair her own flaws. She will not disturb him when he is studying, or watching television, or listening to music. She will do his laundry, cook for him, set the table with flowers, buy him a present, take wonderful care of the children, and remain a lady. She hopes he will see the error of his ways and will be so conscience-stricken that he will apologize and be sweet and solicitous; then they will live happily ever after. Of course, it is all imagination. The beatings continue.

Trying to Get Help

After a few beatings, the Jewish wife may go to her in-laws and tell them their son is having problems of some sort, and is being rough with the children. She will never say that he is beating her. Her mother-in-law asks what she is doing to make him change because nothing was wrong with him before the wedding.

If the battered Jewish wife goes to her own parents, her mother asks what she did to make him hit her, insisting that he is a nice Jewish boy from a good family, he is educated, hard-working, does not drink, and is faithful. She tells her daughter to go home where she belongs. Her father does not say anything; he just looks sad.

If she decides to go to Jewish Family Service or a rabbi, she chooses one far from her neighborhood so she will not be seen; this way neither she nor her husband will be suspect. If she is able to say that she is seeking help because her husband beats her, the rabbi or counselor may express surprise and tell her that she is the first Jewish woman ever to come to them for that reason. But if she is not able to say that she is being beaten, the rabbi or counselor is not able to diagnose the real problem. In either case, she leaves feeling degraded and ashamed, convinced that she is the only Jewish battered wife in the world, and since she is the only one it must be her own fault.

Effects on the Children

The battered Jewish wife will go to any lengths to hide the battering from her children. If they are out of the house and she senses a beating coming on, she precipitates it, rushes into it, to get it over with before they return. If the beating takes place at night when the children are in their beds, she will endure any pain, any humiliation, without crying out, so her children will not hear. Because Jewish children are almost never witnesses to the violence, if they do discover an incident accidentally, the mother apologizes for their father's behavior. Daddy is either sick, or tired, or has money problems, or business problems, and they are reassured that their father would never hurt anyone intentionally. As a result, the children ache for their father's pain, and they love him even more.

Patterns in the Battering Jewish Marriage

To the outside world, the battered Jewish wife and her battering husband appear to be an ideal couple. Neither is an alcohol or drug abuser. They belong to a synagogue and their children are being educated there. They attend business functions together and are cordial in public. The husband appears to be a paradigm of gentleness and charm—the perfect husband. One would not be able to guess there is any difference between his public and private behavior.

But the Jewish wife-beater can push his wife out of the car miles away from home, or even lock her out of her home when she is in her nightclothes. In private, he criticizes everything she does—cooking, cleaning, entertaining—and he blames her for everything that goes wrong. If a child has an accident, she is not a good mother—a devastating criticism. If a record player breaks, she broke it. If there are guests for dinner and he arrives late (deliberately), and her serving schedule is thrown out of whack, she is to blame. If the television set is not working and the repairman cannot fix it and her husband misses a football game, she is at fault because ten years ago she influenced him to buy that model rather than the one he really knew was best. Whatever she does is wrong. If it is not cause for a beating, it is cause for an attack on her intelligence or judgment or common sense.

It is not long before the woman begins to doubt her own veracity. She is in constant turmoil: what is right one time is wrong the next. When she and her husband are in the car together and she is driving, he tells her when the light is red, when it is green, when to stop, when to go, what street to turn onto to get to their own house, and sometimes, even where their own house is. Eventually, she becomes so dependent that she is unable to drive to the store, convinced she will not get there and back safely without getting lost or into an accident.

The battered Jewish wife becomes more and more isolated. People stop inviting the couple to parties because they have cancelled out too often. The husband may refuse to go because she said something to offend him, or because he does not like the babysitter she hired, or because the hosts are boring. And she is left the humiliating task of cancelling at the last minute. She would never go alone. She lacks the confidence to do that, and by this time she is convinced that she has nothing to offer, and they were only invited because the hosts want her husband, not her.

Jewish battered women all report that their husbands are constantly punishing them for something or other. They describe their battering spouses as sullen, morose, and alternating between being exceedingly controlled and volatile. They are bellicose men who dislike any public display of emotions. And they are, at least publicly, horrified by any show of violence toward women.

The husbands are possession-oriented and publicly proud of their wives, and they judge the success of others by how well their wives are dressed and what cars they drive. They operate under strictly stereotypical husband-wife roles, and they control everything. Although they allow their wives access to charge accounts and credit cards, they see to it that the wives have no money of their own, and every penny has to be accounted for. The husbands spend money on themselves and their children (even their wife's money). If their wife displeases them, they do not hesitate to say, "If you do that [whatever it is] again, I'll close our joint checking account," and the wife knows that he will do just that.

Money is important to a battered Jewish woman. Because she is forbidden free access to a checking account, and because even her independent income is controlled by her husband, she saves small amounts of money in secret savings accounts or in hiding places around the house. If she needs medical attention because of the beatings, she goes to a physician or hospital emergency room in a distant neighborhood and pays for services in cash from her savings, and gives a false name so she will not be traced. No matter how viciously she may be attacked, she will not call the police to intercede. The shame of having the police come to a Jewish home would be too great. And she would literally be unable to identify herself as a battered woman to the authorities; the stigma would be unbearable.

Jewish women in battering situations are property-minded in the extreme. They will do almost anything to remain in their homes and hold on to their treasures—silverware, books, furniture. They are also extremely protective of their battering husbands and go to any lengths to keep anyone from finding out the truth about the men's violent behavior. If that means cutting off friendships, they will do so. In their own minds, they are convinced that they are responsible for the violence, and they do not want to risk having their husbands identified as abusers. It is for this reason—the fear of exposing their husbands as well as themselves—that they shove themselves further and further away from anyone who could help or at least understand their situation. And it is for this reason that they return to battering situations when they are discharged from a hospital.

Ending the Battering

Because Jewish women have been socialized to believe that marriage is holy and a Jewish home is sanctified, divorce is usually not considered an option. Occasionally, however, after years of abuse, when the woman is afraid that the beating she has taken may be her last because after the next one she may be dead, she threatens her husband with public exposure, and the beatings stop. Or, if the children are gone, she may leave.

Most of the time, though, she dreams of escape through death—her husband's. She dreams that she is rescued by a long-forgotten boyfriend, or that her husband is killed in a plane crash or an automobile accident, and she gets through the days and nights dreaming of her release and how she will live in peace when her ordeal is ended.

What It All Means

Public and Private Images of Self

It would be easy to assume that Jewish battered women must have masochistic personalities, that they are so property-oriented they would rather be beaten than leave their homes and possessions, or that they think of themselves as so fragile or so superior that they would rather live in terror than get a job or live in surroundings less luxurious—a sort of "Jewish princess" model. Based on the women interviewed, that would be a mistake of the first order. These women *do not* like being beaten, and some do leave.

For others, the reasons for not leaving home have much to do with their image of themselves as Jewish wives and mothers. Because the ideas and values with which they have been inculcated—that engagements and marriages are made in heaven, that Jewish men revere their wives, that their children are God-given—whether they are beaten for the first time early in their marriage or when they are pregnant they simply cannot believe they are actually being beaten. And when the beating is over, they cannot believe it has happened to them. These women suffer from what Harry Stack Sullivan calls "the personification of the not-me," a very intense "negative emotional reaction . . . which has more than a little in common with a blow on the head. It tends to erase any possibility of elaborating the exact circumstances of its occurrence, and about the most a person can remember is a somewhat fenestrated account of the event in the immediate neighborhood."[3]

Guilt and Shame

Their Jewish-family-centered socialization not only prevents such women from being prepared to defend themselves against their husbands and from believing it has happened, but makes them feel guilty and responsible for their husband's actions.[4] That is why all the women reported that during a beating, they would lie there apologizing; they somehow believed they deserved it. If something went wrong in their marriage, it was their fault. When they had been warned against dating and marrying non-Jewish men, the real warning was that if they married non-Jewish men, they would run into rough treatment. Ironically, the opposite now seemed to be true, and the corollary was that when they ran into rough treatment from a Jew, it must be their fault. All the women reported they felt guilty because they had failed their husband, their marriage, and their children.

Because of these perceived failures, these women feel a shame so great and so deep that they are often unable to discuss it with their children, their husbands, their therapists, their families, or their friends. This shame renders them so helpless and so afraid of disclosure that many prefer being battered than run the risk of admitting it. Sometimes this shame begins when they are coerced into going through with a marriage they fear because their parents tell them that social pressures dictate it—it is too late for them to change their minds. All are shamed into staying married because their marriage was "made in heaven," and one cannot undo what God has spent His time arranging. Out of their shame at being beaten, they are unable to tell their parents the real reason they wanted to end the marriage; thus they are further shamed into remaining in an untenable situation.

Whenever they sought help, their shame was reinforced. Their rabbis were not able to help them because they saw wife-beating as not only a "*shonda* for the Goyim" [an act which would humiliate Jews if the Gentiles knew about it], it was also a *shonda* for the Jews. Their in-laws could not help because their shame at producing a son who beat his wife was too great to admit. And their own parents could not help because they couldn't face the shame they would feel at having approved such a marriage, or the shame that would come with divorce.

Shtetl Attitudes in America[5]

Although only half of the women in this study were Orthodox (and even those were modern Orthodox), all believed that their main job or assignment in life was keeping the family close together, and that the main responsibility for the maintenance of the Jewish family rests on the shoulders of the wife and mother. It is what each wife saw her mother do, and what she heard that her grandmother and great-grandmother had done previously.

This principle came from the *shtetl* to America. Although our eating patterns have changed, our clothing has changed, our language has changed, although we have been assimilated and even intermarried, this aspect of ghetto or *shtetl* mentality has maintained itself in the minds of Los Angeles Jews down the generations since their ancestors left the *shtetl*. Other groups in America are subject to much peer influence, and although the boundaries of dating for Jewish girls have expanded quite a bit, in fact Jewish girls are still inculcated with the idea that marriage to a Jew will afford a chance for a better life, and that Jewish women are ultimately responsible for the success or failure of the marriage and family. The question is: How is it that Jewish mothers still have such strong influence? This mechanism which provides all the negative attributes of being Jewish is powerful enough to carry along positive attributes, and reinforces endogamy. Although this mechanism is breaking down, it is safe to say that the major source of influence is still the mother and family.

Some End the Beatings

When each of the women who participated in this study finally decided she had to end the beatings, she did so either by leaving her husband, committing suicide, or threatening her husband with public exposure. Aside from these drastic steps, nothing seemed to work. Her husband was obdurate. She was not able to endear herself to him with favors or make him feel guilty enough to stop the brutality. It is indeed interesting to learn that when some of the wives said, "If you hit me again, I will tell the world about you," the beatings stopped. The good image presented to the outside world by the wife-beating husband is more important to him and gives him more pleasure than beating his wife. At the minimum, it appears that he cares more about his public than his private behavior. Only when the husband was threatened with public exposure did he cease to brutalize his wife.

Conclusion

Because of this study and others like it, we are no longer able to tell Jewish youngsters that Jews are different, that Jewish husbands are superior, that Jews are kinder, more peaceable, less violence-prone. Although it is tempting to teach our children that the Jewish family is superior to all others, or that Jewish husbands are above reproach, parents, rabbis, social workers—indeed, all who are part of the Jewish community—must be ready to recognize and admit that our idealized concept of the Jewish family is just that: an idealized concept, a myth.

NOTES

1. Marriages are made in heaven. *Genesis Rabba* lxviii, 3: "God finds the mating of couples as difficult as parting the Red Sea." Cf. *Genesis Rabba* lxviii, 4: "Since the creation of the world, God has been occupied with matching couples."

2. This article is excerpted from a study conducted for a master's thesis at the School of Jewish Communal Service–Hebrew Union College at Los Angeles. Almost 200 people were interviewed: hospital personnel, psychiatrists, rabbis, social workers, attorneys, women at a shelter for battered women, almost 100 Jewish women married to Jewish men who beat them, and a few Jewish wife-beaters. The portrait of a "typical" American-born battered Jewish wife was drawn from these case studies.

3. Harry Stack Sullivan, *An Interpersonal Theory of Psychiatry,* ed. Helen Perry and Mary Gawer (New York: W. W. Norton, 1953), p. 315. Sullivan discusses the "tripartite cleavage of personifications: good-me, bad-me, not-me."

4. Gwen Gibson and Barbara Wyden, *The Jewish Wife* (New York: Peter H. Wyden, 1969). *The Jewish Wife* is based on depth interviews selected from a national sample of a study conducted to discover if there were differences between 200 Jewish women and 200 of their non-Jewish neighbors. Several of their findings are similar to those of the present study. For example, "Jewish men make better husbands . . . [and] better than average risks" (p. 57). "The primary responsibility for keeping family ties close falls on the shoulders of the Jewish wife" (p. 118). "Most Jewish women insisted on peace in the home at any cost" (p. 133). And "The Jewish wife feels guilty about everything" (p. 239).

5. Solomon Grayzel, *A History of the Jews* (New York: Mentor, 1968) pp. 411 ff. "Many Jews were compelled to live in Ghettos. The Jews will never forget. . . . For as generation after generation spent its life under degrading circumstances such as the Ghetto system imposed on them, the Jews began to show the effects of being harassed and constantly threatened. There were not actually many sharply defined

Ghettos, with walls and gates and guards, but everywhere contempt and disabilities were heaped upon the Jews and the boundaries of their lives were narrowed. Timidity, self-consciousness, suspicion of their neighbors became characteristic of the Ghetto Jew. The term 'Ghetto' came to represent a mental attitude. This attitude spread to the Jews of other lands as Ghetto conditions, though no actual Ghetto spread beyond Italy and Germany into other parts of Europe."

Israeli Women
THREE MYTHS

Lesley Hazleton

THE soft focus of old photographs gives them a lazy, dream-like quality. Beautiful young women, dark eyes shining, smile out at us from seventy years ago. They have pitchforks slung over their shoulders, and wear long cotton dresses and tough work shoes. Standing in the middle of a cornfield, oxen and cart beside them, they glow with health. A lamb under each arm, their faces shine with contentment as they herd the sheep out in the hills.

These are the *halutzot,* the women pioneers who left their comfortable middle-class homes in Eastern Europe to follow a vision of socialism, equality and justice in Palestine. By 1914 there were about two hundred of them, mostly spirited seventeen-, eighteen- and nineteen-year-olds who took the socialist ideology of sexual equality at face value and expected to find it by working on the soil in their new land.

Among them was Rachel Blaustein, later to become one of the major Hebrew-language poets and a national poet of modern Israel. She arrived in Palestine at age nineteen and within the year was working in Kinnereth, an agricultural settlement on the Sea of Galilee, hoping "to make music with the hoe and to draw upon the earth." Such ideas were influenced by "Aleph Daled" Gordon, generally known simply as "the Old Man," who had developed a new mysticism of labor on the soil and the simple agricultural life. It was a natural theme for a young woman just arrived from Russia and elated by the Tolstoyan cult of the laborer. But Rachel Blaustein's dream of agricultural bliss was to be rudely broken by the First World War, which left her stranded on a French training farm, and by illness.

Years later, in 1927, she wrote the swansong of her aspirations in what was to become one of her most popular poems: "Perhaps." In many ways, the poem was to speak for her fellow *halutzot.*

And perhaps it was only a dream after all?
And perhaps
I never really went forth with the dawn
to toil with the sweat of my brow?

Can it be on those flaming and endless days
when we reaped,
that I never gave voice to a song as I rode
on a cartful of sheaves high-heaped?

That I never did bathe in the perfect and placid blue gleam
of Kinnereth, my sea, ah Kinnereth, my own,
were you real, then, or only a dream?[1]

For the majority of the *halutzot,* it was neither war nor illness that shattered their dream, but the resistance of their male "comrades" and the basic economics of earning enough food to live on. In the early years of Degania, a work group later to become the first kibbutz, women were not considered full-fledged members of the group. The men at Degania and at nearby Kinnereth were paid monthly wages by the Palestine Office of the Zionist movement. The women were not. They were not even listed in the annual contracts drawn up between the pioneers and the Palestine Office. When they insisted on being included, the women were told point-blank that they were working for the men and not for the Palestine Office.[2]

The tragedy was that this was true. For every new working group of twenty or so men breaking new soil and planting new fields, there were only three or four women, sometimes just one, and nearly all these women worked in the kitchen or the laundry. They found no music in the hoe and no earth to draw upon, only sixteen-hour days cleaning shirts and peeling vegetables. The men maintained that women in the fields would be an economic liability to the group, since their productivity was lower. A certain number could be taken in only to run the service side of affairs, no more.

But what of the proud philosophy of sexual equality? Surely that was an integral part of the new socialism? It was indeed—so integral a part, in fact, that it hardly needed to be, and therefore rarely was, spelled out. The outcome of avoiding explicitness was bitterly painful for the women.

"In Europe we planned and dreamed about our future in Zion; there, there was to be no distinction between men and women," wrote Sarah Malchin, one of the leaders of the early women settlers, in 1913. On reaching Palestine, however, "our beautiful dreams were destroyed by our hostile surroundings. . . . We girls were met with indifference and scorn everywhere."[3] Ridiculed by potential employers when they applied for agricultural work, the women then saw themselves abandoned by their male comrades. Although they had planned an egalitarian utopia together, the men now thought the women "absurd" for wishing to work alongside them.

The women had two options. The first was to identify with the newfound motherland by claiming a mystic bond between woman's womb and the bowels of the earth, glorifying the mysterious workings of nature which only a female force could contact and understand—a biological mysticism which their granddaughters would develop in the Israel of the seventies. But snakebite, dysentery, typhoid, malaria, and sheer hunger made this option ludicrous. There was no glory here, but a tough and arduous battle against a hostile land. The women were in far too difficult a conflict to indulge in the luxury of mysticism. The leap from the small-town Jewish *shtetl* or the warmth and comfort of more urbane and enlightened Jewish communities to the harshness of pioneering demanded a far greater psychological adjustment from the women than from the men, a more radical break of life-style and self-image. They had farther to fall in coming face to face with the disparity between their dream and its reality. So they chose a second option, incongruous but quick and simple: they tried to identify by dressing, behaving, talking and, wherever they could, working like men. Identification would open the way to automatic equality.

It was an idea that could only fail. A few stouthearted women started a special agricultural school to train women workers who would be an asset to any new kibbutz. They succeeded, though in terms of tens and not hundreds, until the school was shut down in 1921 by the British mandatory authorities "because of the climate." By then the ranks of women pioneers had grown from 6 percent to 17 percent of active socialist Zionists, and the male-dominated kibbutzim firmly refused to accept all of them as members. Some of the newcomers, desperate for work, joined the road-paving campaign run by the British authorities from 1920 to 1922, establishing a reputation as pavers of roads and hewers of rock. In fact, most of the three hundred women who worked the roads performed the same function as the women on the kibbutzim: they ran the kitchens and the laundries. In 1922 they were again out of work, and by 1925 the majority of working women in Palestine were unemployed. "Underemployment was usually their lot even when work abounded," wrote Ada Maimon, the historian of the women's movement in Palestine. "Inequality was the norm."[4]

Young women exchanged their ideals for food, taking work as cooks and laundresses, seamstresses, office clerks and private maids—whatever work there was, wherever it was.

By the nineteen-twenties those women on kibbutzim were fighting a rearguard action. But Golda Meir, then a member of Kibbutz Merhavia, "couldn't for the life of me understand what all the fuss was about." The Merhavia women, she correctly observed, hated kitchen duty, not because it was hard, but because it was demeaning. These were young women who had no more idea how to cook than the men, and whose efforts were often met with derision. Meir saw their struggle "not as one for 'civic' rights, which they had in abundance [*sic*], but for equal burdens. They wanted to be given whatever work their male comrades were given—paving roads, building houses, or standing guard duty—not to be treated as though they were different and automatically relegated to the kitchen." It sounds reasonable enough, though Meir, eagerly feminine rather than feminist, stoutly declared that she "remained more concerned with the quality of our diet than with 'feminine emancipation.' "[5]

The Golda Meirs won the day. Meir's close friend and biographer Marie Syrkin sums up this transient epoch of feminism in her condescending preface to Ada Maimon's history of the movement: "Today the early feminist excesses of the *halutzah,* the woman pioneer, are a matter of the past. . . . The feminist concept of equality has become less literal and more rational."[6]

This "rationalism" helped transmute to myth another facet of the Israeli woman's image: the gun-toting fighter, ready to sacrifice her life for her country. Again there are the photographs from the past, this time from thirty or forty years ago. Now the women look tougher; dressed in fatigues, hair severely pulled back under caps, they train with full concentration and deadly seriousness. They are members of *Haganah,* the Jewish defense organization which fought the 1948 War of Independence and supplied the leadership and manpower for the Israel Defense Forces, formed right after the war.

The *Haganah* women knew how to use a gun. But it was generally the men who did the guard duty and the women who welcomed them home and, if necessary, nursed them. When things got too hot the women would clean and reload the rifles for the men, so that they could increase their rate of fire.

In the first stages of the War of Independence, in late 1947 and early 1948, women soldiers were essential for convoy duties, since they could conceal guns and grenades under their clothes and evade detection by the British troops manning the roadblocks, who did not search women. Some women served in the *Palmach,* the fighting arm of *Haganah,* as well as in the underground organizations of *Etzel* and *Lehi* (the Stern gang), but few were actually involved in combat once the war was under way. The winking condescension with which they were treated is expressed by Yigal Allon, at that time one of the leading *Palmach* commanders, in his history of the Israeli army: "The girls stormed at any proposed discrimination, arguing that it ran counter to the spirit of the new society being built in Palestine to restrict women to domestic chores, particularly since they had proven their competence as marksmen and sappers. In the end, the wiser counsel prevailed: the girls were still trained for combat, but placed in units of their own. Whenever possible, they were trained for defensive warfare only."[7] Allon's "wiser counsel" meant that women served as wireless operators, nurses, quartermasters—exactly as women served in the British army during World War Two. There were women who actually fought, and died, in battle, but it was solely on these exceptions that the rule of the myth was to be based.

Myths compel respect, not necessarily by their truth, but because they are needed by those who believe in them. It is not a rational need, certainly not a conscious need; but it is often vital, since myths lay the basis for a society's perception of itself, for its collective identity and the identity of every member of it. The myths touch, reveal and caress the core of any society's self-image.

The liberation of Israeli women is such a myth. For nearly three decades Israeli women have been the paradigm of women's liberation, the only example of feminism achieved in a world that has yet to awaken fully to the meaning of the word. They have made an essential contribution to Israel's self-image as good and progressive, the antithesis of its notoriously and cruelly sexist Arab neighbors. And the myth of their liberation has benefited Israeli women themselves, shoring up their self-esteem both as Israelis and as women.

It is an inspirational myth, and such myths die hard. They make good journalistic copy. They are exciting. They appeal to the idealist in all of us. Thus Western feminists have been no more immune to the power of the myth than others. The pride in Golda Meir, Israel's premier until 1974, was symptomatic. While nobody attempted to prove that Indian women were liberated by pointing to Indian Premier Indira Gandhi, "Look at Golda" became the slogan of the myth of Israeli women's liberation. The admiration Golda Meir inspired was largely an expression of the longing for women's liberation, a wishful perception of liberation achieved. In this sense, the myth of Israeli women's liberation is perhaps a creative myth, answering deep-rooted needs among women the world over.

But the destructive aspects of this myth far outweigh its creative potential for Israeli women. As the anonymous heroines of the myth, they have been assigned a symbolic existence. Their reality has been subordinated to the accepted image, and they have been relegated to the status of shadows, while the gap continues to widen between their public image and their real selves.

Today the multifaceted manifestations of the myth include the woman soldier just landed from a parachute jump or proudly marching, gun on shoulder, in parade; the tough kibbutz woman working the fields alongside the men or, pistol on hip, driving a tractor; the sexually uncomplicated urbanite who takes what she wants with no misgivings; and of course the tough, wizened politician taking her place in the arena of international politics. But only a few women soldiers are allowed to parachute, and then merely as a morale booster. After basic training, army women rarely hold guns except on parade. One can count the number of Israeli women who drive tractors on the fingers of one hand. The urbanite uses her sexuality more for status than for pleasure. And the politician was an antifeminist who shook her head in amazement at the fact that no other Israeli woman had achieved a comparable level.

Faced with the facts, Israeli women are not fooled by the myth, but they appear to believe in it nevertheless. Open acknowledgement of disbelief would entail a potentially shattering reassessment of their status both as Israelis and as women, a painful shedding of their public image to bring their private pain into the open. Their attitude is one of suspended disbelief, making them willing victims of an empty but soothing ideology. Surrendering their real identity to the "cover identity" ascribed them by ideology, they move in a male world of reality in the false guise of equals.

The ideology of sexual equality was stated clearly in 1948 in Israel's Declaration of Independence: "The State of Israel will maintain equal social and political rights for all citizens, irrespective of religion, race, or sex." It was reiterated in 1949, in the "basic guidelines" of the first government of Israel: "Complete and absolute equality of women will be upheld—equality in rights and duties, in the life of the country, society, and economy, and throughout the entire legal system." Brave words, but empty ones, with neither the commitment nor the intention to carry them toward fulfillment. Neither statement had any legal binding. Both were purely declarative, and within two years both had been utterly compromised by the so-called Women's Equal Rights Law of 1951.

"A man and a woman shall have equal status with regard to any legal proceeding; any provision of law which discriminates, with regard to any legal proceeding, against women as women, shall be of no effect," states the first clause of this law. But three clauses farther down, the law revokes its own edict: "This law shall not affect any legal prohibition or permission relating to marriage or divorce," and "This law shall not derogate from any provision of law protecting women as women." Fully aware of what these clauses meant, the original proponent of the new law, Member of Knesset Rachel Kagan, abstained when it was voted through the Knesset. Within two years it was clear why. The Rabbinical Courts Jurisdiction (Marriage and Divorce) Law of 1953 awarded the religious establishment monopolistic control over marriage and divorce for all Jewish citizens, thus legalizing the sexism of Orthodox Judaism. And one year later, the Employment of Women Law forbade women to work at night on the grounds that this is injurious to their health.

Few bothered to read beyond the titles of such laws, and devotees of the myth could thus remain oblivious to what could qualify as a large-scale political confidence trick. For genuine sexual equality was never a goal of the new state.

The myth of achieved equality was to take the place of real achievement. It resolved the conflict between ideology and emotion by denying the existence of conflict—a defense mechanism of flight rather than fight, which required false constructs to shore it up. For despite an intellectual commitment to women's liberation, the emotional commitment was to the traditional role of women.

By 1948 Israel had been through four decades of experimentation and socialism, fighting and pioneering. Now that the state was founded, it wanted, above all, normalization—and normalization included normal sex roles. The lip service paid to ideology solved problems of conscience by banishing them from public awareness. The everyday contradictions that inevitably arose between ideology and reality were met with the attitude, "We already have laws for sexual equality—if it does not exist in practice, then it is because women are not really interested in it."

The institutionalization of socialist Zionism within the confines of the new state mean the putting aside of ideology in favor of pragmatism. The "Robin Hood role" that political sociologist David Apter ascribes to prestatehood nationalism[8] was both compromised and bureaucratized—and Maid Marian remained where she had been all along, in the forest.

It is a familiar forest. The statistical account of women's involvement in Israel's public life is dismal. There are no women in the cabinet, no women director-generals of government ministries, no women mayors. There are only eight women among the 120 members of the Knesset (parliament). In both academe and government service, women's representation is pyramidal, with many women at the bottom of the ladder and few or none at the top. Women are 48 percent of first-degree university students; by doctoral level, they receive 13 percent of the degrees; and they are a mere 2 percent of full professors. Women make up 39 percent of all civil servants in Israel but only 9 percent in the higher grades.[9]

Women are 1 percent of the country's engineers, 7 percent of its jurists and—the one exception to Western countries—25 percent of its doctors, mainly pediatricians and family doctors. Aside from medicine, women comprise less than 10 percent of professional and managerial personnel. They are 12 percent of Israel's journalists, the vast majority of them snugly tucked into women's pages and magazines. Only 6 percent of working women, as opposed to 24 percent of men, are employers or self-employed.

No more than 51 percent of eighteen-year-old girls are called to serve their "compulsory" two years in the Israel Defense Forces. There are no women generals in the IDF; the highest rank held by a woman is colonel.

Little more than one third of Israel's women work outside their homes (compared with 46 percent in the U.S., for example). Their average annual income is 60 percent of men's, and their average hourly wage about 75 percent that of men.[10] The lower the work status, the greater the difference between male and female wages. The most striking statistic, in a country that has boasted an Equal Pay for Women Law since 1964, is that women working alongside men in plants and offices throughout Israel, doing the same work, may get an hourly wage anywhere from 25 to 40 percent less than that of the men beside them on the assembly line or in the office.

"An employer will pay the same wages to a working woman as he would pay to a man at the same place of work for the same work or for work which is essentially equal," the law says. The two sectors that adhere strictly to the law are academe and the civil service, but the rarity of women at the top in these sectors places in question their commitment to the spirit and not just the letter of the law. Elsewhere, covert discrimination is regularly practiced. Different work titles for men and for women in effect contravene the law, but it is almost impossible to prove that work is "essentially equal." The nationwide federation of labor unions, the Histadrut, quietly sanctions such practices, and has even obstructed attempts to bring cases to court. The law has no authority.

New legislation is easier to create than a change in people's ingrained modes of thinking and relating to others. Attitudes care nothing for legislators' agenda, nor for legal print. Although sexual equality in this instance has the power of the law behind it, the power is meaningless without authority. True authority resides in public assent to the power of the law, and without that assent, the law is reduced to two possibilities: enforcement against the will of the population (which smacks too much of totalitarianism for any country calling itself a democracy), or quiet inefficacy.

Legal change without psychological change alters the surface picture; illusions of progress are created, and legislators can congratulate themselves in the conviction that by pronouncing the problem cured they have actually cured it. At best, however, the psychological situation remains the same. At worst, the laws become counterproductive. By contributing to the myth of sexual equality in Israel, they aggravate the real problem of inequality.

The combination of factors here is unique: an ideology in which few really believed, but which was essential to the self-esteem of the many; a history which glorifies the struggle to realize that ideology, seen through the admiringly telescopic eyes of a later generation that chooses to concentrate on a minority phenomenon; laws which purport to uphold the ideology but which, in phrasing or application, are purposely ineffectual; and a myth which makes true practice of the ideology all but impossible. The myth and the ideology exist in symbiotic union. While the ideology reinforces the myth by giving it rational justification, the myth rationalizes the ideology by assuming it fulfilled. It would be the perfect self-perpetuating system were it not that it takes no account of the reality of experience. Experience—that of the *halutzot* and the women fighters of history, and that of Israeli women today—is negated.

This negation of experience indicates the failure of the ideology. One of ideology's main functions, as the psychologist Erik Erikson expressed it, is "the tendency at a given time to make facts amenable to ideas, and ideas to facts, in order to create a world image convincing enough to support the collective and individual sense of identity."[11] In Israel, the ideology of sexual equality worked perfectly for the collective, the State of Israel, giving it a strong identity as progressive and egalitarian. But it undermined the identity of the individual, the Israeli woman, by placing her experience in complete contradiction to the ideals to which her country subscribed. This clash between ideals and reality, expectations and possibilities, is touchingly expressed by one kibbutz woman, Yael, from Horshim in the coastal plain: "What in fact do the feminists want from us? Do they want to create frustration between aspirations and the reality of possibilities on the kibbutz? Equal rights means equal opportunities, but to push girls toward unrealistic aspirations and expectations will only increase the rate of their leaving the kibbutz."[12] In this sense, the whole of Israel is the kibbutz.

The contradiction between ideology and reality is too great to tolerate consciously; the velvet curtain of ideology hides too harsh a reality. The contrast must be muted so that women can accept it intellectually without feeling that they have merely resigned themselves to it, and so that they can maintain their self-respect as people without forfeiting their self-respect as women.

What women needed was the comfort of an identity that would place the gap between ideology and reality in a happier light. That comfort came offering all the ease and relief of a large, well-padded, old-fashioned armchair after a hard day's work. It was so "obvious" and "natural" a solution to the search for identity that it required just a sigh of relief from struggle, a small step backward, and Israeli women, aided by their government, could relax into a soothing countermythology to the mythology of equality. This was the biological myth, the antidote to the myth of liberation.

The basic assumption of the biological myth is that women are defined, both physically and psychologically, by their biology. This counters the myth of liberation in three major areas. First, it offers an alternative basis for self-esteem by positing that women's child-bearing capacity is of overriding importance, the major factor in any woman's life and therefore a prime determinant of her personality, abilities, and desires. It presents reproduction as women's incomparable and unique contribution as citizens of their state, and as their prime channel for fulfillment as human beings. All else, in comparison, is unimportant. Second, the biological myth justifies inequality as protection. It says that women should not be forced into legal equality lest their biological and psychological vulnerability make their situation harder than, instead of equal to, that of men. Equality is an ideal, but reality demands that women be protected. And third, the biological myth supplies women with a refuge from the struggles and responsibilities of adult life. They are closed in the home, unaware of the main political and social issues which shape their lives. It is the women who create life; but it is the men who shape it.

Theodor Herzl, "the spiritual father of the Jewish state," as he is called in the Declaration of Independence, etched the pattern of liberation overridden by biology in his utopian novel *Altneuland* [Old New Land], written in 1902 and perhaps more accurately prophetic in its description of women's role than on any other point. In Herzl's scheme of things, women in Israel would work until they marry, and then become full-time wives and mothers. In a discussion with the narrator, Kingscourt, the politician hero describes his wife: "She nursed our little boy, and so forgot a bit about her inalienable rights. She used to belong to the radical opposition. That is how I met her, as an opponent. Now she opposes me only at home, as loyally as you can imagine, however." Says Kingscourt, "That's a damned good way of overcoming the opposition. It simplifies politics tremendously." The politician smugly replies, "I must make it clear to you, gentlemen, that our women are too sensible to let public affairs interfere with their personal well-being."[13]

Though Israeli women today do not regard their situation as utopian, they certainly agree that it is sensible. This is how things are; therefore this is how they are naturally meant to be; therefore this is how they ought to remain. For women, the question of equality with men does not arise, for women have different aims in life, different modes of thinking and feeling, and different concepts of what is important. The difference in bodies determines the difference in minds . . . and the difference in legal status.

Hebrew University sociologist Rivka Bar-Yosef, the only top-flight Israeli academic concerned with thorough investigation of the reality of Israeli women's lives, characterizes the Israeli legal view of women as "dissimilar but equal." While paying lip service to the ideology of equality, the law in fact protects the biologically and socially prescribed feminine roles. The legal logic is the tortuous one of the inequality of equality. "These 'ascriptive' laws have a protective tendency," writes Bar-Yosef, "their rationale being the assumption that, due to biological attributes, women are more vulnerable than men. Hence, formal equality based on assumptions of complete similarity results in discrimination."[14] The result is a cynical concept of equality, and a highly paternalistic view of women's place in society.

The 1954 Employment of Women Law limits employment of women at night on the grounds of possible damage to their health. The Defense Service Act of 1959 specifies a shorter period of compulsory military service for women than for men and different kinds of training and employment in service, and it specifically exempts from any form or period of service all women who are married or pregnant or have children. Under the National Insurance Act of 1953, women retire at age sixty and men at age sixty-five, the official explanation being that women still function as homemakers and therefore should not be burdened with a double role beyond the age of sixty. Thus the primacy of women's role as wives and housewives is implicitly sanctioned by law, and the tax authorities concur by refusing to consider a working woman's expenses in payment of other working women (a cleaning woman or a child nurse) as tax-deductible.

None of these laws encourage women to take a full and equal part in Israel's public life. Many women feel that they have little choice in the matter. The paucity of day nurseries, the short primary school day ending at noon, lower pay, and slimmer chances of promotion discourage women from taking a work role seriously. Due to one bright star in the Employment of Women Law, which states than an employer may not fire a pregnant woman and that she is allowed up to three months' paid leave of absence after giving birth (which is covered by National Insurance), employers tend to avoid placing women in positions of responsibility, arguing that women may get pregnant and then disappear from work for three months. The fact that nearly every Israeli working man serves anywhere from thirty to eighty days of reserve military service each year, with his salary also covered by National Insurance, does not occur to them as a reason not to employ men.

It is too much to fight against in a country which has plenty of wars already. So Israeli women tend to work from the time they leave school or graduate from the army until their marriage or first pregnancy, and then drop out. Women are nearly half the work force in the fourteen-to-twenty-four age group (the ratio is high owing to the large number of young women who do not serve in the army and instead work in low-paid jobs until marriage); in the twenty-five to thirty-four age range, women make up less than a third of the work force; by forty-five to fifty-four they are a quarter; and by fifty-five and over they are scarcely more than one fifth.[15] There is no "reentry" phenomenon in Israel as there is in the United States, since forty-year-old women who have spent the last twenty years in the home prefer the role of grandmother to almost certain rejection in the labor market.

Those women who work do so almost entirely out of economic

necessity.[16] What with one of the highest tax rates in the world, booming inflation, and the race to achieve a decent standard of living in a country still wavering precariously between pre- and postindustrialism, an extra income is vital for many families. If a woman does not work, it is a kind of status symbol, a sign to the world that her husband can support his family without his wife's help. The wealthier of such wives may engage in volunteer activities, raising funds for charities, but most of their time is spent around the pool, at the hairdresser's, dressing up to stroll through the shops or linger in a café with friends. These are either the elite, the top of the bunch in the almost entirely Ashkenazi[17] establishment that runs Israel, or the nouveaux riches, wives of businessmen who made it big in the economic boom following the Six-Day War of 1967.

Paradoxically, the other major group of nonworking wives is at the very bottom of the social scale, women from traditional Oriental backgrounds, whose husbands will not tolerate their working outside the home. These are the two extremes of Israeli women: the rich with time on their hands and luxury, and the poor whose lives are a timeless grind of drudgery. And yet both act as showcases of their husbands' ability. The former reflect his professional or social status, the latter his virility in having as many children as possible and his pride and honor in not having to live on a woman's earnings.

The big difference is that the poor work like slaves. Although they are accounted too weak to drive trucks or tanks by the army, and too vulnerable to work night shifts by the government, they lug up to thirty kilos of food at a time from the markets, scrub down tile floors and beat out rugs by hand, wash the dishes and the diapers in iron basins, sometimes without hot water, and spend all of Thursday and Friday preparing food for the Sabbath. Vacuum cleaners, dishwashers, electric mixers and washing machines, even ovens, are generally unknown commodities to these women. Their life is back-breaking, physically tough and mentally exhausting. Says psychologist Shoshana Sharni, who has spent years working with illiterate mothers of large families, all of Moroccan or Yemenite origin: "These women lead monotonous lives and are continually tired, not only physically but mentally, an exhaustion of resignation."[18] Their main burden is extremely low self-esteem, with no faith in their ability to change their situation.

Between the extremes of wealth and poverty, the gap between Ashkenazi and Sephardi Israeli women is still great. Whereas the former marry at an average age of twenty-two and their average number of children is 2.8, the latter marry earlier, at twenty, and their average number of children is 4.6. Some 95 percent of Ashkenazi women have had formal schooling, over a third for more than eight years, and more than half now work outside the home. Only 56 percent of Sephardi women have attended school, less than a third of them for more than eight years, and only 20 percent work outside the home.[19]

But these statistics tell only part of the story, since they include the whole range of Israeli women: mothers and daughters, pioneers, refugees and native-born citizens. What they cannot show is that the daughters are narrowing the gap—in attitude if not yet in concrete achievement—between Sephardi and Ashkenazi. As the Sephardi daughters reach adulthood, for example, their main aim in life, constantly reiterated, is "not to be like my mother." None of the drudgery, none of the burden of many children, none of the waiting on husband as lord and master. These young women are determined to build another kind of life for themselves, and their role model is drawn from the largely Ashkenazi middle class. Thus while the Ashkenazi women have thoroughly feminized the suffragette image over the past three decades, the Sephardi women are trying to move forward into the same modern version of traditionalism. The two groups are reaching toward a consensus on what it is to be a woman, searching for a concept of modern femininity in which biological differences are protected rather than abused or ignored, and being a woman becomes a virtue in itself.

The Ashkenazi role model takes liberation for granted, so much so that there is no need to act on it. "Of course Israeli women are liberated," says Adina, an attractive blonde of twenty-five who, until she married, was a nurse. "It's all there in the laws. If it doesn't show up in your statistics, then it's simply because we don't choose to avail ourselves of it. Look at me, of course I could go on nursing, but I prefer to stay at home and be a good mother instead of trying to do everything all at once. Why on earth should I want to make life hard for myself?"

"Of course all of those things that the *halutzot* did are possible," says Devorah, twenty-nine, who works in the children's house of one of Israel's largest and richest kibbutzim. "But what woman in her right mind would want to do all that? Getting dirty, breaking your back in the fields, sweating under a hot sun, getting old before your time—no thanks, not for me. A woman's role is to take good care of herself so that she can be at her best for her husband and her children."

"Of course a woman should have outside interests, be involved in her society, know what's going on and be able to take an intelligent interest in it," says Ruth, forty-two, lounging among the enveloping cushions of her Danish sofa, with the curtains half-closed against the glare of the late-morning Tel Aviv sun. "But let's face it, a woman's real interest in life is in two things—children and love—and these are what she'll seek for her satisfaction above all else."

"Of course." The theoretical value of the myth of liberation is accepted, but it is the biological myth that governs women's lives. Israeli women use biology as a "masking myth,"[20] a popular ideology which serves to cover and relieve contradictions in the official picture of liberation. But it is inadequate to its task, and only creates further strain as the dissonance between the two worlds of self-image, liberated and biological, sharpens into a potential double bind of schizophrenogenic proportions.[21] An element of choice must be introduced to avert this danger, and it is this element that Israeli women rely on in creating the third of the three main myths which shape their lives: the myth of the "real woman," based not on the vulnerability of femininity as is the biological myth, but concentrating on its privileges.

This development of biology into blessing arises from resignation but transcends it by creating the impression of choice. Choice is a basic assumption of the liberated myth; it does not exist in the biological one. Those women who believe in the liberated myth but live the biological one—the elite and the increasingly affluent middle class in Israel—feel it importatnt to demonstrate that they have chosen, thus retaining at least the illusion of liberation. And yet they see no way to overcome what is known in the kibbutz movement as "the biological tragedy of the woman." The tragedy is therefore raised to the highest level, where instead of being pitied for their femininity, women are to be protected, valued, admired and envied by men. The "real woman" myth places them on a quasi-mystic pedestal to which men can never attain. It emphasizes sexual differences in an attempt to make a virtue out of femininity, to create a positive self-image that would only be demeaned by any suggestion of being put on a level with men. An elusive and closed world of femininity is created. And it would be crazy, given these assumptions, to choose anything other than to be a "real woman."

Betty Friedan's depiction of the feminine mystique accurately portrays the philosophy of this "real woman." "The feminine mystique says that the highest value and the only commitment for women is the fulfillment of their own femininity. It says that the great mistake of Western culture, throughout most of its history, has been the underevaluation of this femininity. It says this femininity is so mysterious and intuitive and close to the creation and origin of life that manmade science may never be able to understand it. . . . The mistake, says the mystique, the root of women's troubles in the past, is that women envied men, women tried to be like men, instead of accepting their own nature, which can find fulfillment only in sexual passivity, male domination, and nurturing maternal love."[22]

In the first two decades of the State of Israel, the realities of life were too harsh for women to swathe themselves in such silk-and-satin wrappings of femininity. But since 1967, when the standard of living began to rise, a growing Israeli middle class has discovered the virtues and vices of a minor but slowly increasing degree of affluence. And as the material quality of their lives has improved, Israeli women have gravitated toward this more affluent version of the biological myth, romanticizing and intellectualizing it to the level of an art.

The real-woman myth offers an aura of feminine self-fulfillment that flatters and glorifies its subject. "Anything I write about real women must read oddly, except perhaps to real women themselves, or the occasional man whom some accident of birth or experience tempts to agree with me," wrote Robert Graves in the sixties,[23] extending an esoteric invitation to a hidden, secret reality, available only to those with the insight and sensitivity to probe beneath the coarse shell of appearances. It is a dangerous little secret. It glorifies the pain of women's lives, praising them for being "real women" despite all the burdens they have to bear. It gives them an insidious pat on the shoulder, together with the time-worn line, "Man's biological function is to do, woman's is to be."

In Israel, where the men defend their country in war after war and the women are the protected, such a philosophy finds easy acceptance. It was tragically and poignantly expressed after the 1973 Yom Kippur War by Naomi Zorea, a member of Kibbutz Maagan Michael, whose second son had died in that war, her first having died in the Six-Day War in 1967. In an open "Letter to the Daughters of Israel" she expressed the woman's role in Israel at war. "No, ours is not an impotent participation in the process of human history," she exclaimed. "We bestow things that are as basic as sun and soil. We bestow life itself, and the first pleasures, food, feel, smell, the beginnings of the capacity to love. . . ." Sitting with other women in mourning, she recalled, ". . . we were five sad, strong women sitting there. It was so sad, yet it was such a marvelous experience. Suddenly I felt as though the five of us sitting there were five mothers out of antiquity, out of mythology, whose power causes them to turn into goddeses." The mothers are the strong, the determiners of fate, not the determined. "If a nation is worthy," Zorea concluded, "its mothers are Graces. If not, they are Destroyers. And the borderline between the two is thin, very thin."[24]

This is part of the role of the "real woman" in Israel, the woman who makes what Yitzhak Rabin, then premier, in a speech for International Women's Year called "the supreme sacrifice"—not her own death, but that of her husband or son.[25] It is a role she carries with the "inborn dignity" that Robert Graves notes as distinguishing real women, but it is also one that can create enormous stress.

With the web of femininity spun tight around her, the Israeli woman is in danger of retreating into a self-spun cocoon, living a rich fantasy life which has nothing to do with the eminently practical accommodations which another part of her is willing to make with her everyday world. Graves' glorification of the feminine mystique and his presentation of women as lost earth-mothers from a previous age, merely acting out their part in modern society, describes a very real phenomenon now growing among Israeli women: the withdrawal from a contradictory reality into a comforting fantasy, not to such an extent as to hinder everyday functioning, but enough to give the woman a personal faith in the meaning of her own existence.

"A real woman somehow avoids suicide or virtual suicide or the mental institution, but is always painfully aware of having been born out of her true epoch," writes Graves.[26] This attitude surfaces sometimes in small signs of a longing for romanticism, harkening to a bygone age of chivalry, so simple and tempting when seen in the misted retrospect of a few hundred years. For instance, fighter pilots, the epitome of Israeli virility, are sometimes called "medieval knights," since they generally fight in close combat, one-to-one. And the paratroopers, nearly as high as the pilots in the Israeli woman's esteem, were referred to as "our noble stallions" during the Six-Day War. A 1976 edition of *Ha-Shavua,* the magazine of the once-radical Kibbutz Artzi organization, illustrated an article on the difficulties of kibbutz women with the romantic drawings of Aubrey Beardsley—flowingly robed ladies gazing longingly at languid knights, and, on the cover, long-tressed women peering down from the turrets of a medieval tower as their knights return from the wars.

This is the new direction of Israeli women's fantasies: not equality, nor motherhood, but a deep yearning for the protected yet vulnerable times of yore, when men indeed "did" and women indeed "were."

And what of the legend of liberation? Dalia Rabikovitz, Israel's leading woman poet, limns its demise in her poem "The Dove," written appropriately in medieval ballad style:

There was once a white dove, once on a day.
Ah, love this dove—
She sprouted a wing and flew away.
Ah, love this dove.

On the way she met the Raven King.
Ah, love this dove—
She met on the way a wolf-pack howling.
Ah, love this dove.

She saw seventy-seven enemies.
Ah, love this dove—
Birds struck at her and had jealous eyes.
Ah, love this dove.

She was white till the day she was devoured.
Ah, love this dove—
From her whiteness and wing a legend flowered.
Ah, love this dove.[27]

NOTES

1. Rachel, "Perhaps," cited in Sholom J. Kahn, "The Poetry of Rachel," *Ariel* 38 (1975). Translated by Professor Kahn.
2. In Ada Maimon, *Women Build a Land* (New York: Herzl Press, 1962), a history of working women in Israel from 1904 to 1954, packed full of information and insight in a field otherwise all but ignored.
3. Maimon, *Women Build a Land.*
4. Maimon, *Women Build a Land.* Some years later the women tried again. By 1930 there were six small training farms for women, which in due time served the additional purpose of immigrant absorption centers for single women, and eventually became general agricultural schools. Meanwhile the *halutzot* also had to struggle for basic political rights against the powerful religious sector of the Jewish community in Palestine at the time. By the late twenties it was clear that women could achieve even the most basic rights only by organizing separately, and from 1928 until 1948 it was the Working Women's Council that led the struggle for women's rights.
5. Golda Meir, *My Life* (New York: G. P. Putnam, 1975).
6. Maimon, *Women Build a Land.*

7. Yigal Allon, *Shield of David: The Story of Israel's Armed Forces* (London: Weidenfeld and Nicholson, 1970) (New York: Random House, 1970).

8. David Apter, in the introduction to *Ideology and Discontent,* ed. David Apter (New York: Free Press, 1964).

9. One of the most useful sources on statistics concerning Israeli women is *Working Material on the Subject of Women in Israel* (in Hebrew), ed. A. Ofek (Work and Welfare Research Institute, Hebrew University of Jerusalem, 1976), a collection of statistics from various sources on women's status in Israel. In English, sociologist Dorit Padan-Eisenstark wrote two articles full of statistical information: "Are Israeli Women Really Equal?" *Journal of Marriage and the Family,* 1973, pp. 538–545; and "Image and Reality: Women's Status in Israel," *Cross-Cultural Perspectives in Women's Status,* ed. R. Leavitt (New York: Hawthorne, 1974). Also useful is P. Lahav: "The Status of Women in Israel—Myth and Reality," in *The American Journal of Comparative Law* 24 (1974).

10. "Survey of Income of Employees," *Monthly Bulletin of Statistics* (in Hebrew; Central Bureau of Statistics, September 1976).

11. Erik H. Erikson, *Young Man Luther: A Study in Psychoanalysis and History* (London: Faber and Faber, 1958).

12. In *The Woman in the Kibbutz* (in Hebrew; Givat Haviva, Kibbutz Research Institute, July 21, 1974).

13. Theodor Herzl, *Old New Land* (New York: Herzl Press, 1960).

14. Rivka Bar-Yosef and Ilana Shelach, "The Position of Women in Israel," in *Integration and Development in Israel,* ed. S. N. Eisenstadt et al. (Israel University Press, 1970).

15. In *Working Material on the Subject of Women in Israel.*

16. See Rivka Bar-Yosef et al., *Women's Attitudes to Family Life* (in Hebrew: Hebrew University of Jerusalem, 1973).

17. Ashkenazi Jews are those of Western origin, generally East European. The early Zionists were almost exclusively Ashkenazi—and from founding the State it was an easy step to almost total control of the political establishment of Israel today. While they were the overwhelming majority of Palestinian Jews in 1948, Ashkenazi are now 45 percent of Israel's population. The majority, the Sephardi Jews (the name derives from the Hebrew for Spanish but applies to all Oriental Jews whose families came from North Africa or the Middle East), are generally socially, politically, and economically inferior, despite their numerical superiority, and are sometimes referred to as "the second Israel"—the Israel behind the successful appearances of the Ashkenazi establishment.

18. Shoshana Sharni, *Characteristics of Moroccan and Yemenite Women with 0–8 Years Schooling* (in Hebrew; Demographic Center, Prime Minister's Office, Jerusalem, 1973).

19. In *Working Material on the Subject of Women in Israel.*

20. See Clifford Geertz, "Ideology as a Cultural System," in *Ideology and Discontent.*

21. The "double bind" theory of schizophrenia poses the following conditions: *a.* two mutually exclusive sets of expectations, presented simultaneously but on different levels of communication; *b.* no way out. A situation, in other words, of "damned if you do, damned if you don't." The theory was first presented by Gregory Bateson et al. in "Toward a Theory of Schizophrenia," *Behavioral Science* 1 (1956).

22. Betty Friedan, *The Feminine Mystique* (New York: W. W. Norton, 1963).

23. Robert Graves, *Mammon and the Black Goddess* (New York: Doubleday, 1965).

24. Naomi Zorea, "Letter to the Daughters of Israel," reprinted in *The Jerusalem Post,* March 11, 1974.

25. Prime Minister Yitzhak Rabin, "Greetings on the Occasion of International Women's Year," speech to the Knesset on February 12, 1975 (Government Press Office Bulletin).

26. Robert Graves, *Mammon and the Black Goddess.*

27. Dalia Rabikovitz, "The Dove," trans. Dom Moraes (Tel Aviv Institute for the Translation of Hebrew Literature).

Women-identified Women in Male-identified Judaism

Batya Bauman

JEWISH lesbian/feminists[1] experience the conflict of living as members of two divergent groups that are often at odds with each other. Judaism is male-centered, while lesbian/feminism is female-centered. Nonetheless, the two groups have much in common.

Lesbian/feminists are women-identified women belonging to the community of women. Jews, of all people, know what "community" means, for Jews have always been a community, and the Jewish people are a community today. *Kol Yisrael haverim.* We have a common history. We have a common language and religion. Our ancient heritage, too, we have in common. We recognize and feel kinship with Jews from other lands whom we have never seen. We have had exile, *galut,* in common. We have anti-Semitism in common.

Women, also, have things in common. We have a common history of misogyny.[2] We have a language different from male language in its images and visions and expressions. We have a religion that centers on the synchronicity of our bodies with the cycles of nature, that has an affinity with all living things, a knowledge of the healing arts, a love of life and a holistic view of the cosmos, an awareness of the waxing and waning of everything in the universe, and the knowledge and vision of an immanent female deity with whom we can identify directly.[3] We are all part of an ecological whole.

The cycles and seasons are very much with us, in both our conscious and our subconscious thoughts and feelings. Biologically we are in tune with nature, as our menstrual cycles coincide with the cycles of the moon and the tides of the oceans. This synchronicity with nature, from which men long felt excluded, is perhaps what men envied, thus imposing the worship of a transcendent male god, a worship in which women can play only minor or secondary roles. With this transcendent male god, men could transcend and conquer nature and women, since women are regarded as closer to nature.

We recognize in other women something of ourselves, even though we may never have seen them before. Men keep us from sisterhood and encourage us to turn against each other by creating myths of the "Jewish Mother" and "Jewish American Princess," for example. We discover and create bonds with the emerging knowledge of our common oppression as women, our suppressed past and future visions and the Zionist movement of women, called Feminism.

Women are in *galut.* We are a community in exile. There was a time when women were not in *galut,* before patriarchy. This is not to imply matriarchy, which is a patriarchal word with its assumption of someone in charge: mother-rule rather than father-rule. If patriarchy is the problem, matriarchy is not the answer. Societies were (and some still are) matrilineal, matrilocal, matrifocal and egalitarian. Some cultures still retain today female images of deity that flourished in earlier history and prehistory. Her names were Innana, Tiamat, Ishtar, Mami, Aruru, Asherah, Astarte, Anat. In cultures outside the Ancient Near East, her names were (and in some cultures remain today) Gaia, Mawu, Songi, Nu Kwa, Danu, Cerridwen, Mu Olokukurtilisop, Pele, Kybele, Hecate, and many more.[4] But in the Western, *civilized* world, our view of divinity comes from the Ancient Near East, where patriarchal Aryan invaders from the north defeated the less militaristic, goddess-worshipping nations, imposing their view of a patriarchal male god[5] conceived in their own image. The Goddess-worshipping Mediterranean and Semitic peoples—some of whom later became the early Hebrew tribes—probably went through a long transition period before finally adopting a patriarchal male god. Later, worship of the female deity was declared evil, immoral, abominable, pagan, and illegal as codified in the Hebrew Scripture, when the ancient Hebrews integrated patriarchy into their own culture. The Hebrews were one of the very few groups to carefully codify this. Perhaps this is the reason so much emphasis has been placed on the role of Hebrew Scripture in the oppression of goddess reverence, when in actuality this oppression was occurring all the way from Europe to India, in all areas invaded by the Aryans.

The essential feminist reaction to Hebrew Scripture is that it is a male book, written by and addressed exclusively to men. Men have created the myths, narratives, and laws that affect not only men, but women as well. Now, this might not be so bad if it did not (as it most certainly does) place men and women in positions of dominance and subordinance. There is no way one can miss the emphasis on male supremacy in Scripture. What is a bit more subtle is that Hebrew Scripture is phallocentric; male sex and male sexuality are viewed as sacrosanct, while female sex and female sexuality are viewed as abominable, unclean, harmful, in need of male control, and expendable when necessary to preserve male purity.

Little Jewish scholarship, if anything of substance at all, addresses the problem of Lot's offering his two daughters to the men of the town to be raped in order to thwart the rape of the two male strangers in the Sodom and Gomorrah narrative. (Genesis 19:4–9).[6] Male gender and sexuality are so sacrosanct that female gender and sexuality are expendable, even when it is that of one's own daughters. Of course, their mother, Edit (Lot's wife), who is later turned into a pillar of salt because she looked back with compassion on the destruction of her home and neighbors and to see whether her two eldest, married daughters were following, had no authority in this matter; if she did, one might speculate that she would have objected to her husband's offer of her daughters to be raped. But not here, since the scenario is created by a masculist mentality.

Elsewhere, in the Gibeah narrative (Judges 19–21) a concubine is raped and murdered to save the Levite, a male stranger in town who brought her into the town with him, from a similar fate. The Levite's concubine is given over to the violent men of the town so that his sexuality might not be sullied!

"Homosexuality" as known in the Bible is not homosexuality as we know it today—love between two consenting adults of the same sex—and Hebrew Scripture addresses only male homosexuality. It has nothing to say about lesbians, probably because it views women's concerns in general as trivial. In addition, there is no conception of women's sexuality without the intervention of men. Hebrew Scripture depicts homosexuality as a violent act, one of dominance and submission. The dominant male treats the subordinate male as men treat women: as inferior. This was considered the ultimate humiliation to which one man might treat another: as he treats a woman. It was a powerful psychosexual way of establishing political superiority; probably this was what the men in Sodom and Gomorrah, and in Gibeah, wanted from the strangers.[7] Fear of being treated like a woman—losing one's manliness—is the source of homophobic feelings and behavior in heterosexual men. Heterosexual men will cease being homophobic when they are ready to accept the absolute and unequivocal equality of women.

And what is the meaning of Deuteronomy 25:11–12?

> When men strive together one with another, and the wife of the one draweth near to deliver her husband out of the hand of him that smiteth him, and putteth forth her hand, and taketh him by the secrets; then thou shalt cut off her hand, thine eye shall have no pity.

The sacred penis cannot be defiled by a woman's touch even in the act of saving her husband!

Attributing sanctity to male gender and phallus initiates the whole saga of the Jewish people with Abraham's everlasting covenant with his god through a mark on his penis. Continuing today, the source of greatest joy in a Jewish family remains when a son joins the covenant with an operation on his penis, his ritual induction into phallocentric Judaism—the *brit milah.* This binds him to the covenant which all Jewish men, starting with Abraham and Isaac, have with their god. Seen in retrospect by the adult Jewish woman, this is the baby girl's first major exclusion from

Judaism. This act is the great divide separating males and their god (the holy) from females (the profane).

The bar mitzvah reaffirms this special covenant as the male child is officially inducted into the Jewish male club—the community of men—when he becomes an adult male and a participatory member of the patriarchy. No women are allowed in that club, the relatively recent contrivance of the bat mitzvah notwithstanding. The bat mitzvah is part of the myth-making process that is supposed to make women believe they are equal participants, when in reality they are not. The bat mitzvah does not carry with it the same weight as the bar mitzvah—and how could it? It is for women and therefore, a minor occurrence as compared with the major event of a bar mitzvah, which is for men. There is no female club in Judaism equivalent to the male club into which a boy is inducted via his bar mitzvah. The latest variation on the bat-mitzvah theme is the bat mitzvah of the adult woman, who, as a child, was deprived of the Jewish education which her brothers received. Upon completing an arbitrary program of Jewish studies, she then goes through a ritual graduation ceremony which is at best just that, a graduation ceremony, and at worst, a pacifying contrivance, a device to perpetuate the myth of equality of genders when, in fact, there is no equality of genders in Judaism.

Most traditional Jewish men (as most men in general) are fearful of feminism, a fear that emerges in joking, trivializing, and at times, rage. They view feminism as a threat, as indeed it is—for once a Jewish woman's consciousness has been sufficiently raised, she inevitably starts to examine the very essence of Judaism and sees it for what it is, patriarchal and male-dominated. Why did it take so long to challenge this state of affairs? Lesley Hazleton's observation about Israeli women applies to all Jewish women: "Their attitude is one of suspended disbelief, making them willing victims of an empty but soothing ideology. Surrendering their real identity to the 'cover identity' ascribed them by ideology, they move in a male world of reality in the false guise of equals."[8]

And so we have the age-old myth of Jewish womanhood as exalted and honored because the Jewish woman is the "queen of her home." Call her a "queen"—and maybe she won't mind so much the relentless drudgery of housework. Put her on a pedestal—and maybe she won't notice her exclusion from meaningful participation in the external world of Jewish life. This myth has kept Jewish women from analyzing their true situation. Moreover, some question must be raised as to who is ultimately "in charge" in the traditional Jewish home when we observe that the Hebrew word for wife is *ishah,* woman, while the Hebrew word for husband is *ba'al,* master.[9] If the woman is queen, then the man is king.

A model of a strong matriarchal figure emerges among Jews of Eastern Europe, but this was a result of external socioeconomic conditions of *galut,* whereby the Jewish male was rendered less *macho* than the picture we derive of his conquering warrior self in Hebrew Scripture. The model, however true or false it may be in actuality, changes nothing in Jewish religious and community life.

Recent attempts try to reform Judaism to make it more palatable for Jewish women—more "palatable," not more "equal," because male-controlled Jewish institutions still want women to willingly accept their roles as assigned by men. Women can now be part of a *minyan,* the Conservative *men* declare. Women can now be rabbis, the Reform and Reconstructionist *men* declare. Even if women rabbis can get pulpits (and it is not so easy) this is simply a method of coopting women into the patriarchy in order to perpetuate it. It remains yet to be seen, for example, whether female rabbis will have as much authority as male rabbis. Will women rabbis, on assuming their roles, instill feminist principles (i.e., entailing some meaningful and powerful uses of *Shekhinah*) into Judaism—a revolution of sorts—rather than carrying on the male-supremacy tradition?

All the recent contrivances of Judaism regarding women, have served to divert women from any real analysis of their situation. Where are the women who can participate fully in the decision-making process of these so-called reforms? Women must wait for the males, who dominate Jewish life, to hand them some occasional token. Certainly, men will offer only those things that will in no way diminish their own supremacy in Jewish life.

And so Jewish feminists face a seemingly insoluble dilemma,

causing much anguish to those women who have been devoted Jews but who are responsive to the imperatives of women's consciousness-raising during the past decade or so. The dilemma and anguish grow geometrically as one realizes how inherent male supremacy is: in fact, reforms that would satisfy us might ultimately render it no longer Judaism. Jewish feminists are confronting the recognition that our Jewish heritage, to which many of us have clung so stubbornly, is totally patriarchal—and in a patriarchy, women, by definition, are subordinate.

Surely, if she had the choice, any self-respecting Jewish woman—let alone feminist—would disavow herself from such a self-negating structure. But even after all that has been realized—and much, much more—is integrated into our consciousness, it is difficult for us to break our ties. We feel that we are a link in Jewish history, a history in which so many women as well as men have suffered and died just because they were Jews and in order to remain Jews. Over the past half century we have seen two monumental events—the Nazi Holocaust and the rebirth of Israel. Both act as epoxies which keep us bound. How can we, after all that has come before us, break the chain? And, we do not want to stop being Jews. In spite of all, many Jewish feminists are feminists because we are Jews. Our Jewish heritage is one of activism in the cause of freedom and justice. Paradoxically, our Jewish experience has taught us the importance of feminist issues. Stripped of male dominance, the Jewish world view may not be so different from the feminist world view.

NOTES

1. Evelyn Torten Beck, Editor, *Nice Jewish Girls: A Lesbian Anthology* (Watertown, Mass.: Persephone Press, 1982).

2. For extensive documentation, see Susan Brownmiller, *Against Our Will: Men, Women and Rape* (New York: Simon and Schuster, 1975); Mary Daly, *Gyn/Ecology: The Metaethics of Radical Feminism* (Boston: Beacon Press, 1978); Andrea Dworkin, *Woman Hating* (New York: E. P. Dutton, 1974) and *Pornography: Men Possessing Women* (New York: Perigee, 1979); Susan Griffin, *Woman and Nature: The Roaring Inside Her* (New York: Harper and Row, 1978) and *Pornography and Silence: Culture's Revenge against Nature* (New York: Harper

and Row, 1981); Ann Jones, *Women Who Kill* (New York: Fawcett, 1981); Sanday, Peggy Reeves, *Female Power and Male Dominance: On the origins of sexual inequality* (Cambridge, England: Cambridge University Press, 1981).

3. See Charlene Spretnak, Editor, *The Politics of Women's Spirituality: Essays on the Rise of Spiritual Power within the Feminist Movement* (Garden City, N.Y.: Anchor Press / Doubleday, 1982); Starhawk, *The Spiral Dance: A Rebirth of the Ancient Religion of the Great Goddess* (San Francisco: Harper and Row, 1979) and *Dreaming the Dark: Magic, Sex and Politics* (Boston: Beacon Press, 1982).

4. See Merlin Stone, *Ancient Mirrors of Womanhood: Our Goddess and Heroine Heritage,* vols. I and II (New York: New Sybilline Books, 1980).

5. See Merlin Stone, *When God Was a Woman* (New York: Harcourt, Brace, Jovanovich, 1978).

6. Louis Ginsberg, in *Legends of the Bible* (New York: Simon and Schuster, 1956), pp. 117–118, claims that "Lot's moral sense was no better than it should have been." Ginzberg notes that Lot was later punished for this, but there seems to be no scriptural reference to Lot's punishment for the intended rape of his daughters. At least the travesty made one Judaic scholar uncomfortable enough to comment on it, however inadequately.

7. Batya Bauman, *The Relationship between Women's Inferiority and Male Homosexual Activity in Hebrew Scripture* (unpublished paper for a seminar on "Homosexuality: A Case Study in Psychoanalytic and Ethical Theory," Fordham University, December 1976).

8. See Lesley Hazleton, *Israeli Women: The Reality Behind the Myths* (New York: Simon and Schuster, 1977).

9. A form of this word, *ba-alah,* means sexual intercourse. This certainly says something about the traditional roles and the implications during sexual as well as other forms of intercourse between a *ba'al* and his *ishah.*

Memories of an Orthodox Youth

Thena Kendall

SIMHAT Torah was for me, as for all ultra-Orthodox children, one of the highlights of the year. I remember going to the synagogue with my parents when I was nine, wearing my best dress and carrying the traditional apple-topped flag. As in previous years, I stood downstairs to watch the processions, mesmerized by the way the usually solemn adults sang and danced and seemed magically transformed. In this large, Orthodox, North London synagogue, the *hakafot* continued until every man had had his turn, and the children were encouraged to dance and sing with them. But that year the dancing had barely begun when a warden came up to me and said firmly: "You are too big to be down here. Go up to the ladies' gallery and watch from there."

It was like being expelled from paradise. Too frightened to protest, I went up to my mother in tears and watched from behind the metal grille. It was the beginning of the realization that there was no place for me in the main body of the Orthodox congregation.

In addition to the usual ineptly taught *heder,* my Jewish education was supplemented by my father, who made a point of teaching me the weekly *sidra,* content on the whole with translations rather than explanations. I was also expected to recite a portion of the morning service before breakfast but had no idea of the meaning. I only knew I got no breakfast until this ritual had been performed.

When I got older, I questioned the meaning of some of the

prayers: Why should I thank God every morning for "making me according to Thy Will," while boys and men gave thanks for not being a woman? I was told that this was because women were not expected to perform a number of the *mitzvot,* and therefore men gave thanks for their opportunities to serve God. It seemed an unsatisfactory explanation, particularly when I saw how much hard work was involved for the women of Orthodox households in running their homes. There was, for example, the annual ordeal of preparing the household for Passover. My mother labored for weeks to get the kitchen reorganized to meet the rigorous requirements of *kashrut.* Every cupboard was cleared out and scrubbed, all the ordinary saucepans, dishes, and cutlery stowed away in cupboards that were not merely locked but tied with string so that no hand should inadvertently tug at a drawer containing *hametz.* The Passover crockery was not allowed to touch any surface on which a *hametz* plate had rested. As a result, in those pre-plastic days, there was a fantastic accumulation of cardboard, wood, and even wire which covered kitchen sinks, draining board, and stove, getting soggier and dirtier throughout Passover.

It was not only the upheaval, but the extra work incurred by the observance of the Passover laws that upset me. Not even a can opener that had been used during the rest of the year could be used during the Passover preparations. One labor-saving device that we did normally use was a mincing machine, but we could not afford to buy another mincer just for the Passover, so (as gefilte fish was one of my mother's specialities) all the fish had to be chopped by hand—a hard and smelly procedure. As it was inconceivable to have a seder meal without guests, we found ourselves cooking on a larger scale with fewer utensils. It was hard work, although my mother never complained. But when I was small I noticed that she invariably fell asleep during the seder ceremony. As a child, I just felt pleased that I was able to stay awake longer than an adult; but later on I appreciated just how exhausted my mother was. As I grew up I found myself increasingly resentful that it was my father who dictated what needed to be done—that surface must be scrubbed; this cupboard must be thoroughly cleaned out before anything could be put into it—but that it was my mother and I who did most of the hard work. Perhaps it gave us a better appreciation of the meaning of slavery, even if there was no sign of freedom.

It was some comfort to me that the kind of squalor inflicted during the Passover on our household was only an annual event. It was a huge relief to see our kitchen free of all clutter, once Passover was over. But in some households more Orthodox than ours, even an ordinary Sabbath inflicted restraints that I found quite unbearable. Some of my girlfriends were not allowed to comb or brush their hair on the Sabbath—breaking up a tangle of hair was considered work—and washing the hands with soap was also forbidden. It was also not permitted to tear paper; but at least these households had the foresight to tear off sufficient pieces of toilet roll to serve the family for hygienic purposes from Friday evening to Saturday night. It all made the day of rest seem unhygienic and unpleasant. At least I began to understand why I was always aware of unpleasant odors in the ladies' section of the synagogue (where no one ever opened a window).

I was not antireligious; I longed for celebration and festivities—but it was only the men and the boys who went to the synagogue toward the end of the Sabbath for *seudah shlishit,* the third meal, at which as far as I could gather there was more merriment than enlightenment. The rabbi did give a talk, but there was drink and refreshment, and everyone seemed to thoroughly enjoy singing table hymns and exchanging stories or reminiscences. I would have liked to have gone too, and so would my mother, who was blessed with a beautiful soprano voice. But the sound of a woman's voice was not allowed to be heard at an Orthodox gathering. So we stayed at home, sitting in the dark (as we were not allowed to switch on lights) and amusing ourselves as best we could. For me the moment the Sabbath ended, and the lights came on, seemed more like a reentry into life than the end of the day of rest. The *Havdalah* prayer which ended *hamavdil ben or l'hoshekh* seemed to be the wrong way around as far as I was concerned. It was the Sabbath that was dark for me—not the week! Somehow holy days seemed to involve drudgery and restrictions but none of the compensating joyousness with which our Hasidic ancestors had celebrated their faith. Once again, as in eighteenth-century Poland, the letter rather than the spirit of the law seemed to dominate.

The older I got, the more the discrepancies between Orthodox practice and Orthodox teachings worried me. The grandfather of one of my closest friends was considered a pillar of our community; he rose at five every morning to devote himself to two hours of Talmud study before going to the synagogue. But as a regular visitor to his household, I knew that he terrorized my friend and her parents. He kept a hairbrush at the dining table in case he needed to administer punishment to his erring granddaughter.

I was only allowed to visit my friend on a summer Sabbath, if we both spent time reading the appropriate chapter from the "Sayings of the Fathers." No one ever offered to discuss with us the implications of the texts we had to read; as these contain some important Jewish thoughts on ethical problems, it seems, with hindsight, an oddly missed opportunity. We amused ourselves by reading aloud the more outrageous names of the learned sages. What teenager could have resisted giggling at Ben Bag-Bag or Nittai the Arbelite? But it also did not escape my attention that the synagogue doyen who insisted on our staying indoors on hot summer afternoons to read about the merit of anonymously given charity, was adamant when called up to the Reading of the Law, that not only the amount but the recipients of one's donations be specified.

It was the static nature of the observance that worried me. I could not accept the immutability of the many rules and regulations that ruled our daily lives. Was it really work to switch on an electric fire on the Sabbath? I could accept that it might have been onerous when it involved making a fire, but now? Nevertheless, my family took seriously the injunction to "build a fence around the Torah." This meant that a number of actions were forbidden, not because they were in themselves sinful, but because they might lead to a transgression. For example, one is forbidden to carry heavy loads on the Sabbath. We were therefore not allowed to carry even a handkerchief in our pockets, as once we carried anything we might forget the prohibition—and goodness knew what we might be tempted to carry! However some Talmudic logic ordained that if we tied our handkerchiefs around our wrists, this was not strictly speaking "carrying" and so was permitted. When I was only six, my parents allowed me to finish off a banana (a luxury in wartime Britain) on the way to synagogue one Sabbath morning. An Orthodox neighbor solemnly upbraided us all for this desecration.

It was the attention to such trivia on the one hand, and more important, the inability to confront the problems of life in twentieth-century Britain on the other, that combined to estrange me from the Orthodox surroundings of my childhood. The crucial break with faith came when I had to come to terms with the fact that my mother had a fatal kidney disease. I remember discussing with an ultra-Orthodox rabbi the ethics of choice presented to doctors involved in the unenviable task of selecting patients for treatment on the few kidney machines then available. What guidance could he give? The answer, evasively phrased, was: "None." This was the most terrifying disappointment of all. Judaism—so it had been dinned into me from my earliest years—was a way of life, and there was a rule in life for every occasion—but for coming to terms with death there seemed to be no help. Death was not even discussed. None of the very Orthodox ministers who visited my mother ever attempted to talk to her about her feelings; they would sit at the foot of her bed discussing abstruse points of Talmud with my father. I remember with particular poignancy one visitor who arrived on the Sabbath and spent his entire visit agonizing as to whether he had desecrated the Sabbath by coming into the hospital through the electronically-operated doors set in motion by his approach. There was also the rabbi who harangued me for allowing my mother to eat, on a plate supplied by the hospital, a minute scrap of kosher chicken brought from home.

When my mother died, I was over thirty and working in a very demanding professional job. Already exhausted by the harrowing months of watching her suffer from an incurable disease, I was not really prepared for the onslaught on my emotions that the funeral preparations inflicted. I was not allowed to see my mother's body nor even to sit watch during the night. A male cousin took on that duty, as my father was too exhausted. I was an only child and we did not have many relatives in England; thus I had actually never had occasion to attend a funeral, but I took it for granted that I would go to my mother's funeral. The Orthodox rabbis were equally adamant that I should not go. This situation was only resolved when my father declared that he wanted me to go. Because of the respect in which he was held, I was allowed to go. Five years later, when my father died, we repeated the confrontation. Quite obviously against the will of the officiating rabbis, I went to the cemetery, accompanied by my husband and his parents. (These practices were quite alien to my in-laws; they belonged to the United Synagogue, which though traditional in its approach was not quite so intolerant.) At the cemetery I was firmly told that I could not go to the grave, and a solid mass of Orthodox gentlemen blocked my way as they followed my father's coffin to his last resting place. However, I knew another route to the grave (which had been prepared next to my mother's) and managed to be standing alongside the grave before the coffin was brought there. No one dared to tell me to leave. But with every clod that was thrown onto my father's coffin, another link that connected me to the Orthodox tradition was broken. I would have liked to have said Kaddish for him, for he had left no son, but no Orthodox congregation would countenance a woman reciting a prayer in front of the congregation. Although a kind friend suggested that I attend the service and recite the prayer quietly to myself, I felt that if the congregation were not prepared to hear my voice I might as well say it in the privacy of my home. It was only some years later when we had become members of a Reform congregation that I realized my wish to recite Kaddish would have been granted without fuss in any Reform synagogue. But my experiences within the Orthodox community left me feeling for some years that my religious needs were better met away from religious institutions. As a teenager, appalled by the constant chatter of the women sitting in the synagogue, I had once ventured to say that I felt it might be easier to achieve a communion with God walking in the open air than in the midst of the gossips comparing notes about their children and grandchildren or moaning about the prices of kosher food. This brought my father's wrath down upon my head. What right had I, a girl, to separate myself from the community? I was bold enough to mention the experience of the Baal Shem, founder of Hasidism, who was reputed to have spent years living in the countryside making his peace with God. That, I was told firmly, was all right for the Baal Shem, but not for us. He had shown us the way; we should be content to follow.

My parents in fact both came from Hasidic families, and I was endlessly reminded of my *yihus*—a Yiddish word that summed up my value based on my ancestral heritage. In the marriage stakes, in a Hasidic setting, I could have become a very hot favorite. It was unfortunate that I did not fit into that world, burdened as I was with an English education and liberated ideas about making my way independently in the profession of my choice, I was hardly destined to be the happy bride of someone just graduated from a yeshiva and hoping to go into some suitable business ideally owned by his father-in-law. It did not bother me that I was a nonrunner in these marriage stakes, but it did bother me greatly when I was fourteen to find that my illustrious ancestry counted for nothing in other circumstances. I was very firmly put in my place when one of my more distinguished relatives, a Hasidic rabbi who lived in New York, was visiting London in order to see his family and meet some of his *Hasidim*. I was allowed to stay up until nearly midnight to greet him. When he first arrived neither my mother nor I were allowed to go near him. For several hours our house was filled with bearded men of all ages—total strangers to us—who were anxious for a glimpse of their *rebbe*. I was banished upstairs. My mother made tea, which one of the men took in to the visitors. Eventually the strangers departed, and my father signaled that we could come in. I rushed into the room, all ready to greet my uncle with outstretched hand. But he stared at me, ignored my hand, and made it quite clear in voice and gesture that he wanted no physical contact with me. No one had thought to warn me that Hasidic *rebbes* did not shake hands with women, even if one were a fourteen-year-old niece with an impeccable lineage. I went to bed shaken and angry, wondering why I had been asked to stay up to greet this man. If he regarded me as unclean I might have served his wishes better by avoiding him altogether. Later on I met his daughter, a married woman who not only wore a wig but had actually shaved her hair off, so that she looked like a convict when I glimpsed her in her bedroom one evening. Once again I was reinforced in my feeling that Orthodoxy and ugliness seemed destined to be linked in my life. I determined never to subject myself to that kind of life-style.

Luckily, I married a man who had not grown up in such an Orthodox household. If both of us had shared these experiences, I suspect we might well have severed all connections with established Jewish communities. As it was, my husband felt rather more benevolent toward Jewish practices than I did. When our first child was expected, my husband took it for granted that if the baby were a boy he would have a *brit.* I felt very equivocal but promised to make inquiries about a suitable *mohel.* I telephoned the Initiation Society (which represents the Orthodox *mohelim* in Britain) and explained that I was expecting a baby shortly, and would like to know of a *mohel* I could contact should I give birth to a son. The man who answered the phone was decidedly unfriendly. He did not reply to my question but posed his own: Why was *I* making this inquiry? Couldn't my husband make the arrangements? I pointed out that in my last month of pregnancy I had leisure to make such inquiries, unlike my husband, who was burdened not only with his own job but with those household jobs I could no longer do. The representative persisted with his questioning. Where had we been married? He was obviously taken aback when I gave the name of the ultra-Orthodox community to which my father had belonged. Nonplussed, he refused to give any more information but told me to ask my husband to contact him if and when we had a son. We did not go back to the Initiation Society for help. A friend of ours recommended a charming doctor who also performed circumcisions. The ceremony took place in the hospital without too much fuss.

Nineteen months later our second son was circumcised in a ceremony held in our own home. This time we broke with tradition. With a friend's help, I prepared a luncheon for twenty friends, nearly half of whom were women. I did not attend the actual circumcision—I could not bear to—but men and women sat around the table and joined together in singing the grace after the meal. I compared the celebration around our family table—men and women together—with a conversation I had had some months earlier when I had gone back to visit some young women who were members of my parents' community. They all had been younger than I, and they had been obsessed, as all mothers are, with concern about their children and their houses. But the central focus of conversation was the expected birth, around Passover, of one young woman's second baby. There was long and agonized discussion about how she should prepare for this event: Should she cook lots of food *pesachdik,* so that if the *brit* took place on Passover she would be all prepared with the correct food? On the other hand, this would be difficult to do in March when the kitchen was not suitably prepared. But if she prepared ordinary kosher food to put into the freezer, what would they do after the birth if the baby's *brit* had to be held on Passover? The discussion raged interminably over the most amazing details of *kashrut.* I had forgotten the hours of discussion over what was kosher and what was not kosher, that was invariably on the agenda whenever members of the community met. It all seemed a long way from religion. I just felt grateful that I was free of the need to attend to such trivia and gave thanks with all my heart for being blessed with two healthy children. The Reform congregation that we had joined shortly before the birth of our first child held a baby-blessing ceremony involving both parents. It was a very moving experience to stand together before the Ark holding our little son and recite the prayer of thanksgiving. At least now I was allowed to speak in a synagogue.

It was partly the personality of a particular Reform rabbi, and partly the atmosphere of real worship that I experienced in his congregation that led us to align ourselves with this less traditional approach to Judaism. In this synagogue women are actively involved in all parts of the service, and in recent years two women have become rabbis in Reform congregations. I can sit alongside my husband and sons during any service, and I can now touch or kiss a Torah scroll when it is carried around the synagogue. This year I was even invited to carry a Torah on Simhat Torah. However, I did not feel worthy of the honor and refused. Here my Orthodox upbringing lingers; I feel that unless one observes the law one cannot claim the privileges, and as a not very observant Jew, I felt it was right to refuse. But even though I myself have no desire to lead a congregation—despite my ancestry—I am delighted that other women have the opportunity to do so.

A Feminist Path to Judaism

Gail Shulman

WHAT does it mean to be a Jew? Ever since we were children, most of us have had to deal with this question. In fact, I have only to hear the words to be reminded of the books well-meaning adults gave to bat and bar mitzvahs and of all the serious discussions we had in confirmation class or young adult groups. We talked about Jewish identity, the importance of continuing the tradition, both at home and in synagogue, our sense of chosenness, the importance of opposing injustice with courage and strength, the implications of suffering, and, of course, the Holocaust. Those discussions undoubtedly still go on, but for a Jewish feminist ten years after the woman's movement began, the question of what it means to be Jewish has been replaced by another, namely: Why does a feminist bother to ask the question at all?

A child in a family with any Jewish consciousness cannot avoid growing up with a sense of uniqueness. Looking at my own childhood (in a medium-sized city in southeastern New York state), I can see how my feeling of specialness was intensified by the fact that the Jewish population was relatively small. The message was conveyed to me that I was not like everyone else: Living in a kosher household, staying out of school on the High Holy Days, eating special foods on special dishes at Passover, making Hanukkah cards instead of Christmas decorations (along with the two other Jewish kids in my third-grade class)—all were powerful expressions of the specialness of being Jewish. In the synagogue I felt in awe at being in a holy place, as though God might actually speak to me, and I thought I understood what it meant to be a member of the chosen people. Yet for a Jewish female child, the sense of being different exists within Judaism as well and is made clear to us in the sex roles we are shown and the expectations with which we grow up. From childhood on, I have seen my parents living out traditional sex roles—my mother keeping kosher and maintaining a gracious Jewish home, my father participating regularly in the *minyan* and the life of the synagogue. Although I don't remember questioning the polarity of those roles until I was a young adult, I do remember becoming aware of the restrictions placed on women when my grandmother described her mother: "She loved to study Torah, and she had long discussions with the rabbi. Everyone said she would have been a rabbi if she had been a man." I also remember that along with my perception of the synagogue as a beautiful, holy place, there were less positive feelings—the sense that I, as a female, was allowed only limited participation in the synagogue, that I must be silent, obedient, and hang back and watch as the men led and participated in the service. Even though women and men sat together in our Conservative synagogue, there was an obvious sense of separation. We *watched* while they *did*.

Years later, the feminist movement provided me with a context and a supportive community in which to articulate my anger and frustration with patriarchal traditions. Jewish feminists came to see that the treatment of women as "separate but equal" was the thinly veiled rationalization of a real fear of women—as other, as unclean, even as evil. Six years ago in the Jewish feminist movement, our anger was mingled with hope that Judaism contained more than just a niche for us as wives and mothers, nurturers and transmitters of tradition, that we could be participants, leaders, equals who could change and reinterpret *halakhah,* demand inclusion in the *minyan* and the rabbinate, create new rituals that would welcome girl babies into the covenant as ceremonially as boys, develop special ceremonies for women, and rediscover female imagery and symbols in Judaism. Those were and continue to be very important issues, but despite many important changes in the various denominations (and within individual synagogues as well), Jewish leaders often respond to a narrowly defined "woman's role," rather than to women as real people. A telling example of this kind of response has been the recent concern of Jewish leaders over the declining birth rate and the effect the Zero Population Growth movement has had on Jews. The message is quite clear, and the reaction seems to be more to Jewish feminism than to Zero Population Growth—while Jewish women participating in the *minyan* and serving as rabbis may be tolerated, uppity Jewish women disavowing the primacy of their place in the home will not:

> Many "liberated" young Jewish women no longer regard the opportunities and responsibilities for rearing children, keeping a home, and engaging in constructive social or philanthropic work as sufficiently fulfilling. . . . Even mothers of small children with successful husbands arbitrarily elect to return to the labor pool, leaving much of the vital influence of early childhood training to maternal surrogates and day centers. . . . The dramatic decline in the fertility rate of young women with greater educational background and higher family income . . . has been thoroughly documented.[1]

Not all the responses are as blatantly sexist. Many rabbis and Jewish leaders express the fear that reluctance to produce large families presents a threat to the survival of Judaism itself, and they appeal to Jews to show concern for the future of Judaism before thinking of themselves. But it is immediately apparent that such an unselfish gesture would affect a woman more than a man. This seems little more than an attempt to arouse a woman's guilt for jeopardizing the future of Judaism by daring to consider her own needs first.

There is indeed a threat to Judaism here; but it is not so much a threat to future generations as it is a challenge to the basic patriarchal structure of Judaism, which condemns us when we refuse to accept the role of wife and mother and mocks us as Sophie Portnoys when we do. The result of such strong-arm tactics will not be to bring Jewish feminists back into line but rather to force many of us—single women, women with families and careers, lesbians, single mothers, and married women who are childless—to ask the painful question, "Why bother with Judaism at all?" For years I've asked that question, alone and with other women, and for some time I have known that even if I could view my personal and religious history as part of my past, important but *past,* that I could actually put away from me, I would still face a more difficult obstacle. Despite my being a feminist who is not a traditional Jew, it is my very Jewishness which is at the root of my feminism. Feminism is a prophetic movement concerned with justice for the oppressed, compassion for those who suffer, a sense of history, of community, of righteousness, and the courage to live in opposition. Oddly enough, Sigmund Freud, an avowed atheist (and certainly no feminist) acknowledged a similar debt of gratitude to his Jewish ancestry: freedom from prejudices that narrow the use of the intellect and the readiness to live in opposition.[2] If this has been a positive discovery, it is also ironic—my feminism is enriched by and rooted in my Judaism, and so the two are in a sense inseparable; yet I do not feel accepted by the very tradition that has formed and informed me, for it fails to support and affirm the women that I and many other feminists have become.

In the spring of 1979, I went to Newport, Rhode Island, with a friend who is not Jewish. After we had toured one of the mansions, we decided to see the Touro Synagogue, the oldest synagogue in the United States. We arrived an hour or so before sunset; the air was clear and still, the synagogue was beautiful and I felt as though I were on a pilgrimage. But when we reached the main entrance we found a neatly lettered sign that politely but firmly reminded "ladies" that they were to use the side entrance. My friend and I did not enter the Touro Synagogue that day (although ironically he, a non-Jew, could have walked through that front door simply because he was male), and I left having heard once again the fundamental *no* that Judaism offers to women. Judith Plaskow's words came to mind: "Every time I let myself be lulled into thinking that I as a whole person am a member of this community, some event lets me know in no uncertain terms that I am wrong."[3]

And so the task of Jewish feminism is not as simple as it seemed ten years ago. It is not merely a matter of changing and reinterpreting *halakhah* and gaining inclusion in the *minyan;* rather, it is a much more complex process, bringing with it the hope (and threat) of profound change. Feminism challenges the patriarchal nature of Judaism and demands recognition of women as full persons rather than only in male-defined roles. It is clear that a logical extension of this recognition would be the affirmation not only of traditional families, but of many other kinds of family units and life-styles as well. Without these fundamental changes in the patriarchal structure, many feminists who do not fit into the traditional roles will continue to feel estranged from Judaism. My own examination of my life as a feminist has resulted in the positive discovery that one source of my feminism is my identity as a Jew. But the irony here is that I affirm my Jewishness in a way Judaism seems unable and unwilling to accept or return.

NOTES

1. H. L. Roberts, "Endogenous Jewish Genocide—The Impact of the ZPG-Nonparenthood Movement," *The Reconstructionist,* November 1974, as quoted by Shirley Frank in "The Population Panic: Why Jewish Leaders Want Jewish Women to be Fruitful and Multiply," *Lilith,* vol. 1, No. 4, p. 16.

2. Sigmund Freud, "Ansprache an die Mitglieder des Vereins B'nai B'rith" (1926), *Gesammelte Werke,* vol. 16 (London: Imago Pub. Co., Ltd.); quoted by Erik Erikson in *Childhood and Society* (New York: W. W. Norton, 1963), p. 281.

3. Judith Plaskow, "The Jewish Feminist: Conflict in Identities," *Response,* Number 18 (Summer 1973), p. 12.

Part Two

FORGING NEW IDENTITIES

Introduction

FEMINISM has not been easy for Jews. The examination of Judaism's treatment of women in its laws, customs, and teachings makes many of us question whether it is desirable—even possible—for a feminist to be a Jew. Theologian Dorothee Soelle has written that "the more a person perceives his [sic] suffering as a natural part of life, the lower his self-esteem . . . To be caught up in one role, without flexibility, predisposes one to suffer." Belief that one's role, however unhappy, grows out of the natural order does not encourage change, but instead fosters an inability to recognize and articulate frustrations and unhappiness. When a role is believed to be ordained by God, to whom one must submit willingly and with joy, it becomes even more difficult to question it. The questioning of Jewish tradition and teachings and the initiation of a search for clearer understanding of women's and men's roles takes great courage, particularly since the outcome of the search is still unknown. The feminist struggle with Jewish identity reflects stages remarkably similar to those outlined by Elisabeth Kübler-Ross in describing the mourning of one's own impending death: denial, anger, bargaining, depression, and acceptance. The parallels are not really surprising, since feminists are mourning the loss of a part of their internalized identity by rejecting the socially normative, stereotyped images of the kind of women they were raised to become.

Many women—and certainly many men—still deny that there is anything wrong with the role assigned women by Jewish law and tradition. Usually, a sense of oppression and injustice arising from personal experience is the initial spark for most who question Judaism's values, customs, structures, and beliefs. The response is anger, a feeling of betrayal by one's people, by religion, and by God. As several of the contributors to this volume indicate, experiences such as being forbidden to dance with a Torah on Simhat Torah, being forced to say Kaddish hidden behind a curtain, or praying a liturgy that knows only male language and imagery—these give Jewish women a sense of false consciousness, of being forced into a mode of existence that is not an authentic expression of self-understanding.

A common and seemingly constructive reaction to this anger is to bargain for improvements. Many feminists thought that eliminating the most obvious signs of discrimination would resolve the problem. Many community leaders thought that permitting women responsible positions within national organizations or counting women in the *minyan* would settle the matter. To be sure, the bargaining was highly successful, and many gains were made, particularly in recent years, although not without serious compromise. Some women still bargain, demanding *aliyot* to the Torah while renouncing any desire to be ordained rabbis.

But for many feminists, bargaining only brings about an even greater sense of alienation. The process of fighting for certain simple changes often makes women aware of their broader exclusion from the formation of Jewish law, tradition, interpretation, and application. Learning, for example, that it was for the sake of the "honor of the congregation" that women do not lead certain prayers in the presence of men, brings the more painful knowledge that the very concept "congregation" refers exclusively to male Jews. Further and deeper study of Judaism makes feminists aware that the problem is not individual prayers, but the entire range of liturgy; not particular rituals, but the entire symbol system; not today's community, but the entire course of history. The problems seem eternal and insurmountable, and many feminists feel unable to make the necessary changes. Worse is the realization that feminists struggle not within a foreign body, but within their own people and religious heritage, as Jews among Jews. The treatment of women in Judaism represents the subjugation of a people by their own brethren: "A loss numerically greater than a hundred pogroms; yet Jewish literature and history report not one wail, not one tear," writes Cynthia Ozick.

Acceptance of Jewish identity by feminists can begin with the formulation of constructive new interpretations of Jewish tradition. Ozick describes the conflict in identity that arises when women are excluded from the normative Jewish experience: "When my rabbi says, 'A Jew is called to the Torah,' he never means me or any other living Jewish woman. . . . My own synagogue is the only place in the world where I am not named Jew." Yet the treatment of women in Judaism derives not from Torah, Ozick argues, but from its misinterpretation by rabbis throughout the centuries; it is a social, not a sacred question. While the Torah is ultimately concerned with eternal and immutable principles of justice, it contains no commandment stating, "Thou shalt not lessen the humanity of women," Ozick points out. But precisely because it stands for justice as an absolute requirement—even to the extent of opposing aspects of the natural and social order—the Torah provides its own basis for radical change of women's position within Judaism, change that is necessary, Ozick concludes, "to preserve and strengthen Torah itself."

The disjunction described by Ozick between the affirmation of her Jewish identity by non-Jews and the negation of it within the synagogue extends beyond the religious community. Deborah Lipstadt reviews the attempts by Federation organizations to allow only minimal, low-level positions to women, primarily as volunteers, and to reserve the most important decision-making positions for men. She argues that the reality of contemporary American Jewish life makes such role-divisions within Federation anachronistic. At a time when women are being accepted into high-paying professions and can attain some degree of economic and political power, they continue to be relegated to subservient positions within the Jewish community; this is intolerable to women and stifling to a community in need of talent and leadership. The voluntarism expected of Jewish females today is simply a continuation of the self-sacrifice traditionally expected of women, Lipstadt claims. Yet the power of Federation, with its huge financial resources, must be fully open to women if they are to become equal partners in the Jewish community. Relegation to a separate women's division or to menial tasks guarantees exclusion from self-determination and from changes necessary to support new roles of women and men.

Yet even when apparent signs of separation of women and men are removed, attitudes may remain. Rosa Kaplan examines the position of women who are single, divorced, or widowed, and who often have difficulty integrating into the family-oriented synagogue and community. The problem, Kaplan explains, is that while today's community has broken down the physical barriers between women and men, its members' attitudes still reflect the expectation that traditional family roles will be maintained: "Even if an unattached woman were interested in joining the usual woman's activities, the hours such activities are scheduled most likely would not be convenient for a working woman." The problem in the Jewish community is not only conflict between men and women, but among the varying life-styles: "Unless individuals learn to relate to each other inside and outside the family as human beings rather than as role-occupant, the family that stays together may well decay together."

The conflict between the demands of feminism and Judaism is great because the two constitute inseparable identities; one cannot be sacrificed for the other. Alice Bloch describes her move away from the Jewish community as she grew involved with a lesbian community. Yet despite Judaism's vehement rejection of homosexuality, she does not reject her Jewishness: "Jewish identity is important to me because being Jewish is an integral part of myself: it's my inheritance, my roots. Christian women sometimes have a hard time understanding this, because Christian identity is so much tied up with religious beliefs. It is possible to be an ex-Catholic or an ex-Baptist, but it really is not possible to be an ex-Jew. A Jew doesn't have to believe any particular doctrine: she just *is* a Jew."

Often feminism, rather than turning Jews away from Judaism, creates the possibility for women to identify as Jews. Before the feminist movement, women who felt alienated from their allotted positions simply left the community. A crucial difference lies between the solutions of Dorothea Mendelssohn (1765–1839) and Lily Montagu (1873–1963), both of whom were intellectual forces in their generations. Mendelssohn found no intellectual or spiritual satisfaction in her role within Judaism, and so converted to Christianity, while Montagu, influenced by the women's movement in England, became a founder of Liberal Judaism.

Feminism provides options. To those who remain to struggle within the boundaries of a particular community, it offers support; for those who move to a new community, it is a vehicle for new contacts. Sara Reguer does not seek a synagogue that will be more accepting of her, but seeks changes within Orthodoxy, the community in which she grew up. She describes in her essay the lack of understanding and even hostility that greeted her when she said Kaddish at her mother's funeral and for the next eleven months at daily services in Orthodox synagogues. While there is no explicit rabbinic injunction prohibiting women from saying Kaddish, widespread belief holds that women are exempt or even barred from the ritual. For Reguer, the primary goal is education of the community concerning its own tenets, as well as the encouragement of other women in mourning who need the support of joining a daily *minyan* to say Kaddish. During her year of mourning, Reguer writes, "It was saying Kaddish . . . that enabled me to keep my sanity. If I had not *had* to get out of bed at 6:30 A.M. in order to be on time for the beginning of services, I can guarantee that I simply would not have left my bed at all."

For others, the *Havurah* movement has been important in its efforts to balance traditionalism with creativity, while striving for equality of women and men as its goal. Reading from the Torah for the first time at a *Havurah* gathering was, for Arleen Stern, "a moment in the process of coming to terms with a troubling part of my tradition, the part that would consign me to a role of passivity, that tells me I have no place in leading others. By publicly reading in a *havurah* service, I moved a step closer to feeling I have a place and a home as a Jew."

Whatever paths are chosen within feminism, Jewish identity clearly remains important. Many feminists claim that precisely because they are Jews they become active as feminists, and often because of feminism they are motivated to retain positive affirmations of their Jewishness. Carolyn Heilbrun writes in her book, *Becoming Woman:* "To be a feminist one had to have had an experience of being an outsider more extreme than merely being a woman. . . . Having been a Jew, however unobserved that identification was, however fiercely I had denied the adamant anti-Semitism all around me as I grew up—still, having been a Jew had made me an outsider. It had permitted me to be a feminist."

While being a Jew fostered Heilbrun's identity as a feminist, being a feminist often encourages women to strive for a deeper understanding of Judaism. Rejecting traditional images of women, feminists are beginning to examine Jewish teachings from a new perspective, creating interpretations that allow, even demand, radical changes in outlook and behavior. According to Claire Satlof, the key to such interpretation lies in ritual and language, the central themes of Jewish feminist fiction. Rituals establish the ordering of individual lives and make profound statements about our understanding of the social and religious order, an assumption basic to both Judaism and feminism. For example, the difference in traditional Jewish rituals for naming baby girls and baby boys clearly indicates the different positions that children will grow to occupy as adults within the community. In creating new rituals to celebrate the birth of a baby girl or her attainment of puberty, women enhance their own self-esteem as well as establish a new position for themselves in the community.

Language is particularly crucial, Satlof argues, because it is "the means by which we conceive and perceive the world." Since texts are central to Judaism, men have held power by controlling the writing, interpreting, and study of those texts. "Women were powerless to alter the situation as they were denied the means—language—of controlling their world," Satlof writes. By composing new texts, women tell their own stories, retell the stories of history, and set forth patterns through which they henceforth shape the world. Writing becomes an agent for change within Judaism, "not merely redistributing roles but realigning and revaluing the realms of rituals and history."

In this way, the significance of feminist fiction lies beyond the stories it tells and the rituals it describes. Their real intent and power are "the wresting of linguistic control from men and a literary revisioning of Jewish reality." The unique nature of this genre of literature makes possible, according to Satlof, a ritual reenactment through reading. The readers "participate in and perform that text . . . reconstituting themselves through the proffered new beginnings."

That participation in ritual can lead to a new sense of oneself is echoed in a personal vein by Deborah Lipstadt. She went to say Kaddish on her father's *yahrzeit* at afternoon services in a local synagogue which does not ordinarily count women in the *minyan.* When only nine men had arrived and the sun began to set, the rabbi decided to accept Deborah and begin the prayers. Services over, she was about to leave for an appointment, when she suddenly realized her presence was necessary for the others to make a *minyan* for the evening services: "I felt a wonderful wash of warmth and fulfillment. . . . You see, they *needed* me for the *minyan.*"

Not only individual women, but all participants in Jewish communal life are affected by the changing roles of women. Laura Geller reports in her essay that her appearance as rabbi on a pulpit leading synagogue services disturbed many of her congregants' expectations, leading them to question many of their theological assumptions. Some began to explore their understanding of God more deeply, finally rejecting male, anthropomorphic images, while others began to take a more active role in synagogue services after seeing what obstacles Geller had been able to overcome in becoming ordained a rabbi.

Such questioning is both necessary and welcome as feminists challenge Jewish traditions and teachings in writing and action. For Jewish women who do not see themselves reflected in the images and roles of women set forth by classical Judaism, the task is to develop an identity that will combine the values of feminism with those of Judaism. The problem is not limited to women, but extends to the entire community, which is often not at all eager to participate in the search for answers. The goal is to reconsider not only individual identity, but the self-understanding of the community as well.

Notes toward Finding the Right Question

Cynthia Ozick

Is the Right Question "Theological"?

The philosopher Suzanne K. Langer somewhere observes that every answer is concealed in the question that elicits it, and that what we must strive to do, then, is not look for the right answer, but attempt rather to discover the right question. The danger in the present discussion—the relation of women to the Jewish Way—is that the wrong question will be asked, inexorably leading to answers that are as good as lies.

How can one learn whether one has asked the "right" or the "wrong" question? From a consideration of the answer. By way of illustration: we have lately heard a complaint that Jewish mainstream tradition, being devoid of female anthropomorphic imagery, not to mention female deity-figures, is an obstacle to the self-esteem of women. Jewish women, we are told, lack idealized larger-than-life "models." The "female nurturing principle" is absent from Jewish cosmic notions.

Formulated as a question, the complaint emerges as follows: how shall we infiltrate into Jewish thought an adumbration of divinity which is *also female*?

One of the most frequent answers is to tinker with the language of liturgy. For instance, for the phrasing of "Blessed art Thou, O Lord our God, King of the Universe," we are advised to substitute the term "Queen of the Universe."

The answer stuns with its crudity. It is preposterous. What? Millennia after the cleansing purity of Abraham's vision of the One Creator, a return to Astarte, Hera, Juno, Venus, and all their proliferating sisterhood? Sex goddesses, fertility goddesses, mother goddesses? The sacrifices brought to these were often enough human. This is the new vision intended to "restore dignity" to Jewish women? A resurrection of every ancient idolatry the Jewish idea came into the world to drive out, so as to begin again with a purifying clarity?

The answer slanders and sullies monotheism. The answer has tested the question; the question fails. Without an uncompromising monotheism, there can be no Jewish Way; it becomes, then, somebody else's way; but not the Jewish one. Not for nothing does a Jew fervently recite, morning and evening, "Hear, O Israel, the Lord our God is One," in order to reaffirm daily the monotheistic principle.

A second answer, less coarse, seemingly more "philosophical," is offered to the same question. This second answer proceeds as follows:

"If the phrase 'Queen of the Universe' is too scary, too suggestive of Caananite *baalim* [gods] or Greek statuary or Christian madonnas, then why not draw on the Female Principle latent in certain historical byways of the Jewish experience itself? How about the *Shekhinah,* the female shadow or emanation of the Godhead, whom we encounter in Kabbalah? No one can accuse *her* of incurring idolatry; like God, she is without form; we know of her only that she is She. The *Shekhinah* admits, among ideas of formlessness, the idea of the female."

Subtle. But again an assault on monotheism.

"Wait! Before you jump to conclusions about my position," says this second answer, "let me go forward a bit. You are about to tell me that the God of the Jews has no incarnation, no human form, no human attributes in addition to no shade whatever of duality or plurality. Why then, all the human imagery we already encounter in liturgy?"

"Because of the limitations of the human mind," replies the answer's interlocutor. "Who can conceive of 'grasp' without 'hand'?"

"But the Lord's outstretched hand, symbolic though it is, is always a symbolic *male* hand. If, in your toleration of the limitations of the human mind and the poverty of our human language, you already tolerate a *male* anthropomorphic image, why won't you tolerate a *female* anthropomorphic image?"

The interlocutor is silent.

"Or to say it otherwise," continues the answer, "if you are unyielding in the purity of your uncompromising monotheism, why do you tolerate a *male* monotheism?"

The answer has turned into a question, and the question, it seems, is improving. It is improving because it has left behind goddesses and female Emanations and is approaching the problems of language, not in the tinkering sense, but elementally. What helpless babies our tongues are! It is as foolish to refer to the Creator-of-the-Universe as He as it is to refer to the Creator-of-the-Universe as She. (Nor is the compassionate Voice of the Lord of History a neuter.)

The question, even in the improved version of its answer, can take us only to quibbles about the incompetence of pronouns. It remains the wrong question. It leads nowhere. It has no fruit. It is dust.

Why Isn't the Right Question "Theological"?

Why, really, is any question about the nature of divinity not the right kind of Jewish question?

For two reasons: first, "the nature of divinity" is a theological question, and Jews traditionally have no theology. Concerning the nature of God, we are enjoined to be agnostic, and not to speculate. "You will see My back, but My face you will not see." And when Moses asks God about the nature of divinity, the reply is only: "I am that I am." In Deuteronomy we encounter a God who asserts that the mysteries of the universe belong to God, and that it is our human business only to be decent to one another, steering clear of what we have not the capacity to fathom.

Secondly, when the question concerning the nature of divinity is pointed toward issues of female consciousness, then it becomes simply irrelevant. Here, with regard to women, it is overwhelmingly the wrong question. *The status of women is, in any Jewish context, by no means a "theological" question. It is a sociological fact; and that is a much lighter load to carry.*

To see what the difference is, consider one aspect of the problem for women as perceived by Christianity and Judaism. Consider Eve.

In both the Jewish and Christian views, Eve, the First Woman, is an inferior moral creature; she cannot keep a promise to God, and she inveigles the First Man, also an inferior moral creature, into a similar betrayal. Both are punished—as equals—by expulsion from Paradise, and by the imposition of two kinds of labor.

Now that may be a nasty portrait of the First Woman, but—in the Jewish view—that is pretty much that. The human race continues, under realistic—i.e., non-paradisic—conditions. You can take Eve out of Scripture and the nature of divinity continues as before: I-am-that-I-am.

Not so in the Christian scheme. There, Eve's "sin" leads to Adam's "fall." The Fall of Man is not a Jewish notion; it is purely Christian. And without that Fall, there would be no need for Redemption; and without a need for Redemption, there would be no Crucified Christ and no Vicarious Atonement. In short, for Christianity, if you take Eve out of Scripture, Christianity itself vanishes.

Eve, the bad woman, is theologically crucial to the survival and continuation of Christianity.

Eve, the bad woman, is irrelevant to the survival and continuation of Judaism.

The Approach of "Simple Justice," and How It Is Thwarted

The feminist Letty Cottin Pogrebin: "A life of Torah is embodied in Hillel's injunction, 'Do not do unto others what you would not have them do unto you.' Men would not like done unto them what is done unto women in the name of *halakhah*. For me, that is that."

Within the scheme of *halakhah*, however, that is not that, although *halakhah* is above all a system of jurisprudence founded on the ideal of the practical attainment of real, not seeming, justice. Developed over centuries by schools of rabbis through precedent after precedent, *halakhah* evolved through application of general principles to urgent practical cases. *Halakhah* is deemed to be flexible, adaptive, attentive to need and actuality—the opposite of the dry bones of uncaring law. And why this should be is clear—*halakhah* is founded on and incorporates scriptural aspirations toward decency of daily conduct and the holiness of the ordinary. A deep halakhic premise is that the individual's well-being is enhanced, through reasoning compassion, by the communal good.

Juridical systems also pay attention to classes. Under *halakhah,* women *qua* women are seen as a subdivision of humanity, not as the main class itself. Now a subdivision is, by definition, not the fundamental rule, but rather a somewhat deviating instance of the fundamental rule: a step apart from the norm. Under *halakhah,* the male is the norm, and the female is a class apart. For instance, there is a Tractate entitled *Nashim,* "Women"; but there is no corresponding Tractate called "Men"—because clearly all that does not apply to women falls to men. Men are the rule, and women are the exceptions to the rule.

Nevertheless, the explicators of *halakhah* (one hesitates to use the term apologists) claim that the biblical "Male and female created He them" means, quite simply, equality of the sexes in the eye of the Creator; and so far, so good. It is only when we come to examine "equality" halakhically that we discover that it is meant to signify not equal, but complementary. Male and female are viewed as halves of a whole, goes the argument, and each half has its own separate rights and responsibilities: there are distinct roles for men and women, which overlap very little.

When "complementary" is taken to be the relation between the norm and its deviation (or call it the rule and its exception), then the role of the norm will be understood to be superior to the role of the exception.

When "equal" is defined as "distinct," then simple justice is thwarted.

On Not Being a Jew in the Synagogue

Item: In the world at large I call myself, and am called, a Jew. But when, on the Sabbath, I sit among women in my traditional shul and the rabbi speaks the word "Jew," I can be sure that he is not referring to me. For him, "Jew" means "male Jew."

When the rabbi speaks of women, he uses the expression (a translation from a tender Yiddish phrase) "Jewish daughter." He means it tenderly.

"Jew" speaks for itself. "Jewish daughter" does not. A "Jewish daughter" is someone whose identity is linked to, and defined by, another's role. "Jew" defines a person seen in the light of a culture. "Daughter" defines a relationship that is above all biological. "Jew" signifies adult responsibility. "Daughter" evokes immaturity and a dependent and subordinate connection.

When my rabbi says, "A Jew is called to the Torah," he never means me or any other living Jewish woman.

My own synagogue is the only place in the world where I, a middle-aged adult, am defined exclusively by my being the female child of my parents.

My own synagogue is the only place in the world where I am not named Jew.

On Not Being a Juridical Adult

Though we read in Scripture that Deborah was a judge in Israel, under postbiblical halakhic rules a woman may not be a witness. In this debarment she is in a category with children and imbeciles.

In the halakhic view, a woman is not a juridical adult.

She is exempted from liturgical and other responsibilities that are connected with observing a particular practice at a specific time. This, it is explained, is a compassionate and sensible ruling. What? Shall she be obliged to abandon the baby at her breast to run to join a prayer quorum at a fixed hour?

The so-called compassionate and sensible ruling perceives a woman exclusively as a biological figure. Time-fixed communal responsibility is left exclusively to males—as if milk were the whole definition of parenthood; or as if, in fact, milk were the whole definition of a woman; or as if in each marriage there is to be only one reliably committed parent, the one with the milk; or as if a mother, always and without exception, is in charge of sucklings only.

If the context should change from functional to intrinsic, from the identity of relationship to the identity of essence, from the ideal of extenuation to the ideal of inclusiveness—ah, then compassionate exemption is transmogrified to demeaning exclusion.

To exempt is to exclude.

To exclude is to debar.

To debar is to demote.

To demote is to demean.

Young girls, older women, and unmarried women do not have babies at their breasts. Where is the extenuating ideal for them? They are "exempted"—i.e., excluded, debarred—from public worship all the same.

The halakhic rationale for universal female exemption, however, is not based on compassion for harried mothers, nor is it, as some erroneously believe, related to any menstrual taboo. It rests on a single phrase—*kavod ha-tzibur*—which can be rendered in English as "the honor [or self-respect] of the community." One infers that a woman's participation would degrade the community (of men).

I am not shocked by the use of this rationale. (I *am* perhaps shocked at a halakhic scholar of my acquaintance who refers to the phrase "the honor of the community" as a "concept that seems to defy comprehension.") Indeed, I welcome this phrase as wonderfully illuminating: it supports and lends total clarity to the idea that, *for Judaism, the status of women is a social, not a sacred, question.*

Social status is not sacral; it cannot be interpreted as divinely fixed; it can be repented of, and repaired.

Women, Debtors, and Thieves

The biblical practice of debtors' servitude—applied also to thieves—was unusually large-minded in that, when the debtor's or the thief's term of work had expired, he was obligated to return to his former status as an ordinary citizen. A debtor or a thief who refused independence after the expiration of his servant's term had a hole bored in his ear—a mark of contempt for one who declined to take on the responsibilities of a higher status.

Under *halakhah,* as presently viewed, there is no way for a woman to achieve a change in status. Her present status (according to my halakhic scholar-acquaintance) "appears to defy emendation or modification within the halakhic context."

What the Jewish juridical genius could once do for a thief, it cannot now do for a woman?

A Man, Too, Is Sometimes Exempted

There is at least one other category of person—besides a woman—who is exempted, under *halakhah,* from the *minyan,* the quorum of ten required for a public worship service. This is a man in a state of new bereavement. He is regarded as being unable to perform in a condition of deep grief.

Only a visit from the Angel of Death can reduce a man to the quotidian, unextreme, situation of an exempted woman. How shall one parse this odd equation? To enjoy the public status of an ordinary woman, claim a death in your family. Or, when a *minyan* is forming, if you would learn what it is to be a woman, go into mourning. Or, to push it still farther: a woman is like a man who has suffered an irreversible loss. Ah, Freud!

On the Denigration of the Synagogue

The desire of women to participate in public worship in traditional congregations—to be "counted," literally, as a member of the quorum of ten—is often met with a lecture explicating American Jewish sociology. It is only under the influence of the ministries of our Christian neighbors, we are told, that the synagogue has become central—whereas it is, in fact, not at all central, and never was: the true matrix of Jewish life is in the family and in the home.

In all the history of the synagogue—one of the oldest institutions in the world—there never was a time when the synagogue was, if not slighted, then as aggressively diminished as it is now. And why is it only *now* that "The synagogue is secondary!" becomes a battle cry of the traditional rabbinate? The emphasis on family and home has not diminished; why, then, should the significance of synagogue worship quite suddenly be reduced?

Answer: *The synagogue becomes a focus of disparagement only at that moment when women begin to make equal claims on it.*

On the Diminution of Prestige

Item: In liberal synagogues, where women may carry the scrolls of Torah for the festival of Simhat Torah, fewer and fewer men come forward to receive this honor.

Item: In liberal congregational structures, where women may become congregational presidents, fewer and fewer men come forward to vie for this honor.

The "honor of the community" may mean, no more and no less, jealousy over prestige: prestige is always reduced when a lower caste is given access to it.

Women's Devotional Literature: On the Discovery of Hacks and Forgers among Those Who Mock Women

Glückel of Hameln, the remarkable seventeenth-century Yiddish-language memoirist, thought of herself mainly as a businesswoman and as a mother recording her life for her children. But anyone who encounters her miraculous book knows better. In a wonderful introduction to a new Schocken edition of *The Memoirs of Glückel of Hameln,* Professor Robert S. Rosen remarks, "Glückel, although she would not have known what to make of this, was an artist."

She would not have known what to make of this. How could she know she was an artist? How could she know that what she was expressing was a lust for storytelling, a gift for the moral lyric? In another body, in another society, she might have turned out to be Wordsworth. In another body and in another society she did, in fact, turn out to be Heinrich Heine, who was one of her descendants.

Thinking about Glückel of Hameln quite naturally leads to thinking about Rebecca Tiktiner and Toibe Pan. They were both poets, and they both lived in Prague. Beyond this we know nothing, since, unlike Glückel, they left no memoirs. Their names are associated with the composition of *tehinot,* lyrical devotional poems.

The famously brilliant Beruriah, celebrated not only as the wife of Rabbi Meir but also in her own right, was known to speak satirically of those rabbinic passages which make light of the intellect of women. To punish her for her impudence, a rabbinic storyteller, bent on mischief toward intellectual women, reinvented Beruriah as a seductress. She comes down to us, then, twice notorious: first as a kind of bluestocking, again as a licentious woman. There is no doubt that we are meant to see a connection between the two.

No one dares malign the creators of the *tehinot.* Of course, they are usually termed poetesses rather than poets, but that is something else—their characters are never called into question. The authors of the *tehinot* are models of piety. But because the *tehinot* are traditionally projected as being the work of women poets, it is the *tehinot* themselves that are maligned for their literary quality. We shall never be able objectively to determine whether Rebecca Tiktiner and Toibe Pan of Prague were good or bad poets; simply because they are known to have composed *tehinot,* they are by definition bad poets.

Consider the subject matter of the *Seder Tehinot,* published at Basel in 1609. There are prayers for taking away the priestly portion of the *hallah* dough, for baking Sabbath cake, for putting on Sabbath clothing; there are prayers for immersion in the *mikvah,* for pregnancy, and for the moments just prior to childbirth; there is even a prayer for wise philanthropy for the use of a well-off woman. There is a prayer for lighting the Sabbath candles, and another for the approach of the new moon.

All these devotionals reflect exactly the religious situation of women, then and now. Half of them are biological; the other half concern themselves with the limited religious space offered to women.

But it was not only the artistry of the *tehinot* that was ridiculed;

it was also the limitations of their subject matter. And yet the subject matter was ordained by the restrictions inherent in the religious opportunities of women. It is as if you put a poet in a steel cage in the middle of a desert and left him with pen and paper. If he is by nature a religious poet, he will find ways to praise the Creator in writing devotional lyrics about the only matter available to him: steel bars, a tract of sand, the roof and floor of his cage, and his own body. And then, having done all this to your religious poet, you mock at him for the paucity of his images and observations. Rather than mock, one should marvel: the aspiration to praise the Creator becomes more and more artful with less and less opportunity. "To see the world in a grain of sand," Blake wrote, and that is the mode of the *tehinot* written by women. Restricted to their own bodies, they saw the divine impulse in the only cage allotted to them.

That cage was summarized in the word חנ"ה (*hnh*), an acronym that evokes the biblical Hannah, but refers to three precepts especially applicable to the religious life of women: *hallah, niddah, hadlakah,* giving the priestly share of dough, observing the period of menstruation, and lighting the Sabbath candles.

While the authors of the *piyyutim*—a vast rollcall of poets—explored a variegated landscape of themes, and reached toward both cosmos and eros for their imagery, the authors of the *tehinot* had only these three coarse bars to their cage: *hallah, niddah, hadlakah.* As a consequence, they were universally scolded, ridiculed, and condemned for their coarseness and their paucity and the sentimentality of their vision.

But what about that other branch of "women's literature," also written in Yiddish, the *Tsena Urena* (containing the portion of the week and folk tales)? We may call it a "branch," so ambitious, rich, and abundant it is, although the *Tsena Urena* is the work of a single teeming, twinkling, original, joyfully pious mind, combining scriptural stories both in translation and paraphrase, legend, myth, tale, homily, and a vivid storyteller's style. It is true that the *Tsena Urena* is not taken seriously either, but, unlike the *tehinot,* it is not reviled or snickered over. It is an amalgam of enormous erudition and an energetic poetic imagination: what could have motivated any ordinary scholar to undertake such a work? Jacob ben Isaac Ashkenazi, though he was in possession of all the attributes of an "ordinary" scholar of the seventeenth century, had nevertheless a secret motivation for the composition of the *Tsena Urena*. We will come to it in a moment. His public motivation, however, was noble enough: it was to raise up and enlighten the minds of women; to make Torah accessible in the vernacular. The author of the *Tsena Urena* appeared to take a different view from the Rambam: Maimonides frequently uses the phrase "women and the ignorant," denies women the right to be appointed to communal office, and recommends wife-beating. It is clear from the tone of the text that the author of the *Tsena Urena* did not hold such vulgar views of his readership: in fact, we may guess that he was both in love with his readership, and at the same time gave little thought to its sex, only to the *tabula rasa* of its mind. Why did Jacob ben Isaac Ashkenazi turn to a readership of women? The answer is deliciously intoxicating: where else should he, could he, turn for the expression of the mandate of the storyteller's imagination?

The secret of the *Tsena Urena* is that it was written out of the desire to play with Story. We may think of it as the first Yiddish novel; the first *Jewish* novel, in fact, in an age when to invent such a thing was impossible. What the *Tsena Urena* did was, in a manner of speaking, to smuggle Dickens into the community of women; women, Jacob Ashkenazi's sole readers, were artistically enriched as the other half of the community was not.

But if the *Tsena Urena* was regarded with a certain tolerance because it was taken to be—though without value—good enough for women, it was still perceived as a debased literature. Not so debased, however, as the *tehinot:* the *Tsena Urena* was after all, written by a man for the edification of women; its very premise (though not its secret imaginative essence) was patronization; its ostensible raison d'être was looking down one's nose at a lesser mental breed in order to refine and elevate it, and as such the *Tsena Urena* earned a modicum of grudging respect.

The *tehinot,* on the other hand, were tendered no respect at all, because they were purported to be written by women for women; they were themselves womanly products, the debased works of minds of limited capability and seriousness.

The *Tsena Urena* was not written for the sake of women; it was written for the sake of its own form and possibility, for the freedom it granted the writer. But if the *Tsena Urena* contains a delightful irony—that, pretending to cater to women, it was in actuality the only outlet in its time for an imaginative artist—so too do the *tehinot* reflect an irony, though a mordant and cruel one.

I quote verbatim this remarkable passage from the *Jewish Encyclopedia:*

> The names of the authors [of the *tehinot*] are nearly all fictitious and high-sounding, and have been affixed in order to make the *tehinot* salable. It is known that some of the *tehinot* were written by indigent students of the Rabbinical Seminary of Vilna or Jitomir (among others, Naphtali Makil le'Ethon), and by Selekowitz, for nominal sums, and that the publishers stipulated that the writers should fashion the composition in tearful and heart-rending phrases to suit the taste of women readers. This forced cultivation of devotional feeling rendered the *tehinot* exaggerated and over-colored, and this did not escape the criticism and ridicule of the men against the women who were such devotees of the *tehinot.*

Extraordinary. What we learn from this wipes out altogether the metaphor of the religious poet caged in a desert, with only his bars and his body and the desert sand to inspire his devotions. It is not that women were limited in the kind of poetry they sought to write; it is that they only rarely wrote at all. What we are examining when we look to the *tehinot* to discover a history of unsung women poets is, instead, a long history of forgery and corruption; a history of a manipulated reader's market; a history of opportunistic publishing. While in English and French literature women had to adopt the names of men—"George Eliot" and "George Sand"—in order to be accepted as salable, in order *not* to be reviled as lacking in literary worth, here we discover a condition wherein men adopt the names of respectable though perhaps mythical women—for instance, "Devorah, wife of Naphtali, formerly Nasi of Palestine"—in order to be accepted as salable, and *on purpose* to be reviled as lacking in literary worth. In short, the very women's literature which was regarded as debased because it was written by women turns out to have been written instead by hungry male hacks in the employ of cynical commercial forgers. And the ridiculed intellectual work of women turns out instead to be the purposefully purple prose of contemptuous rabbinical opinion given over to commercial exploitation.

Rebecca Tiktiner and Toibe Pan, poets of Prague, suffer under a double burden: first, we do not know whether they were real poets or merely names invented for a pittance; and second, even if they really lived, even if they composed the most glorious devotional lyrics of their age, their poetry would be found to be inferior.

When women are condemned for the intellectual and artistic standards that are imposed on them, how are we to judge the moral nature of the hacks and forgers who condemn them?

On the Depth of the Loss and the Absence of Grief

Theorists of American Jewish sociology claim that the current women's agitation within the synagogue and in all parts of Jewish life is a response to the stimulus of the general women's movement. The traditional rabbinate tends to define feminist views as forms of selfishness, narcissism, and self-indulgence, all leading to what is always called "the breakdown of family life." It would be hard to deny the presence of selfishness, narcissism, and self-indulgence in a society much given over to these (and they are not confined to the women's movement); it would be hard also to deny the effect of the women's movement in stimulating more women to examine their lives as Jews.

But the sources of Jewish women's claims are more profound than simple external impingement. It is true that some of these claims appear to coincide with popular influence, and undoubtedly some are directly derivative. Indeed, one wants to join with those rabbis who take unhappy note of rampant faddism and superficiality—because the protests and claims of Jewish women are too serious to be classed with any intellectual fashion, or even with any compelling current movement.

That these protests and claims are occurring in this generation and not in any earlier generation is *not* due to the parallel advent of a movement. The timing is significant: now and not forty years ago: but it is not the upsurge of secular feminism that has caused the upsurge of Jewish feminism.

The timing is significant because the present generation stands in a shockingly new relation to Jewish history. It is we who have come after the cataclysm. We, and all the generations to follow, are, and will continue to be into eternity, witness generations to Jewish loss. What was lost in the European cataclysm was not only the Jewish past—the whole life of a civilization—but also a major share of the Jewish future. We will never be in possession of the novels Anne Frank did not live to write. It was not only the intellect of a people in its prime that was excised, but the treasure of a people in its potential.

We are the generation that knows more than any generation before us what mass loss means. It means, for one thing, the loss of a culture, and the deprivation of transmission of that culture. It means lost scholars of Torah—a lost Rashi; a lost Rambam; a lost Baal Shem Tov; a lost Vilna Gaon. The loss of thousands upon thousands of achieved thinkers and physicians, nourishing scientists and artists. The loss of those who would have grown into healers, discoverers, poets.

Now the moment we introduce the idea of mass cultural loss through excision, then the "timeliness" of the feminist movement, and even its very juxtaposition with Jewish aspiration, becomes frivolous.

But first let us agree on certain premises—obligatory premises, without which it is debasing to proceed. Let us agree, first, that the European cataclysm has no analogies, and that it is improper to draw any analogy from it. And then let us agree that the European cataclysm is not a metaphor for anything; it is not "like" anything else. And, further, let us agree that the European cataclysm is not to be "used," least of all for debating points. It is not to be used, but it is imperative that it should, as far as that is possible, be understood. It is also imperative that we derive particular lessons from it. The lessons are multitudinous and variegated, and we cannot yet clearly imagine even a fraction of them.

Yet we must dare to imagine.

Having said all that—that the European cataclysm is no analogy, no metaphor, no rhetorical instrument—let us then begin to think about Jewish mentality in the wake of the cataclysm. We are not as we were. It is not unnatural that mass loss should generate not only lessons but legacies. An earthquake of immorality and mercilessness, atrocity on such a scale, cannot happen and then pass us by unaltered. The landscapes of our minds have shapes, hollows, illuminations, mounds and shadows different from before. For us who live in the aftermath of the cataclysm, the total fact of the Nazi "selection" appears to affect, to continue to affect, all the regions of our ideas—even if some of those ideas at first glance look to be completely unrelated issues.

Indeed, it may be that for Jews like us, who come immediately after the Nazi period, there *are* no "unrelated issues." And surely there is a connection between, say, the whole pattern of impediments and distinctions that stop up Jewish passion in women, and the Jewish passions of Hannah Senesh and Anne Frank and the poet Gertrud Kolmar and all those young women (whose names are not so accessible as these) who fought in the Warsaw Ghetto. In the ragged battlements of the Warsaw Ghetto there was no *ezrat nashim,* no women's gallery.

The connection I am about to make is not one we reflect on every day; yet it has infiltrated us, it is a legacy and a lesson, and its mournful language is as follows: *having lost so much and so many.*

To think in terms of *having lost so much and so many* is not to "use" the Holocaust, but to receive a share in its famously inescapable message: that after the Holocaust every Jew will be more a Jew than ever before—and not just superficially and generally, but in every path, taken or untaken, deliberate or haphazard, looked-for or come upon.

The consciousness that we are the first generation to stand after the time of mass loss is knowledge that spills inexorably—how could it not?—into every cell of the structure of our lives. What part of us is free of it, or can be free of it? Which regions of discourse or idea or system can we properly declare to be free of it? Who would risk supposing that the so-called "women's issue" can be free of it?

Put beside this view, how trivializing it is to speak of the "influence" of the women's movement—as if Jewish steadfastness could be so easily buffeted by secular winds of power and pressure and new opinion and new perception. The truth is that it would be a blinding mistake to think that the issue of Jewish women's access to every branch and parcel of Jewish expression is mainly a question of "discrimination" (which, if that were all, *would* justify it as a feminist issue). No. The point is not that Jewish women want equality as women with men, but as *Jews with Jews*. The point is the necessity—*having lost so much and so many*—to share Jewish history to the hilt.

This lamentation—*having lost so much and so many*—produces not an analogy or a metaphor, but a lesson, as follows:

Consider the primacy and priority of scholarship; scholarship as a major Jewish value; scholarship as a shortcut-word signifying immersion in Torah, thought, poetry, ethics, history—the complete life of a people's most energetic moral, intellectual, spiritual, lyrical soarings and diggings.

Or look for a moment to Adin Steinsaltz's definition of that aspect of Torah called Talmud:

> From the strictly historical point of view the Talmud was never completed. . . . The final edition of the Talmud may be compared to the stages of maturity of a living organism; like a tree, it has reached a certain form that is not likely to change substantially, although it continues to live, grow, proliferate. Although the organism has taken on this final form, it still produces new shoots that draw sustenance from the roots and continue to grow. . . . [The Talmud] is the collective endeavor of the entire Jewish people. Just as it has no one protagonist, no central figure who sums up all discussions and subjects, so it has continued throughout the centuries to be part of a constant creative process.[1]

There is a single sentence in the foregoing description that is—eschewing critical or interpretive subtlety, playfulness, rhetorical chicanery—a plain whopping lie on the face of it. I will come back to put a finger on it very soon.

First, though, let us suppose—bringing to the supposition the vigilant Jewish mentality developed in the aftermath of mass loss—let us suppose that a group of Jewish scholars uncovers an egregious historical instance of wholesale Jewish excision. The historical instance is open, obvious, in everyone's plain sight, and has always been; but we have averted our eyes. The excision has barely been noticed, and among Jewish scholars and guardians of culture (whom the excision most affects) has not been noticed at all.

The nature of the excision is this: a great body of Jewish ethical thinkers, poets, juridical consciences—not merely one generation but many; in short, an entire intellectual and cultural organism—has been deported out of the community of Jewish culture, away from the creative center. Not "deported" in the Nazi sense of being taken away to perish, nor in the sense of being deprived of natural increase, but rather in the sense of isolation, confinement away from the main stage of Jewish communal achievement.

And this isolation, this confinement, this shunting off, is one of the cruelest events in Jewish history. It has excised an army of poets, thinkers, juridical figures; it has cut them off and erased them. It is as if they were born to have no ancestry and (despite natural increase) no progeny. They have been expunged as cleanly, as expertly, as the most thoroughgoing pogrom or Inquisition imaginable: an Inquisition designed to rid the Jewish people of a mass of its most vital and vitally contributing and participating minds. And all, it should be noted, sans bloodshed.

I began, you will have observed, with the words "let us suppose." But we need not suppose this melancholy history. It has already happened, generation after generation; and we know it, and have always known it (knowing is different from noticing); yet we, who weep at the loss of Jewish thinkers denied fulfillment through pogrom after pogrom, century after century—here, with regard to the one mass loss I speak of, we have always been stonyhearted. We are indifferent. We display nothing so much as an absence of grief at the loss. We have not even noticed it.

And there they are—rank after rank of lost Jewish minds: Jewish minds whose books were not burned; rather, they were never in possession of books to begin with.

When Adin Steinsaltz, the eminent contemporary scholar and interpreter of Talmud, writes that the Talmud "is the collective endeavor of the entire Jewish people," he is either telling an active and conscious falsehood; or he has forgotten the truth; or he has failed to notice the truth. The truth is that the Talmud is the collective endeavor not of the entire Jewish people, but only of its male half.

Jewish women have been omitted—by purposeful excision—from this "collective endeavor of the Jewish people," which has "continued throughout the centuries to be part of a constant creative process."

A loss numerically greater than a hundred pogroms; yet Jewish literature and history report not one wail, not one tear.

A loss culturally and intellectually more debilitating than a century of autos-da-fé; than a thousand evil bonfires of holy books—because books can be duplicated and replaced when there are minds to duplicate and replace them, and minds cannot be duplicated and replaced; yet Jewish literature and history report not one wail, not one tear.

On Jewish Repair and Renewal

Although there has been a curious absence of grief over the mass loss of half the available Jewish minds, there begins now to be some nervous notice, some dry-hearted attempt at repair.

"We must encourage more women to enter fields of Jewish scholarship, where they will be able to assume positions of respect traditionally accorded to the scholar," my halakhic scholar-acquaintance writes. At last—although it is clear it is a "we" admitting a "they" to the "collective endeavor." It is not yet a genuinely collective "we." Nor could it be, at so early a stage of recognition of the need for repair.

But what—in traditional congregations—are some of the suggestions for repair? They are, among others, *women's* Torah study groups, *women's minyanim, women's* holiday celebrations. Repair through traditional activities under continuing segregation. Isolation goes on, but scholarly air is let in. This is plainly an improvement over the centuries-old habit of deportation out of study. The halakhic scholar who advises these improvements considers them to be advances under the sheltering boughs of "the Torah's spirit and truth, the Divine Truth of Torah." And these suggestions, he points out—segregated study, segregated *minyanim,* segregated celebration—do not violate *halakhah,* because they flow from the halakhic premise of separation, which in turn flows from the notion that, in his words, "different rights and responsibilities do not necessarily imply inferior value."

Is study by women, now to be "encouraged," equal to study by men, or is it of inferior value? If it is not of inferior value, why is it to be kept apart? The same questions logically apply to prayer and celebration. When women are discouraged and isolated from the centers of study, prayer, and celebration (by virtue of certain categories of eligibility), then separation of the ineligible from the eligible makes, in its own frame, sense. (A circular kind of sense, however, since mostly it is the rule of separation itself which determines ineligibility!) But once eligibility for study is declared to be universal regardless of sex, then what rationale continues to impose isolation? It is a detriment to study when good minds are kept apart.

Return for a moment to Steinsaltz's discussion:

> One of the great Talmudic commentators, the Maharsha, often ended his commentaries with the word *vedok* [continue to examine the matter]. This exhortation is an explicit admission that the subject has not been exhausted and that there is still room for additions and arguments on the question. To a certain extent the whole Talmud is rounded off by this *vedok,* the injunction to continue the search, to ask, to seek new aspects of familiar problems.[2]

If recent history has made us vulnerable to grief over mass loss; if we consider how we ourselves have amputated from the Jewish cultural body so many philosophers, historians, poets, scholars; if we reflect on the excision of generation after generation of Jewish students (we who are so proud of our joy in study, of our reverence for holy study!); if Jews in their full, not amputated collectivity, are drawn in awe to "the Torah's spirit and truth," then why do the sincerest scholars of Torah appear to offer Jewish women stopgap tactics, tinkerings, placebos and sops, all in the form of further separation and isolation?

These recommendations for study and prayer within a frame of continuing segregation fail to address the one idea that calls out to be addressed. They are not solutions arrived at by means attentive to the Maharsha's injunction toward *vedok,* toward continuing to examine the matter; they are, instead, obstacles to examining the matter; they are evasions of the matter. They are the very opposite of "a constant creative process," which can never proceed through evasion, but must endure a head-on wrestling with the sinew of the dispute.

The deepest sinew of the dispute concerns the premise that has, up to and including our time, deported women out of the houses of study: "Different rights and responsibilities do not necessarily imply inferior value."

It is that premise which needs search, examination, renewed scrutiny—because everything follows from it, and to tinker with its consequences is to evade the very essence of one of the most urgent Jewish questions of our generation: the loss of an army of Torah scholars. If *halakhah* aids in suppressing the scholars who can grow to create it, that is a kind of self-decimation. If the Jewish communal conscience continues to amputate half its potential scholarship, that is akin to cultural self-destruction. When half the brain is idling, the other half is lame.

Until Jewish women are in the same relation to history and Torah as Jewish men are and have been, we should not allow ourselves ever again to indulge in the phrase "the Jewish genius." There is no collective Jewish genius. Since Deborah the Prophet we have not had a collective Jewish genius. What we have had is a Jewish half-genius. That is not enough for the people who choose to hear the Voice of the Lord of History. We have been listening with only half an ear, speaking with only half a tongue, and never understanding that we have made ourselves partly deaf and partly dumb.

Footnote: An Objection to the Foregoing, from the View of the "Pious"

It is so foolish one wants to omit it. Still, it might as well be mentioned: a pious view of women is that they are dangerous temptations to men. A man cannot sit near a woman—not for prayer, not for study—because he is inherently weak and she will arouse him sexually: he will be "distracted."

The woman, on the other hand, is not considered to be a sexual creature, easily aroused or "distracted" when close to males. At the same time, a woman in public is regarded solely as a sexual provocation.

(The apologists for walling in women claim that the wall in traditional synagogues is to protect men from their own weakness. But if the wall is made necessary by a male deficiency [which women are said not to share], then why are the males not walled in? Logically, it ought to be the sick who are confined, not the well.)

Much of the vast structure of Jewish segregation of the sexes rests on the fear of male temptation, on the so-called weakness of males in the face of "distraction."

Yet all Jewish practice requires restraint, dedication, and concentration. A Jew restrains himself from following the eating of meat with the drinking of milk. He restrains himself from driving a car on the Sabbath, or putting on an electric light, or carrying money. Clearly, this is not the place to draw up a list of all the things a Jew restrains himself from doing; but anyone who knows even a little of the life of observant Jews is aware of how very long that list would be.

Is an observant Jew, whose life is nearly defined by the practice of restraint, a more libidinous creature than other males?

In the secular American community, we see conferences of physicians, chemists, writers, teachers, etc., where males and females sit next to one another discussing the merits of an argument, and the males are not prevented from, nor suspected of, "distraction" by physical walls of separation. Non-Jewish males and nonobservant Jewish males—who do not have the benefit of the observant Jewish male's daily regimen of self-restraint—are able to study side by side with women, apparently with sufficient concentration. Indeed, this is a premise of almost the entire American university system.

Is the pious Jewish male more subject than other males to sexual arousal under inappropriate conditions?

In fact, observant Jewish men are without doubt better prepared than others for sexual self-restraint, and it is not pious Jewish males who are weak in the face of women—only their arguments.

Seven Conclusions for the Attention of the Traditional Rabbinate

1. The question of the status of the Jewish woman is not "theological." To alter the status of the Jewish woman is not to change one iota of the status of Jewish belief.

2. Therefore the question of the status of Jewish women is "merely" a sociological issue.

3. As a sociological issue, the status of women is the consequence of human decisions amenable to repair by human institutions.

4. In order to satisfy the most traditional members of the community, and also to place the responsibility for injury where it most belongs, the repair must emerge out of *halakhah,* the judicial machinery for change.

5. The difficulty has been not that principles of *halakhah* are being applied, but precisely that they are *not* being applied.

6. As a result of halakhic inaction, Jewish life is in a condition of internal, self-inflicted injury, and justice is not being done.

7. It is the most traditional elements of the community who should set the example for the rest in doing justice. Why? Because it is they who make the claim of being most in the mainstream of authentic Jewish expression; of being most representative of historic Jewish commitment; and finally it is they who dedicate themselves to being models for Jews who are less stringent in striving to live conscientiously within the frame of Torah.

The burden of leadership in repairing injury rests with those who are a) most responsible for the injury; b) most in possession of the means of repair, i.e., *halakhah;* and c) most conscientious as practicing Jews.

But Suppose the Question Is *Sacral? The Missing Commandment; The Two Walls of Scandal*

Sometimes I feel ashamed. The problem—the status of Jewish women—shames me with its seeming triviality, its capacity to distract, its insistent sociological preoccupation, its self-centeredness, its callous swerve away from all those hammer blows dealt to the Jewish people as a whole.

Especially after lifting my eyes, as, a few moments before undertaking this paragraph, I have done, from documents and meditations which concern themselves with the Great Destruction that came on us in Europe between the years 1933 and 1945—especially then, I smart under the apparent hollowness of this theme. And it is not only by comparison with the worst that this sense of hollow triviality is aroused. There are other walls, more recently erected, that contrive to shut off, and justifiably, thinking-about-women-as-Jews: the continuing brutalities in the Soviet Union; the active resurgence of anti-Semitism in England, Germany, and France; the stunning erosion of American moral urgency toward Israel; the shock of discovering nests of self-designated Nazi groups in every major American city; above all the assault of commotion, danger, and dilemma tirelessly impinging, always and always, on Israel—confronted with all of these, how small, how indulgent, how without large meaning, how shallow and weak the question seems!

The desire to raise it, in the shadow of all these desolating anxieties, strikes one as a scandal: as a thick wall of scandal between oneself and the priorities of Jewish interest.

And yet there is another scandal. This second scandal has an even greater capacity to shock. It is a second wall, huger and thicker still, immensely high and powerfully built, that throws its shadow across the whole of Jewish history. If the first wall seems to separate Jews from necessity, this second wall is even more dangerous: it separates Jews from the Covenant.

The second wall must be scaled by everyone who has dissented from the drift of all my remarks so far. Up to this point, in these *Notes toward Finding the Right Question,* I have taken the position that the issue of the status of Jewish women flows from societal, not sacral, sources. But suppose this position is dead wrong? And suppose the opponents of this position, who believe that the status of women is in fact a sacral question, are right?

Clearly it would be narrow-minded, as well as metaphysically risky, not to pay close attention to those who insist that one cannot look at the question of women without the imperative of looking simultaneously into the profoundest intent, deeper than social practice merely, of Torah itself.

And clearly one cannot reflect on the meaning of Torah without also reflecting on justice and injustice.

What is injustice? We need not define it. Justice must be defined and redefined, but not injustice. How to right a wrong demands ripe deliberation, often ingenuity. But a wrong needs only to be seen, to be seen to be wrong. Injustice is instantly intuited, felt, recognized, reacted to. That there is injustice with regard to women is well understood; otherwise there would be, to take only three illustrations centuries apart, no *halitzah,* no *ketubah,* and no current agitation over *agunah.*

The fact that injustice can be instantly identified raises a strange question. Each of the great offenses is recognized and dealt with in the broadest way in the Decalogue by means of a single all-encompassing "Thou shalt not." But the Decalogue is silent about the status of women except insofar as women are perceived as part of the web of ownership. We are not told not to covet our neighbor's husband; a husband is not property. And the injunction against adultery, while applying to both women and men, is to protect husbands from theft. But just as "Thou shalt not covet thy neighbor's wife" is a refinement of "Thou shalt not commit adultery," so are both of these refinements of "Thou shalt not steal."

In the most fundamental text and texture of Torah, the status of women, except insofar as women are defined as property, is not recognized as an offense or an injustice.

So the question arises: if, in the most fundamental text and texture of Torah, the lesser status of women is not worthy of a great "Thou shalt not," then perhaps there is nothing inherently offensive in it, then perhaps there is no essential injustice, then perhaps the common status of women is not only sanctioned, but, in fact, divinely ordained?

Yet, if this were so, why are there any attempts at all in rabbinic history to repair the status of women? It is as if the Oral Law is saying to the Written Law: *there is something missing.* In fact, whoever believes that the Oral Law is implicit in the Torah is already saying that something is missing: obviously if the missing element were explicit, the Oral Law would not have to derive it.

What we receive through Torah is the eternality and immutability of certain moral principles, beyond social custom and even despite nature.

When we accept this standard—that Torah gives precepts for the elevation of humanity—as endemic in Torah, and when we posit the giving of such precepts even as a kind of general definition of Torah, as in effect the essence of Torah, we run into a wall of scandal.

Consider: murder, robbery, false witness, abuse of the elderly, adultery, and a thousand other examples of victimization and dehumanization fill our planet. There is no moment when the Commandments are not applicable. "Thou shalt not steal" is timeless, no matter how the social and economic and political orders have changed or will change. No argument from progress or modernity can efface the force of "Thou shalt not steal." "Thou shalt not steal" carries within it the blinding clarity of simple justice in the face of simple injustice. No matter how high the wall of property rises around the clear principle of "Thou shalt not steal," no matter how dusty the cloud of *pilpul* that may through various imaginable systems obscure it, the precept can be discerned at the center, untampered-with, untainted, unmolested, clear, pure, with the force of timelessness. The precepts of Torah criticize the world and sit in judgment on its ways.

Of course, Torah is not always alone in acknowledging timeless moral principles. Other religions, including those which are not Torah-derived, make some of the same acknowledgments. But Torah *is* alone in asserting the timelessness of the Sabbath as a day set aside for the elevation of humanity. Nature does not recognize the Sabbath; to nature, all the days are alike. And it may be that, to nature, every act is alike; do the laws of biology distinguish between the cessation of breath in a sheep the wolf has just killed, and the cessation of breath in a man the murderer has just killed and robbed?

So, with regard to moral principle, and also with regard to the Sabbath and other days delimited for sacral and moral purposes, it is no use saying, "Well, but the world isn't like this." The *point* of the Commandments is that the world isn't like them, that the Commandments are contrary to the way the world really is. That is why we value them; that is how they come to elevate us above merciless nature and unjust social usage. It is because Torah makes us and our usages different and separate from the way things appear to be given, that we have found meaning in being human.

How, then, does all this relate to a wall of scandal? It would seem that, in every instance, Torah can be trusted to say its timeless and holy "Thou shalt not" to the lenient, cruel, and careless indifference of both society and nature—to the way human beings unmediated by conscience behave, and even to the continuum of conscienceless nature as it passes through its undifferentiated days.

With one tragic exception. In one remarkable instance only there is lacking the cleansing force of "Thou shalt not," and the abuses of society are permitted to have their way almost unchecked by Torah.

With regard to the condition of women, we speak of "the abuses of society"—but these abuses are so wideflung on our planet that they seem, by their undeviating pervasiveness, very nearly to have the sanction of nature. If we look only into Torah, we see that the ubiquitousness of women's condition applies here as well, with as much force as elsewhere. Women's quality of lesser-ness, of otherness, is laid down at the very beginning, as a paradigm and as a rule: at the start of the Creation of the World woman is given an inferior place. In Scripture, it is true, whenever we hear her speak in her own voice, she is uttering a protest against being put upon: Sarah arguing with Abraham, for instance, over Hagar, or Zelophehad's daughters arguing with Moses over their inheritance. In each case God is moved by injustice and enjoins both Abraham and Moses to redress the abuse. In both accounts the injustice-contradicting texture of Torah prevails over the offenses of the ruling social order.

But mostly the social order as given—woman dehumanized, woman as inferior, woman as chattel—remains untouched by the healing force of any grand principle of justice. Probably the worst scriptural instance is the drinking of the bitter waters, the trial-by-ordeal for a woman suspected of adultery. If there are no more bitter waters for women to drink, if trial-by-ordeal, a commonplace of the ancient world, has been allowed to lapse into disuse, it is because the rabbis, after the Destruction of the Temple, applied the injustice-contradicting impulse of Torah to the social order as given.

Many of the disabilities of women in the given social order have been related to property; women themselves have been regarded as property; and often enough the desire for property clashes with justice as plainly seen. And on occasion justice-carrying Torah has been rabbinically applied to the world-as-given—as, for instance, when polygamy was banned, and before that by some centuries, when the levirate law that forced a woman to marry her husband's brother was ceremoniously circumvented. The *ketubah* [marriage contract] was instituted for the protection of women, the emphasis being, of course, on the protection of the legally lesser by the legally greater.

Citing such examples, Judith Hauptman, a teacher of Talmud at the Jewish Theological Seminary, is moved to apologetics:

> We renounce the view held by many, both men and women, that the Jewish tradition, having been shaped by men, is totally biased in their favor. It was the rabbis, members of the very class of people who were more equal than others, who voluntarily extended some of their privileges to those who were not so fortunate.[3]

But the difference between justice and injustice is that justice is a requirement, a Commandment, not a voluntary ceding of a privilege; while injustice is presided over by tyranny, and tyranny is sometimes, though never consistently or reliably, benevolent. To honor "the very class of people who were more equal than others" for *the leniency of their tyranny over women* is to honor injustice.

On the whole, it turns out, the status of women under Torah is not remarkably or radically different from the status of women in the world at large. And when we consider the world at large, what we see is steady and incontrovertible. A society of Amazons and primeval matriarchs is a fantasy, a myth, one of those wishful dreams that result in sphinxes and gryphons and that inner universe of poetical fancy against which Torah turns its face. As far as we can tell, history, archaeology, and anthropology combine to persuade us that in every place, in every time, in every tribe, women have been set aside as lesser, and in that assumption of inferiority have suffered dehumanization: because inferiority *is* dehumanization.

When so-called "progressive elements" in Jewish religious life call for change on the ground that "times are different now," "those were ancient practices," "what applied then doesn't apply in our modern society today," "the religious participation of women is an idea whose time has come," and so forth, one can only shrug at the smallness and irrelevance of such comments. They do not grow out of justice, or rather, out of the texture of injustice-contradiction; they come out of the impulse for alleviation that the strong arbitrarily offer to the lesser—the benevolence of tyranny. Such views are, like the *ketubah* in its period, green vines growing on the wall of scandal. One is glad enough to see green growth and life at any time, but one would rather not have to endure the weight and presence and shadow of the wall at all. The difference between justice and alleviation is similar to the difference between justice and injustice: alleviation is a now-and-then thing, and justice is forever and immutable, neither age-bound nor society-bound. Alleviation is what nowadays is sometimes called "situation ethics," an ad hoc poultice applied to a particular wound; but justice is a cure, and obviates the need for partial measures. Wherever justice blazes, apologetics vanish.

What Torah has occasionally offered (as in the case of Moses and the daughters of Zelophehad, as in the case of the rabbis who abrogated the levirate law and conceived of the *ketubah*) is alleviation. What, among the urgencies of the deeper moral life, would this be equivalent to? It would be equivalent to having a jerry-built set of sometimes applicable, sometimes inapplicable circumstances in which thievery, say, would not be allowed. Instead of the now-and-again alleviation of the worst effects of thievery, we have the thunderous once-and-for-all Commandment: "Thou shalt not steal." Instead of alleviation for the victim of robbery, in short, we have a grand, high, pure, uncompromising, singular principle of total justice. A precept.

Why did "Thou shalt not steal" come into being? It came into being because in every place, in every time, in every tribe, then or now, whatever the social or economic or political order, there have been thieves. It came into being because it was necessary to set a precept against the-way-the-world-ordinarily-is.

And that is the salient meaning of Torah, to give precepts against the-way-the-world-ordinarily-is.

With, as I have said, a single tragic exception. We look at the-way-the-world-is with regard to women, and we see that women are perceived as lesser, and are thereby dehumanized. We look into Torah with regard to women, and we see that women are perceived as lesser, and are thereby dehumanized. Torah, in this one instance, and in this instance alone, offers no precept to set against the-way-the-world-ordinarily-is. There is no mighty "Thou shalt not lessen the humanity of women!" to echo downward from age to age. There is no immutable moral principle to countermand what humankind will do if left to the willfulness and negligence and indifference and callousness of its unrestraint.

This is the terrifying wall of scandal built within the tower of Torah itself. In creating the Sabbath, Torah came face to face with a nature that says, "I make no difference among the days." And Torah made a difference among the days. In giving the Commandment against idolatry, Torah came face to face with a society in competition with the Creator. And Torah taught the Unity of the Creator. In making the Commandment against dishonor of parents, Torah came face to face with merciless usage of the old. And Torah ordained devotion to parents. In every instance Torah strives to teach *No* to unrestraint, *No* to victimization, *No* to dehumanization. The Covenant is a bond with the Creator, not with the practices of the world as they are found in actuality.

With one tragic exception. With regard to women, Torah does not say *No* to the practices of the world as they are found in actuality; here alone Torah confirms the world, denying the meaning of its own Covenant.

This wall of scandal is so mammoth in its centrality and its durability that, contemplating it, I can no longer believe in the triviality of the question that asks about the status of Jewish women. It is a question which, reflected on without frivolity, understood without arrogance, makes shock itself seem feeble, makes fright itself grow faint. The relation of Torah to women calls Torah itself into question. Where is the missing Commandment that sits in judgment on the world? Where is the Commandment that will say, from the beginning of history until now, *Thou shalt not lessen the humanity of women?*

If it were shown to us that we might have had a Commandment ordering the Sabbath day, but that Torah failed to give it to us in our great need, we would not for a moment accept such a premise; we would cry out, "But of course there is a Sabbath! How can it be otherwise under the Covenant!" It seems unthinkable to imagine a week without the Sabbath; it is unspeakable to imagine a Torah that did not give us the Sabbath.

But suppose it were so. Suppose the Sabbath-Commandment were missing. Perhaps then we would look into Torah to try to invent a Sabbath for ourselves. This mind-play is not so fantastic or offensive as it may at first sound—we have a vigorous paradigm. When the Temple was destroyed, we did not languish or die. Instead, lacking Jerusalem, we came to Yavneh, and invented the Synagogue in order to save Torah—to preserve it and to transmit it. When Torah seemed frayed, we ran to repair it.

That is our present condition with regard to women. It is as if a commandment of the stature and holiness of the Sabbath-Commandment were lacking. It is not a fantasy or an imagining to say that Torah is silent, offers no principle of justice in relation to women, no timeless precept of injustice-contradiction, and in general consorts with the world at large. Torah does not make a judgment in this instance; it consorts. The Covenant is silent about women; the Covenant consorts with the world at large. The Covenant does not make a judgment; it consorts. With regard to women, the Commandment separating Torah from the world is the single missing Commandment. Torah—one's heart stops in one's mouth as one dares to say these words—Torah is in this respect frayed.

So what we must do is find, for this absent precept, a Yavneh that will create the conditions for the precept.

The Oral Law, with its rabbinic piecemeal repairs, is the first to inform us that such a precept is implicit though absent—otherwise whence would the Oral Law derive its repairs?

There was no Commandment that said, "When the time comes, go and preserve Torah through Yavneh." But when that was done, when we came to Yavneh and devised means and purpose to preserve Torah through our long Exile, we saw that what we had done was in accord with the Covenant, and in fact showed itself in all clarity to be the voice of the Covenant.

The Destruction of the Temple—the Temple that seemed fundamental to Torah—appeared to call Torah itself into question; there was no ready precept for that barren moment; and what was our response? To strengthen Torah by discovering the strengthening precept.

The dehumanized condition of women within Torah appears to call Torah itself as a source of precept into question; the precept is missing; and what then shall our response be? To strengthen Torah; to contradict injustice; to create justice, not through the fragmentary accretions of *pilpul* but through the cleansing precept of justice itself; so that ages hence, our progeny will look back on us as we look back on Yavneh; and they will be able to say, as we say of that other green growth out of barrenness, "What was done was done in accordance with the voice of the Covenant."

To do this is necessary—but it is not necessary for the sake of a more harmonious social order; it is least of all necessary for the sake of "modern times"; it is not necessary for the sake of women; it is not even necessary for the sake of the Jewish people. It is necessary for the sake of Torah; to preserve and strengthen Torah itself.

NOTES

1. Adin Steinsaltz, *The Essential Talmud* (New York: Basic Books, 1976), pp. 272–73.
2. Steinsaltz, p. 273.
3. Judith Hauptman, "Women's Liberation in the Talmudic Period: A Reassessment." in *Conservative Judaism,* Summer 1972, p. 28.

Women and Power in the Federation

Deborah E. Lipstadt

NEARLY a decade has passed since Jacqueline Levine stood before the General Assembly of the Council of Jewish Federations (CJF) and called upon it to grant women access to the "highest levels of decision and policy making" and to end token female representation within its ranks. For too long and "all too often," Levine declared, "women have been relegated to being mere observers when they should be participants."

In issuing this clarion call to the organization that is the broadest embodiment of the organized Jewish community to reassess the role it granted women, Levine was asking for something far more significant than just increased power for women. Since 1969 CJF, which is the closest thing to an umbrella body within the American Jewish community, had been steadily opening its ranks to previously unrepresented segments of the community. Students, young adults, and a number of other groups had asked for and been granted a role in the decision-making process. New institutions and avenues to facilitate greater access and input into policy formulation had been established. The leaders who had realized these changes recognized that could the Jewish community—already then quite concerned about its shrinking demographic and philanthropic base—could no longer afford to close the door to any group that stood ready to play its part.

In asking that the same be done for women, Levine and those who supported her did not have as their ultimate objective the imposition of a particular agenda, feminist or otherwise, on the organized Jewish community. Their goal was the increased democratization of American Jewish life. In analyzing the changing role of women within the Federation structure, therefore, we are really looking at something far greater than just the question of one particular group's access to power. We are looking at one change among a broad spectrum of changes in the structural composition and ideological dynamics of the organized Jewish community. Together they reflect the new tenor that in the past decade has come to characterize Jewish communal life in America.

In her address to the General Assembly of the CJF, Levine acknowledged that since 1965 there had been a significant increase—50 percent—in the number of women who served on Federation agency boards, held Federation officerships, and were members of Federation committees. But rather than allow her audience to rejoice at this development, she dismissed such changes by noting that the actual number of women serving in official positions was "so low [that] this kind of increase loses any real significance."[1]

Levine's talk contained nothing new. What made it noteworthy was the setting in which she issued her challenge. This was not a single organization being asked to open its ranks. The American Jewish community is a political entity founded on a "multidimensional matrix of institutions and organizations." Within this matrix Federation encompasses the greatest number of organizations, represents the largest number of Jews, supervises and funds the most diverse types of programs and institutions and, most significantly, raises the greatest percentage of communal funds. The local Federations house the "real powers of communal governance." CJF, whose powers are growing, represents the nationwide network of Federations and is "chief among the countrywide [Jewish] organizations."[2]

Federation not only supports its constituent agencies—e.g., Jewish Family Service, Jewish Centers Association, and Jewish Education Bureau—but in most communities also raises funds for the United Jewish Appeal (UJA), which is responsible for the overseas needs of the Jewish community. Ultimately, Federation controls 75 percent of the public expenditures of the American Jewish community. The Federation/UJA fund-raising apparatus has resulted in a

> system of interlocking, hierarchically structured networks centered around different loci. The most prominent givers are part of a continent wide network. They in turn are among the top leaders of local networks which in turn are comprised of circles of givers built around particular industries or trades or around institutions such as synagogues or communal agencies or around residential neighborhoods.[3]

This was the entity that was being asked to change. And the person who was asking it to do so was not an outsider. As national president of the Women's Division of the American Jewish Congress, Levine had access to the highest levels of policy making. She was not one who had been shut out; but as she pursued the national scene, she saw that numerous others had. (An example of this fact was provided in a 1976 survey of six midwestern communities that revealed that 90 percent of the persons on executive boards/committees of Jewish fundraising organizations were men.[4])

Federation provides for women's participation in the form of a Women's Division, which conducts its own campaign and runs an array of educational and cultural activities. The vast majority of women involved in Federation activities—certainly most non-working women—are involved through Women's Division. Men generally participate in the fundraising campaign through trade and professional divisions. Although generally regarded as "highly energetic," many consider Women's Division "separate but not equal," and contend that women within its confines "work on a successful but secondary level."[5]

The funds raised by Women's Division constitute, in fundraisers' parlance, "plus giving."[6] They are, in other words, funds that would not have otherwise been donated by the male head of the household. In 1982, Women's Division raised one hundred million dollars, 17.5 percent of the total amount raised. Clearly, women have had a role, an important one. However, as Levine noted, too often a woman who worked hard and successfully in the Women's Division or in various constituent agencies found herself "locked out at the level where her decision may mean something, namely, as it is put, 'with the men.' " If anything, women have worked at "executing policy rather than formulating it."[7]

During the past decade the Jewish community has responded in a variety of modes to the feminist critique. The most noteworthy and "revolutionary" changes have come in the spiritual or religious realm. It is there that the most famous battles (e.g., the ordination of women as rabbis) have been and are being waged. In contrast, the focus of this article is on a sector of Jewish life generally categorized as secular.

However, applying Robert Bellah's concept of "civil religion" to the activities of Jewish organizations, it can be argued that communal endeavors, although ostensibly secular, actually constitute a spiritual expression of Jewish life.[8] Many Jewish communal leaders devote extraordinary amounts of their creative energies to Jewish communal work. They are actively and totally immersed in Jewish activities in a way which is reminiscent of a pre-modern model of Jewish life. They are unlike most contemporary Jews who, irrespective of the particular segment of the religious community with which they are affiliated, relegate their Jewish activities to well-defined and rather limited spheres. Within the Jewish community there are only a few select groups (e.g., Lubavitch *Hasidim*) for whom Jewish life is as all-encompassing as it is for these secular Jewish leaders. For them communal work becomes a "sacred mission" and a means of insuring Jewish survival. Although they may not observe *halakhah* in any way, they are in a certain respect passionately religious Jews.

Given this interpretation of communal activities, it can be said that we are examining women's roles in an aspect of the spiritual, not secular, realm of the American Jewish community. This explains in part why some women have pursued the effort with such commitment and have not abandoned the organization despite their seemingly limited success. It is not simply an organizational issue but a quest to spiritually participate in Jewish life.

In the aftermath of Levine's critique, several analysts of the social structure of the Jewish community predicted that the increasing influence of the feminist movement would force existing barriers to fall and that, as a result, women would gain access to power.[9] Others were more pessimistic about the potential for change. They discerned far more formidable obstacles in women's path. The organized Jewish community, they contended, "looked only to men for its top leadership."[10] They foresaw a continued attempt by men to maintain control. In fact, those who predicted change were correct. The changes, however, have been slow, sporadic, and hesitant. Nonetheless, increasing numbers of women are involved in the leadership positions or are on the way to them.

Before trying to analyze the extent of these changes and the reasons for them, we will find it instructive to isolate some of the reasons why women have been excluded from the decision-making sanctum in the past. One must acknowledge—and both female and male leaders of some of the largest Federations in the country do so—that there existed and still exists an inherent refusal on the part of certain male leaders to accord women positions of power simply because they are women. Many capable women *have* been locked out. Often the refusal was—and is—justified by the argument that Federation's raison d'être is fund raising and the Federation is able to solicit donations through the example set by its leaders.

Women, particularly nonworking women, generally do not have the same fund-raising capacity that men have. Women, data shows, earn less than men even when both occupy the same position. Most women are, in fact, employed in positions at the lower end of the salary scale. Consequently, women have less access to funds than do men. This is one of the arguments used to explain the refusal to grant women top leadership positions. Although there is some legitimacy to the argument, the statistics reveal that the exclusion is far too rampant to be explained totally by it.

There are, in addition, other reasons responsible for preventing women from gaining access to leadership. These are barriers that women, responding to age-old societal expectations, have placed in their own paths. Educated to be passive, particularly in the company of men, women have been unwilling to engage in the power politics necessary to achieve success in a political entity—Federation included. The Federation functions as a political body. Achieving one's objectives can mean brokering, arguing, fighting. Women, far more reluctant to engage in confrontation than are men, are fearful of being labeled as "aggressive." Their fears are compounded by the existence of a double standard: those qualities which produce an "aggressive woman" make for a "forceful man." Yet it is often forcefulness which is necessary to effect change.

Social scientists argue that men and women have long adhered to significantly different leadership styles. These styles are probably the result of psychological factors that have socialized each of the sexes into traditional roles and behavior modes. Men, according to this theory, emphasize solving the issue at hand and completing the task in as expedient a fashion as possible. Less attention is generally paid by them to the emotions that might have created the problem. Women, sociologists contend, tend toward the intuitive and make decisions after meshing both the apparent and the real. Less tolerant of conflict, women will try to avoid it by using a "collaborative mode" to achieve consensus. The decision-making process may take more time, tangential issues are considered, and emotions are both evaluated and often come into play. Institutions and organizations, particularly those with a profit motive, tend to value the male leadership and decision-making style. These are those who question whether the modus operandi in which men tend to engage is best suited for communal, philanthropic and social welfare institutions.[11] Obviously each style has both its positive and negative aspects. An approach that is useful in one situation may be detrimental in another.

Embedded in these styles of leadership are stereotypical roles that have long differentiated male and female modes of behavior. Women who break out of the stereotype in order to achieve their goals are often subjected to severe criticism. One of the ultimate ironies is that some women who adopted the male style of leadership—whether by choice or lack of choice—in order to achieve their objectives have come to recognize that in so doing they have lost valuable qualities and characteristics inherent in the female mode.

How extensive, then, are the changes that have occurred since Levine's call? In a number of cities (e.g., Los Angeles, Boston, and New York) women serve[d] as Federation Presidents or chair[ed] the general campaign. There is a notable increase in the number of women filling these roles. However, their success should not be interpreted as indicative of sweeping changes. These talented and capable women are, in many cases, the exceptions originally mentioned in Levine's talk. In absolute terms there are still few of them. They are in many cases "very wealthy women" or the wives of very wealthy men.[12] They have long served in the inner circles of leadership, but now they are being granted the top positions. On the other hand, even if their numbers are small, there are many more of them than there were ten years ago, and some occupy extremely prominent positions—such as president of the New York Federation. Their voices are being heard, their talents being used.

It is on the lower and younger levels of leadership that the more sweeping changes are taking place. In recent years a new avenue for active participation and for access to positions of power has developed in the form of Young Leadership programs. They are designed to attract and train promising young [under forty] communal leaders. Individuals involved in Young Leadership generally have their own income. Women have become increasingly active in Young Leadership programs. In certain cities, e.g., Los Angeles, the most prestigious leadership development programs were restricted to men until a few years ago. Women now participate fully, serve on the executive committees, and play an important role in local and national leadership development.

At the national level there has also been a change. One of the most blatant signs of women's exclusion in the past was the all-male United Jewish Appeal Young Leadership Cabinet, composed of men under forty who have been singled out by their communities as outstanding leaders—men who have already made, or have the potential for making, significant communal contributions of time and money. They are expected to go on to fill important local and national roles. They commit substantial amounts of energy to the Cabinet and Cabinet related activities. Social, educational, and cultural programs are arranged for them.

For many of its members the Cabinet provides an intense sense of camaraderie and bonding, much like the feelings that develop among fraternity brothers.

A number of attempts were made to try to admit women to the Cabinet. They all failed. Many of the men feared that the special relationships they shared would be threatened by the presence of women. Some argued that their wives would oppose the presence of women on the Cabinet retreats. Ultimately, in order to stave off what increasingly appeared as the inevitable, a Women's Cabinet was formed.[13] The Women's Cabinet is composed of both working and nonworking women or, to use Cabinet terminology, business/professional women and professional volunteers. In most communities, the Cabinet women have not been given the same responsibilities in the general campaign as have the men, in part because the Men's Cabinet is more established and the men on it have an already proven track record of fund raising. However, some of the women on the Cabinet do hold important and impressive posts in their communities and at the national level. The role the Women's Cabinet will create for itself depends on the members' willingness to struggle for recognition and the lay and professional infrastructure's willingness to accommodate them.

A recent study in Los Angeles reveals that on the local level of the Federation changes are also taking place. This is particularly obvious on the committee level. (It is, in fact, on the committees that some of the most significant and important work is done. In many communities the Board of Directors serves mainly as a validating body, accepting, rejecting or modifying the recommendations of the various committees.) Committee chairpeople (who assist the president in selecting people for the committees) can be said to occupy some of the more powerful positions in the organizational structure.

In Los Angeles, during the past decade, there has been a significant increase in the number of women serving on committees. In 1970 13 percent of the Board of Directors were women. In 1980 women constituted 22 percent of the Board. Membership in the Leadership Development Committee has increased from 21 to 44 percent. Some committees have remained fairly constant, but most have shown considerable change. Twenty-three percent of the committees are chaired by women, among them two of the more powerful committees.[14]

Currently there is nothing even mildly resembling parity. But the community has begun to seriously deal with the issue. A committee was established in 1980 to study the role of women in Federation and in its constituent agencies. Its mandate was to review the lay structure of Federation and its agencies and to assess the nature of women's involvement in leadership. Its goal was to increase the opportunities for women to serve at all levels of the Federation and its agencies. Attempts are being made to determine whether the existence of a Women's Division excludes women from other Federation activities, and to what degree women have been prevented from achieving leadership and upward organizational mobility.

Only a few other communities appear to be engaged in such sweeping efforts, despite the fact that it is nearly ten years since Levine called for the establishment of just such a committee. Despite the fact that it took Los Angeles nearly a decade since this issue was first articulated to seriously analyze the role of women, it is not surprising that it is one of the first and only Jewish communities to do so. Daniel Elazar, one of the foremost analysts of the political and social structure of the organized Jewish community, recently described the Los Angeles Jewish Federation as the "cutting edge" of the organized Jewish community.

The executive vice president of the Los Angeles Federation recently described this as one of the three most exciting developments currently taking place within the organization. The other two are the attempt to forge closer relations between synagogues and Federation and efforts to decentralize the Federation itself in order to accord greater powers of governance to those in outlying geographic areas. All these efforts—geographic regionalizations, closer synagogue-Federation relations, and increased access for women—reflect a desire to democratize the power structure and grant roles in policy making to those who previously had been shut out.

Similar changes have taken place in other cities in the United States. To what might they be attributed? Feminist arguments probably have had some impact, though an indirect one. Amy Stone's biting article "The Locked Cabinet" was probably a major factor in the creation of a Women's Cabinet, if only in that it called national attention to that which in 1977 seemed both immoral and anachronistic.[15]

Young leadership activities have brought about change, as has the fact that increasing numbers of women are entering the job market. Women in business or professions generally have limited amounts of time for leisure activities. If those activities are either unfulfilling or nonproductive, it is likely that they will not be pursued.[16] Federations now recognize that they must offer these women tasks no less challenging than those offered to their male counterparts.

But it is not only the existence of increasing numbers of business and professional women that is forcing a change. Feminist attacks on volunteerism have put many nonworking women on the defensive. The National Organization of Women (NOW) charged about seven years ago that "volunteer work reinforced the economic dependence of women by occupying them with unpaid service rather than gainful employment." In the aftermath of this attack, women's organizations were forced to reevaluate their programs. Although it is estimated that significantly more American Jewish women are members of Jewish women's organizations than are women in the general population, increasing numbers of them are in the process of leaving or have left the volunteer arena. Organizations have been forced to make logistic and substantive changes in their programs in order to retain these women. As a staff member of the American Jewish Congress recently noted, "a viable strong person wants to be involved with issues, not in being the recording secretary."[17]

The Federation is reacting pragmatically to two different but interlocking factors: the changing nature of women's expectations and the eroding base of the Jewish community. The shrinking demographic composition of the community is compounded by recent statistics on patterns of philanthropy, which reveal that "young people are giving less often, professionals do give appreciably less than businesspeople, and less identified Jews give less than their more involved counterparts."[18] These developments, whose advent veteran fund-raisers have long feared, make it incumbent on the Jewish community to draw upon the talents and resources of all its members.

From a structural perspective the changing role of women will have the greatest impact on Women's Division. It will increasingly become the locus for nonworking women, while working women will be found only in entry-level leadership groups. They will choose—and are already choosing—to serve in their appropriate trade and professional divisions. This results from issues of self-image as well as self-interest. Professional and business contacts made through Jewish communal activities often provide financial rewards—lawyers and doctors, for example, frequently refer clients to colleagues with whom they work in their division of the campaign—and women in business are as anxious as their male counterparts to garner these rewards.

The activities of Women's Division will also change. They will become increasingly issue-oriented as those women who are professional volunteers demand constructive use of their time and energy. Nor will Women's Division be alone in changing. A number of Jewish women's organizations have already found it advisable "to alter their basic structure to obviate opposition and encourage growth."[19]

Fears have been expressed that as a result of the increasing numbers of women in the Federation structure the allure of the organization will be diminished. "Prestige," it is argued, "is always reduced when a lower caste is given access to it."[20] To buttress this hypothesis, there are those who contend that once women began to serve as synagogue presidents, participate in the *minyan,* and fill positions as congregational officers, men began to consider the synagogue "women's work" and turned to other pursuits.

If it is true that men have turned away from synagogue activities to communal ones in recent years, this shift probably has less to do with women's participation than with the nature of the synagogue. The influence of a Federation, the funds it raises, the size of its operation, and a spectrum of power-related factors make it far more enticing to many than the limited (however important) sphere of the synagogue. It could therefore be argued that women found it easier to achieve leadership roles in synagogues because men had already moved on to community-wide or nationwide activities. In reality, however, relatively few large, prestigious synagogues are led by women. In the Conservative movement less than 10 percent, or 68 out of 753 Conservative synagogues, currently have women presidents.[21]

Most importantly, even if women attain increased power in Federations, men will not move on because, in the words of one leading Federation executive, "this is still the biggest game in town." The denigration argument is as fallacious as saying that now that women are increasingly being elected to public office politics is no longer as enticing because it has been feminized. The issue, ultimately, is not the sex of the person who leads but the tasks the organization performs.

The most critical implication of increasing women's involvement in Federation is in the realm of the nature of the leadership. The ability to set an example—particularly a financial example—has always been a criterion for leadership. Although women are gaining economic power, they are far from having achieved economic equality. What, then, are the implications of making leaders of those who cannot set an example, at least financially, worthy of emulation?

This question extends far beyond the issue of women's involvement. It touches upon the fundamental issue of communal democratization. The very nature and objectives of Federation predicate against total democracy. There always will be a hierarchy of leadership based *in part* on the ability to give both time and money. The issue, therefore, is twofold: Given a person's—man or woman—limited ability to donate funds, is there nonetheless an avenue for that person's voice to be heard, opinions articulated, and influence felt? Are there leadership positions that they can assume? Secondly, for those women with giving ability equal to men's, is there equal access to the decision-making process and the power *situs*?

The question of democratization is not a new issue. Federations have been moving in this direction for over a decade. Ever since the 1969 student protest at the General Assembly of the CJF, younger voices have been heard and *listened to* throughout the land. Leadership development programs recognize that talent and commitment are characteristics equally as important as (if not more important than) wealth.

In certain cities the entire structure has been decentralized in order to allow those in outlying geographic areas increased responsibility and power. In all cases these have been both bold and pragmatic decisions: bold, because power has been given to those who did not have it before thereby diminishing the top leaders' freedom to act at will; pragmatic, because had these changes not been made many of these groups would have either abandoned Federation or found their own independent avenues for participation in Jewish communal life.

The course of future change will depend on a number of factors. Initially, Federations must engage in an analysis of the current situation in their local communities. Have women been accorded increased access to power in the past decade? Has the change been more apparent than real? Often just gathering statistics has made both men and women aware of the problem and has served as an impetus for change.[22]

In addition, it must be recognized that there are no "women's issues," but that questions such as day-care, fertility, single-parent families are *community* issues. Most women work, statistics reveal, because of economic necessity. Day-care within a Jewish framework is therefore not a women's luxury but a family necessity and, in the broader sense, a community necessity.[23]

As the process of change occurs it is mandatory that those demanding change remember that Federation is an entity which operates on the basis of consensus. It is both evolutionary and reactive. Change evolves slowly, filtering up and down. Federation does not anticipate societal change but follows it, particularly when it is called upon to do so.

Critics should not expect revolutionary alterations in the Federation structure; but neither should they accept excuses as to why the *status quo* must be maintained. Eventually change will come, affecting not only women but the entire decision-making process. The community will recognize, as many of its members already do, that opening up the power structure is the right thing to do—not simply because it is moral, but because it is a pragmatic necessity. It must be done if the American Jewish community is to function in the coming decades at its optimum strength and draw on the manifest talents within its midst.

NOTES

1. Jacqueline Levine, "The Changing Role of Women in the Jewish Community," *Response* 18, Summer 1973, pp. 60–62.

2. Steven M. Cohen, "American Jewish Feminism: A Study in Conflicts and Compromises." *American Behavioral Scientist,* Vol. 23, No. 4 (March–April 1980), p. 522; Amy Stone, "The Locked Cabinet," in *Understanding American Jewish Philanthropy,* ed. Marc Lee Raphael (New York: Ktav Publishing House, 1979), p. 46. [Originally published in *Lilith* magazine]; Vera Margolis, "Today's Jewish Women: The Challenge of Change," *Journal of Jewish Communal Service,* Winter 1975, p. 149.

3. Daniel J. Elazar, *Community and Polity: The Organizational Dynamics of American Jewry* (Philadelphia: Jewish Publication Society, 1976), p. 127.

4. Steven M. Cohen, "Will Jews Keep Giving? Prospects for the Jewish Charitable Community," *Journal of Jewish Communal Service,* September 1978, p. 60.

5. Raphael, *Understanding American Jewish Philanthropy,* p. 4.

6. Stone, "The Locked Cabinet," p. 41; Margolis, "Today's Jewish Women," p. 149.

7. Stone, p. 43.

8. Levine, "The Changing Role of Women," p. 63; Kenneth D. Roseman, "The Men of the Power Structure," in *Understanding American Jewish Philanthropy,* p. 54.

9. Robert Bellah, "Civil Religion in America," in *Beyond Belief,* ed. Robert Bellah (New York: Harper and Row, 1970), pp. 168–192. For a fuller discussion of this type of analysis as it pertains to the leadership of the American Jewish community see Jonathan Woocher, "Civil Judaism in the United States" (Philadelphia: Center for Jewish Community Studies, 1978).

10. Elazar, *Community and Polity,* p. 281.

11. Stone, "The Locked Cabinet," p. 41.

12. J. Dennis, "Support for the Party System by the Mass Public," *American Political Science Review,* 1966, pp. 600–615; Irene H. Friese et

al. *Women and Sex Roles: A Social Psychological Perspective* (New York: W. W. Norton, 1978), pp. 345–348.

13. Anne Lapidus Lerner, "Who Hast Not Made Me a Man: The Movement for Equal Rights for Women in American Jewry," *American Jewish Year Book, 1977* (Philadelphia: Jewish Publication Society, 1978), p. 31.

14. Stone, "The Locked Cabinet," pp. 41–51.

15. *Study Committee on Women in Federation and Agency Leadership of the Jewish Federation Council of Greater Los Angeles.* December 10, 1980. Many of the conclusions and hypotheses presented in this section grew out of discussions with Sherri Weiner Bernstein.

16. Stone, "The Locked Cabinet."

17. June Sochen, "Jewish Women as Volunteer Activists," *American Jewish History* (September 1980), p. 32.

18. Nadine Brozen, "Volunteerism: New Paths," *New York Times,* June 3, 1979.

19. Cohen, "Will Jews Keep Giving?" p. 69.

20. Lerner, "Who Hast Not Made Me a Man," p. 33.

21. Cynthia Ozick, "Notes toward Finding the Right Question," *Lilith* 6, 1979, p. 22; p. 120 of the present volume.

22. The 1981 United Synagogue Yearbook and Directory (New York, 1980).

23. Lerner, "Who Hast Not Made Me a Man," p. 33.

The Noah Syndrome

Rosa Felsenburg Kaplan

THE Fall 1974 issue of *Davka,* which focuses on "The Forgotten Jews," carries in it two articles that seen in conjunction point to yet another group of forgotten Jews—the unattached woman. In his article "Jewish Theology and the Sexual Revolution," Dr. Harold Schulweis clarifies the Jewish point of view which emphasizes the importance of fusion of body and spirit in the sexual experience as well as of marriage as a basic social institution. In her article on "Jewish Singles," Marcie Lincoff talks about a group which, for one reason or another, has elected not to be married, or to at least delay the assumption of the normative pattern to which Dr. Schulweis refers. Neither of them touch on the fate of the individual who has entered into the state of matrimony at one time, but who no longer finds him or herself in this state: the divorced, separated, or widowed.

Early Jewish writings say little about individuals who do not fit the normative pattern, nor do they discuss community attitudes toward those no longer married. Grief at the loss was to be expected, and provisions were made for their support. In some instances, particularly in the event of divorce, the women returned to the patrilocal household. To be sure, such a step was a painful one, and the status of a returned woman or a widowed woman was not enviable. It might be conceivable that Ruth preferred to go whither Naomi went out of a sense of fear of return to the parental household after abandonment of her particular ethnic group. (As a child, I was troubled by the injustice to

Vashti of Purim story fame who had to choose between *two* fates worse than death.)

In a society in which marriages were arranged (even after polygyny came under a *herem*), the nonmarried state could easily be remedied and the interim period could perhaps be tolerated. Moreover, the traditional separation of men and women during ritual and social occasions created a bond among the gender groups which made it possible for the unattached woman to live with the situation. In any case, it would appear that until the advent of modern medicine, there must have been any number of unattached adults simply because the death rate was high and life expectancy low. A household very often consisted of a number of individuals other than conjugally or nuclear related family members—uncles, aunts, cousins, grandparents and partially parentless children—because of this factor.

The woman in traditional Jewish society had a place different from that of the man but, as the Proverb suggests, a position of equal stature. In contemporary society, on the other hand, with a lower death rate, there is a greater possibility of maintaining the Noah's Ark pattern of coupling. Moreover, although both male and female animals were created to be equal, some are "more equal than others." The fate of the unattached woman appears to be a lot more trying than that of the man.

Though we may rail against the limitations of a closed society, we tend to forget that the open—or opening—society, too, has its discontents. The Women's Movement may object to the definition of the "Woman of Valor" in terms of her household obligations, but it tends to forget that this woman had a very secure place in the traditional Jewish community. This society was organized in such a way that almost every female child could aspire to become a "Woman of Valor," a status not to be erased by the loss of a mate and guarded against capricious termination by divorce through a series of customs around the maintenance of *shalom bayit,* or the obligation to resolve conflicts.

The enforced separation between men and women during prayer, festivities and other social events (usual at the turn of the century and still observed by some Orthodox groups) created a situation in which it was possible for a very close relationship among the women to develop so that every woman had a secure place within the community. Widowhood tended to intensify the relationship, particularly during the initial period. Divorce was frowned upon, to be sure, but was not necessarily a barrier to integration into society. In instances where the blame was considered to lie with her husband, some of the women even rallied to the support of a divorcee. All unattached women, and particularly the single ones, of course, became the object of the arranging of matches—a mixed blessing, depending upon the sensitivity of the matchmaker. Regardless of marital status, however, each woman could attend services and participate in community activities—the *hevrah kadishah* or the *bikur holim* societies—to the extent of her ability, regardless of marital status.

Conservative and Reform Judaism, with their emphasis on the cohesion of the nuclear family (following the modern, but somewhat Protestant, principle that "The family that prays together, stays together") have changed this situation for the unattached woman. Now, when a widow or divorcee attends services, the joyful interaction of intact families in adjoining pews reminds her only too painfully that she has lost her mate. What is more serious, in the push toward greater family participation and cohesion, many community centers and synagogues have been oriented to the family and collect dues based on family membership, at rates which may be prohibitive for the unattached woman, particularly one responsible for the care of children. A request for scholarship or reduced membership fee is humiliating. Thus temple or community center membership may be "out" for financial reasons, as well as psychological ones.

When it comes to membership in community activities of the temple, the single woman tends to be out in the cold again. A widow might continue to belong to the sisterhood if she joined it while her husband was still alive, but a widow, divorcee, or single woman will hardly be *invited* to join the sisterhood or the "Young Matrons" or any of the other groups organized along gender lines. And, to be sure, sex separation continues in synagogue organizations despite an ideology which makes women more equal. The fact that women may be counted as part of a *minyan* but that some Conservative congregations still wait until ten men arrive is of less consequence than the fact that extra-ritual activities are segregated. Even if an unattached woman were interested in joining the usual women's activities, the hours such activities are scheduled would most likely not be convenient for a working woman. This is, in part, a function of the needs of the child-rearing woman—the normative woman in the congregation.

The *havurah* does not solve the problem. Most *havurot* are *collections of families.* The more intimate group of the *havurah,* consisting of families, tends to make it difficult to absorb an unattached woman or two. The alternative of the *havurah* of singles, of course, perpetuates the pattern of "no place for the unattached."

The challenge is to eliminate the institutional and cultural lags which maintain the *mehitzah* in a society which does not offer the social support of traditional society. The solutions are not simple. As we move to the year 2001, we obviously cannot return to the early 1900s. We have gone too far socially to resurrect the *mehitzah,* and marriage is no longer as universal or permanent as it used to be. The number of unattached women continues to be sizable. A possible option is the development of coeducational or non-gender-specific and non-marital-status-specific educational and community action groups which meet at a time convenient for most working people. Such groups could allow for casual contact around areas of mutual interest and the development of intimacy among members when the requisite feelings exist. The question of financing of synagogues and community centers would also need to be reviewed with a view toward making inability to pay a sizable membership fee less disgraceful than it has been in the past. Child-care programs and vocational and personal counseling might ease the lot of the female head of a single-parent household.

Attempts at social engineering will not change the situation sufficiently, however, unless they are accompanied by far-reaching attitudinal and behavioral changes. The normative nuclear family must not and cannot be maintained at the expense of those who, for one reason or another, do not fit the pattern. If women are to be truly equal to men, they have to be included in communal activity on a par with men. This requires not only that men "accept" their contribution, but also that women accept themselves and one another regardless of marital status. Unless individuals learn to relate to each other inside and outside the family as human beings rather than as role-occupant, the family that stays together may well decay together.

Scenes from the Life of a Jewish Lesbian

Alice Bloch

1947—I was born in Youngstown, Ohio, and was named Alice Doreen, after my grandmother Elka and my great-grandmother Drayzel, both of whom had died shortly before. (Anglicizing Yiddish names was common practice among American Jews at the time.) My parents, Norma (Nehama) and Bernie (Benyomin), and I lived in the home of my mother's parents, Laura (Leah) and Nat (Nachman).

1952—We moved to a house outside the city limits, in an area that was changing from farm community to suburb. The minister across the street had failed in his attempt to convince all property owners on the block not to sell to Jews.

1953—My parents joined the Conservative synagogue so that I could attend Sunday School. This synagogue was the natural choice; my grandparents had joined it after their oldest son had married a Catholic. I liked Sunday School. I began to question my parents: Why weren't we keeping kosher? Why didn't we observe the traditions I was learning about?

1954—My father decided to switch to the Reform temple. I heard him defend his choice to my grandparents: the Reform temple was more modern and more suited to American life, and I wouldn't be learning one thing in Sunday School and doing another thing at home.

1955—For the Purim pageant, I dressed as Ruth (who said to another woman, "Whither thou goest, I go") in a beautiful ivory-

and-turquoise-colored garment my grandmother made for the occasion. I liked that, but I hated the rabbi's hypocrisy: he despised children and was nice to us only when our parents were around, because they were the ones with the money.

1956—My mother died. Someone at school told me that she was in heaven. I said I didn't think so, because heaven was for Christians. That same year a boy in my class called me a dirty Jew.

1960—I became best friends with the only other two Jewish girls in my class. We joined a girls' club at the Jewish Center together and went together to bar mitzvah parties, where we usually danced with each other. Everyone thought I was weird because I wouldn't play spin-the-bottle.

1964—I attended a Friends' meeting with my college roommate. I liked the quiet and meditative quality of meeting better than the Hillel services.

1967—I went to Paris for a year, I rented a room in the apartment of an anti-Semitic woman. She said I was different from other Jews (who were crass, money-grubbing, lustful, and filthy) because I didn't go to synagogue. I began to attend an Orthodox synagogue there.

1968—I became a part of the university Orthodox Jewish community. I kept kosher, observed the Sabbath, and went to synagogue. I began to sleep with Orthodox Jewish men. My father and stepmother were worried that I might never marry at all. I felt a real connection with my Jewish roots for the first time. I begged my grandparents and great-aunts to tell me stories about their early lives, the same stories that had bored me before. I took great satisfaction in knowing that Jews all over the world were following the same customs and saying the same prayers as I.

1969—I moved to Jerusalem, where I lived among Orthodox Jews. I spent every Sabbath with a group of friends, and I was "adopted" by two families. Every Israeli I met wanted to know why I wasn't married yet. I was worried too: all my relationships with men were terrible. I entered psychoanalysis with a German-born Orthodox Jewish Freudian male psychiatrist recommended by my friend Judy, to whom I was very much attracted.

1970—My closest friend, Risa, and I began to study the Bible and pray together every day, and to learn the *nigunim* [melodies] for reciting prayers and reading the Torah aloud. We tried to reinterpret prayers and laws that seemed anti-woman. We both hated the enforced passivity of women in synagogue, and we developed the idea of starting a women's *minyan,* a group of women who would pray and study together, without men, and would perform every part of the Jewish services.

1971—For my birthday Risa gave a party for which she and I prepared commentaries on two verses from Exodus. All of my Orthodox friends came, and this was probably the first time that any of the men had ever sat quietly to hear women's interpretations of the Bible. I was thrilled to show off my new knowledge. About the same time, I was becoming intensely aware of lesbian feelings. I quit psychoanalysis and began to think seriously about what kind of life I could have as a lesbian. Clearly there would be no place for me in Israeli society or in the Orthodox Jewish community. I was in terrible conflict. I returned to the United States and became engaged to a gay man who had been my friend since college. He too was trying to live as an Orthodox Jew, and we decided that marriage would keep us on the path of heterosexuality and Orthodox Judaism. He asked me to stop studying the Bible until he could catch up with me; he didn't want his wife to be more learned than he. I refused. Within a month we broke the engagement. I came out as a lesbian and rejected Jewish law and religion altogether, though I maintained a strong identity as a Jew.

1976—I attended the Kol Nidre service at Beth Chaim Chadashim, the gay synagogue in Los Angeles. In a way I felt comfortable, at home, knowing I could be a part of a Jewish service as a lesbian. In another way I felt alienated: the service was both too similar to and too different from the prayers I had cherished in my Orthodox days. A part of me wanted this gay ritual to be entirely new and original, with no roots in patriarchy, and another part of me wanted the service to be the rich and meaningful Hebrew ritual I had learned in Israel, rather than the watered-down Reform version. Both parts were frustrated.

1977—Today is the first day of Passover. Last night I went to Alix Dobkin's concert ("Why is this night different from all other nights? Because tonight is an all-women's concert!"), and I just ate a bagel for breakfast. Last month I sent for a subscription to *Lilith,* a Jewish feminist magazine, and I am waiting for the first issue to arrive. I feel heavily the waste of learning and the denial of real need in my neglect of Judaism, but I feel equally strongly the rejection of religious practices that are based on patriarchy and heterosexuality. For now, I am more or less comfortable identifying myself as a Jew but not comfortable practicing the Jewish religion. In the future, I hope to join with other Jewish lesbians to develop rituals that would flow from our womanhood, our lesbianism, and our Jewish roots. I am also interested in searching the past for Jewish women who studied and reinterpreted the traditions and who started all-women study and rituals groups (like the one Risa and I were going to start in Israel).

I take pride in my Jewish heritage, and I am tired of hearing women dismiss Jewish identity as "oppressive" and "patriarchal," without knowing anything about it. I am tired of feminist books that sum up all Jewish thought in that one stupid prayer, "Blessed art Thou . . . who did not make me a woman," that has probably been invoked more times in this decade by Christian women to condemn Judaism than by Jewish men to thank God. And I am tired of the popular belief in the women's community that Jewish women have had no first-hand experience with racism. Anti-Semitism is a form of racism, and so is the assumption that everyone is Christian. I have encountered both of these forms of racism in the lesbian community as well as in the outside world.

Jewish identity is important to me because being Jewish is an integral part of myself; it's my inheritance, my roots. Christian women sometimes have a hard time understanding this, because Christian identity is so much tied up with religious beliefs. It is possible to be an ex-Catholic or an ex-Baptist, but it really is not possible to be an ex-Jew. A Jew doesn't have to believe any particular doctrine; she just *is* a Jew.

In talking with Jewish friends, I've discovered that our families somehow transmitted to us many values that are traditionally Jewish, even when our families were trying hard to assimilate into Christian America, even to disguise their Jewish identity. In

Europe, the Hebrew scholar held the place of greatest honor in the Jewish community; in America, Jews have placed great importance on their children's education. I see a similar inheritance in the area of social responsibility: my great-aunt Sarah was sent to America by her parents because she was active in the Bolshevik movement and they were afraid for her life; in America, she and her children became active in the civil rights movement; now, I am active in the lesbian movement. It's no accident that disproportionately high numbers of Jews are involved in most social action movements in the U.S.

Of all the values I acquired from my Jewish background, today I especially prize two: an emphasis on actions rather than beliefs, and a sense of the privacy of a community.

Jewish law is permeated with the philosophy that it is more important to live properly (by treating other people well) than to think or even worship properly. This emphasis on ethics shows up in the laws for Yom Kippur, the Day of Atonement, which is the most important holiday of the year. On this day all Jews are supposed to "clean the slate" by fasting and going to synagogue to pray for forgiveness for the misdeeds of the past year. However, in the days before Yom Kippur, a Jew is supposed to make appropriate amends to all the people she has hurt or cheated during the year; in some cases, an apology is sufficient, but in other cases, restoration of damages is required. Unless she has first made amends to other people, she does not have the right to ask God for forgiveness.

Now, many Jews in this century don't know or obey the specific laws of Judaism—and many of these laws don't deserve to be obeyed, in my opinion, because they are outdated and patriarchal—but the central principle remains and is passed from parent to child: what you believe is less important than how you act. Today, I find myself applying this principle within the women's community; I am less interested in purity of feminist politics than in quality of woman-to-woman interaction. In judging whether a particular woman can be trusted, I try to look at her behavior, the way she treats other women, rather than at her rhetoric or her political line.

Jews have always had a community, with its own intense internal life, and a feeling that what goes on inside is nobody else's business. Conversely, Jews have respected the privacy of other ethnic and religious groups, and have made no effort to convert non-Jews to Judaism. Jews have never been missionaries. I feel that this attitude has done much to shape my politics as a lesbian. I have a strong desire to join together with other women who share my interests, but I feel little urge to transform the others.

At a recent meeting of women who teach at the Los Angeles Women's Building, I heard one woman say that her goal in teaching was to convert and organize housewives, to make housewives into activists. This really rubbed me the wrong way; I felt that her attitude toward her students was condescending, and I couldn't imagine why she would want to teach women she obviously didn't respect. Later, I realized she had been brought up as a Christian, and very possibly had been taught to convert the nonbelievers. I am certain that my being Jewish and her being Christian has a lot to do with our political differences.

Writing this article has been a very preliminary exploration for me of my Jewish background and the ways in which this background has affected my life as a lesbian. I feel that there's a lot more to come!

Kaddish from the "Wrong" Side of the *Mehitzah*

Sara Reguer

TODAY is the first anniversary of my mother's death. She died suddenly, in the prime of life, and the void left in my life is immeasurable as well as indescribable.

Jewish laws and customs concerning death are infinitely wise. Without knowing the psychological terminology, the laws teach the need of facing the reality of death—hence in Israel, in particular, no coffin is used for the burial, so that you cannot pretend that the shrouded figure is not what it is. The laws first recognize the need to have time alone during the immediate aftershock of death as well as the need to have people come to comfort you so that you do not feel totally alone; and then the laws gradually push you, first after seven days, then after thirty days, and finally after eleven months, to rejoin the world.

But what if you are, as I am, an Orthodox Jew as well as a feminist? How do you deal with the dilemma of burying your mother outside Jerusalem where the burial societies, the *hevrah kadishah,* are run by men who still think they are living in the ghettos of the late Middle Ages? Let me add one more personal note. I stem from an Orthodox family of note (i.e., I have *yihus*); therefore, what I do tends to have wider ramifications than if I were merely acting on my own. I can also get away with what some consider outrageous behavior because I have the backing of my father, a man well trained in the rational Lithuanian *yeshivot* of the previous generation.

There we were, in our grief—my father, one of my brothers, and myself—standing in front of the body of my mother. Without even thinking, I joined the two men as we mumbled through the first choking Kaddish of the funeral service. After about three repetitions of the Kaddish, as we moved from the chapel toward the grave, the head of the *hevrah kadishah* suddenly realized that I was saying it aloud with the men. Before the next one, he ordered the men only to say it, repeating this order in Hebrew, then in Yiddish, and finally in English. I looked straight through him and continued in an even louder voice. At the grave site, the same thing happened. He handed the shovel to my father to shovel some dirt into the grave, then gave it to my brother, and then pointedly gave it to a male cousin. I ignored the man, bent down to scoop up some dirt with my hands, and threw it into the grave, as is required of all close relatives of the deceased, in keeping with the traditional attitude toward the reality of death. By now the man was livid, especially as he saw he had no backing from any of my family.

After the body is buried, Jewish custom dictates that attention then turns from the dead to the living and the process of comforting begins. This is traditionally symbolized by the formation of a double row of people through which the mourners pass. The head of the *hevrah kadishah* cornered me as the lines were being formed and said that I was absolutely forbidden from passing through the two rows. Why, I asked. Because it was not modest for women to go between two rows of men. (Until that point I had not even noticed that the lines were male.) I retorted that this had nothing to do with men or women but with mourners, and if it bothered him so much, he should have two rows of women for me. The logic of the statement, I later found out, made the rounds of the ultra-Orthodox communities in Jerusalem, with many rabbis agreeing with my statement. Unfortunately, many of my sister-Jews do not have the internal fortitude to follow what I did, but remain cowed by the *hevrah kadishah* and "custom," that old excuse for not allowing women to follow ritual.

During the week of sitting *shiva* I continued to say Kaddish with the *minyan* that came twice daily to the house. I studied the laws of mourning with my father, and he backed my resolve to continue the practice for the required eleven months. Yes, daughters too should say Kaddish for their parents. The rabbis, in their wisdom, knew the pyschological benefits of going to the synagogue daily to perform this duty, and they did not discriminate against women. What seems to have happened—here as with a long list of other practices—is that certain *mitzvot* [commandments] have luck and others do not. An example of a lucky *mitzvah* is candle lighting.The law states that a house must have candles lighted in it in honor of Shabbat: if there is a married couple in the house, the wife lights the candles, and if a married woman is not there, then a man lights them. This *mitzvah* regarding candle lighting has been expanded by certain sects of Judaism to include all females, young and old, with all sorts of mystical overtones given to it. Few women attending Brooklyn College have not been accosted by Lubovich men who ask them first whether they are Jewish, and if so, whether they are willing to light the free candles in the holders Friday night.

An unlucky *mitzvah* is Kaddish. Too bad. It was saying Kaddish for the past year that enabled me to keep my sanity. If I had not *had* to get out of bed at 6:30 A.M. in order to be on time for the beginning of services, I can guarantee that I simply would not have left my bed at all. Depression is a terrifying experience partly because one is virtually unable to fight it.

Did I mean what I was saying? Was I really reaffirming my belief in God's greatness (which is the meaning of the words of the Kaddish prayer)? Not for the first few months. Rather, I battled God every inch of the way. Catharsis came suddenly, violently, but it took almost the full eleven months before I again really meant the words I was pronouncing—meant them on the internal level.

Externally, there were some very interesting aspects to my Kaddish-saying career. I had my "home synagogue," the one that I attended most often, and after the initial shock of my appearance wore off and the old men agreed among themselves that I was right in saying Kaddish, I became one of the gang—or almost. For I sat behind a separation, in the corner. My anger at this particular *mehitzah* grew to the point that one rainy day, when a man came in and unthinkingly draped his wet coat over my "cage," I growled aloud. He jumped at the sound and looked at me questioningly. I said, "If you treat me like an animal, why the surprise if I growl like one?" He excused himself and removed his coat. I later found out from some of the men that this particular man did something unusual a few days after that incident. I was away for five days or so, and each morning during my absence the old gentleman I had growled at sat behind the *mehitzah* to see what it felt like. He agreed with my dissatisfaction and frustration, but neither of us could come up with a solution to the problem.

Most daily services are not held in the main synagogue but in a small room either downstairs or to the side of the main hall. Since women do not usually come to weekday services, most synagogues do not have facilities for them. When I appeared, the solution to the problem this posed was usually my standing to pray outside the room through the open door. Inevitably, there would be a scramble to get me a *siddur,* a chair, a Bible, and an embarrassed apology for the lack of a women's section. Inevitably, also, there would be a moment of stunned silence as I would rise to say Kaddish out loud. Some would come and ask if I had a brother, I would reply that it made no difference if I did or did not, for all children were obligated to say Kaddish for parents. Some would offer to say it for me. I repeated what I said about brothers. I also said that if it offended anyone for me to say it alone, they were welcome to say it with me, but not for me. A rush to the books, or to the rabbi, brought the usual—albeit sometimes reluctant—affirmation of my deed.

In one Hasidic synagogue, one man almost shouted at me to say Kaddish silently because my chanting aloud was against the injunction of *kol ishah;* the singing voice of a woman is considered by some to be sexually arousing to men and therefore is forbidden. I asked the man whether he spoke to women in public. He said yes. I said that I was merely speaking in public also, but to God. And if it still bothered him, he had no business sitting right near the *mehitzah* to start with.

Then there was the time I visited Boston and was praying in an Orthodox school attended by one of the most outstanding Jewish scholars and rabbis of our day. The sexton was nervous because I had already told him what I would be doing. He insisted on saying Kaddish with me. But I saw a flurry of activity in the corner where the rabbi sat, and when it came time to say it, I said the Kaddish alone and all answered, as they properly should have.

It has not been easy. This past year has been the worst of my life. It has been eased somewhat by my Kaddish-saying and by the positive reactions of most of the men I met at the services. On Sabbaths and holidays, women often came over to ask about what I was doing, usually adding that it was too bad they had not known about this during their own year of mourning, when they too had needed desperately some sort of ritual to lean on.

After much soul-searching, I decided at the end of this past semester to share my ideas and thoughts with my class at Brooklyn College, where I gave a course on "The Jewish Woman." At first I had hesitated; even though I felt strongly about the validity of my actions, I did not want to influence my students, who tend to be very much impressed by what I do. But if someone like myself is not going to teach this, who will?

Learning to Chant the Torah
A FIRST STEP

Arleen Stern

BROWSING through the long list of offerings in the program of the Second Havurah Summer Institute, I found my attention caught by one course: "Torah Trop for Beginners." "Starting from the beginning," the description said, "this course will culminate in students' preparing and reading the Torah at the Shabbat services."

My attraction to the idea of reading the Torah in public had to do both with my newly serious interest in Judaism and with my commitment to feminism. In an essay in *Havurah,* a newsletter published by the National Havurah Coordinating Committee, Martha Acklesburg points to the problems experienced by Jewish feminists, particularly those from traditional homes, when they are confronted by the male monopoly over communal ritual roles. "The tensions and confusions aroused in many women and men by these confrontations were severe," she wrote. "Some left active participation in the Jewish community."

That fit my own experience. Raised in an observant home, I found meaning and satisfaction in the ritual; yet for some years I found it actually painful to attend traditional synagogue services solely as passive consumer, barred by my gender from assuming any public role.

Still, I had my hesitations. The day before the class was to begin I chanced to meet Ellen Frankel, the teacher of the course, on campus. I told her I was thinking of attending but that it would be quite a step for me, since I had never even had my own *aliyah*—public calling up before a congregation. She encouraged me to come.

The next day, thirteen people gathered in the assigned room; eleven women, two men, ages ranging from the mid-twenties to late seventies. And we began. Learning to chant the Torah requires two initial skills. First one must sing the line, consisting usually of two to four notational signs, over and over to gain familiarity with the melody. Each notational sign is sung by name. Then the chanters must memorize the signs that appear above or below each word. This may sound simple, but there are approximately twenty notational signs to be mastered, ranging from simple to complex. Luckily, some notations are used much more often than others. When the notations are learned, those tunes are sung to the actual text being chanted.

We spent much class time chanting the melody lines, first in unison, then solo. As our repertoire grew, we chanted more than a single line at a time. The challenge grew as we attempted to chant with only the notational songs as guide. From the first day, I found myself humming the melodies to myself and asking classmates for the correct progression of lines.

On Friday, we had our fourth and final session (only three had been scheduled, but we requested an additional session). The moment of truth arrived when Ellen asked who would like an assignment to prepare for Shabbat. After a heavy dose of encouragement from our mentor-teacher, three of us, all women, agreed to take assignments. One woman and I divided a portion, and I took two *pesukim* [sentences] to prepare.

The previous evening I had had one of my few glances into a Torah. It was intimidating. When the scroll is opened, one views a literal sea of words. The Torah is handwritten in columns several inches wide. There are no commas, no periods, few divisions of any kind—and no vowels at all! Moreover, there are none of those helpful notational signs one sees when following the reading in the synagogue *humash*. Before I ever thought about reading from the Torah, I had regarded the pointer used, the *yad,* as an aesthetically pleasing device. Now I realized that it was a simple necessity: each reader must mark his or her progress and show the next reader where to begin.

After dinner Friday night, I absented myself to begin preparing. Unfortunately, I cannot read Hebrew written without vowels at sight, so that I began by memorizing the pronunciation of each word. Ellen had assured us that no one would stop us if we sang a note inexactly—there are many variations in the tunes. It would be different if we mispronounced a word; after all, we would be reading sacred text, and we would have to be corrected.

Finally, I was able to begin chanting the actual text. We had each been given a photocopied page of our reading from the *tikkun,* a book with the Torah script on one side and the same text complete with vowels and notational signs on the other. Eventually I began practicing the chant from the unmarked side. From time to time as I practiced the two other women came by with their assignments and we chanted to each other and exchanged encouragement.

In the morning I awoke with melodies going through my head. At breakfast, I ran through my portion with a woman who had read many times before. She gave me the best advice. "Take the practice sheet up with you," she said, "and if you need it, use it." I don't know how kosher the advice was, but it saved my life.

After several more practice runs, I joined the traditional *havurah* service in progress. About forty people attended this service (others were offered as well). I began to alternate between extreme confidence and total terror. Confidence because I was sure the people I knew in the group would be completely supportive; terror because I thought I might earn only their commiseration.

When the Torah was taken out, every person in the room received it with outstretched arms and then passed it on to the next recipient. Then the reading began, and I was told to come forward. The first new reader chanted her portion and it was my turn. I faltered a few times, but the words came out and it all happened fairly quickly. Luckily, Ellen stood next to us as promised, and prompted as necessary. As I finished, I encircled my fellow student with one arm in exaltation. We were four women standing before everyone.

The readings finished, Ellen announced that we had all learned trop this week and had just read for the first time. She suggested that everyone say *sheheheyanu,* a blessing chanted to commemorate significant first events, and the group did so. The feeling of relief and exhilaration brought me close to tears. Not only had I read a most sacred text publicly, I had done so among people to whom I felt close, of whom I was a part.

It was the high point of the Institute for me, and as should be with meaningful events in our lives, marked both a culmination and a beginning. It was a moment in the process of coming to terms with a troubling part of my tradition, the part that would consign me to a role of passivity, that tells me I have no place in leading others. By publicly reading in a *havurah* service, I moved a step closer to feeling I have a place and a home as a Jew.

History, Fiction, and the Tradition
CREATING A JEWISH FEMINIST POETIC

Claire R. Satlof

IN *Bread Givers,* one of the first novels ever published by an American Jewish woman, the narrator's father reprimands his wife in words that leave no doubt as to her spiritual status, or his. "Woman!" he commands, "Stay in your place! You're smart enough to bargain with the fish-peddler. But I'm the head of this family!"[1] Clearly locating himself as the spiritual rather than the domestic head of the family, Reb Smolinsky reveals the traditional Jewish assessment of the two roles. His duty as spiritual guide demands that his wife and daughters recognize his otherworldly significance by freeing him of the need to support himself financially. In return for supplying him with the physical necessities of life—such things as women are fit to provide—he, the father and husband, promises the ritualized spiritual support that only a man can offer. "Am I not their light?" he asks in rhetorical self-righteousness. "The whole world would be in thick darkness if not for men like me who give their lives to spread the light of the Holy Torah."[2] If a woman like Sara, the novel's narrator, rebels against the male-dominated religious tradition that leaves women effectively powerless, she can only be, in the words of her outraged father, "a toad, . . . a thing of evil, . . . a denier of God,"[3] a spiritual outcast in a world in which spiritual status mandates social roles.

Books and stories by such American Jewish feminists as

Esther Broner, Joanne Greenberg, Rhoda Lerman, Cynthia Ozick, Nessa Rapoport, and others[4] self-consciously attempt to end the division of the world into a male-controlled spiritual realm and an everyday, profane, women's world. By confining women to the physical world while offering men passage into the higher sacred order, traditional Orthodoxy has denied women the opportunity to establish a sense of autonomous self, or even a strong sense of self as Jew. Consequently, any Jewish feminists' attempt to create a literature of their own must ground itself in the area of Jewish ritual activity—the area most immediately in need of change.

Esther Broner's *A Weave of Women* reflects the Jewish feminists' rebellion against women's systematic exclusion from the sacred, and presents one way in which they seek to end it. Replete with visions of new ritual forms, this novel portrays a community of women who seize control of the traditionally male-oriented ceremonies and, more notably, create female-oriented ones. A kind of counterlife, the novel opens with the birth of a baby girl and proceeds through the cycle from woman's birth to woman's death and woman's resurrection. In the first pages, the women perform a hymenotomy on the newborn infant, a counterritual to the male circumcision. Calling this ritual "a ceremony on the throne of Miriam" (a feminist answer to the chair set for Elijah at a *brit milah*), the women sing "of *women's* chairs [emphasis added]: the birthing stool, the throne of Miriam, the chair of the longing woman at the window, of the cooking woman at the table, of chariots of war and chariots of angels ascending."[5] Here, women control the liturgy, and the liturgy reflects the power of women. However, the ceremony is much more than a recast male ritual, as the women's prayers indicate: the women perform the hymenotomy to fulfill women's needs as determined by their own social history. "Terry, the godmother, says, 'May all orifices be opened,' " while Dahlia says, "May she not be delivered intact to her bridegroom or judged by her hymen but by the energies of her life."[6] In each blessing, the symbolism of the ritual marking merges with the symbolic rejection of the historical treatment of women as vessels for male sexuality and vassals for the home. Far from denying God in these pages, the women seek new ways to embrace Him—or Her, for women, too, are created in God's image, as these authors affirm.

The relation between ritual activity and the social status of Jewish women is basic to an understanding of theology and religious community. In anthropological terms, a theology is shaped by certain sacred stories—myths—that are both of belief and to be believed in. Members of a particular religious community demonstrate their belief in a given theology by performing certain ritual activities that, in turn, give meaning to—and so establish the legitimacy of—their everyday lives. In Judaism, all ritual activity involves the ordered repetition of mythic acts of original, archetypal ancestors such as Abraham, Isaac, Jacob, Moses, or, especially, God, the primal "ancestor." Individual Jews and Jewish communities relive the myths, the sacred stories of these ancestors, by following their exemplary models for all aspects of human behavior—in diet and marriage, work and education, ceremony and ritual. Religious observances such as circumcision, recitation of the seder, celebration of Shabbat (a repetition of God's rest) or laying *tefillin* are all acts of *imitatio Dei,* ritual imitation and reenactment of archetypal events. With each performance, the participants assume the holiness and power of the original ancestor, reasserting Jewish belief and history. As mythically ordained behavior governs every hour of the Jew's day, the community is continually reestablishing its unique identity as Jews.[7]

For women, however, some rituals are forbidden, others carefully circumscribed. Full participation in the wide realm of rituals that delineate the Jew is necessarily closed to women. The injunction "Ye shall be holy for I the Lord your God am holy" is fulfilled by performing the commandments, and it is this holiness which establishes Israel as a nation. But women may not become *Kohanim,* may not lead in communal prayer, may not have access to the sacred texts. The religious activities open to women are performed in private, at home, cutting them off from the communal striving for holiness and severely limiting their participation in and identification with that realm of the sacred so central to Judaism. The very world of women—the world of the physical, the bodily, *gashmiut*—is separated from that of the spiritual, *ruhniut,* and only men have traditionally inhabited the latter.

As Broner implicitly acknowledges, if rituals always accompany—and, more importantly, effect—the transition from one cosmic world to another (from the physical everyday to the sacred), so they provide a transition from one social world to another.[8] Consequently, in each newly devised (or revised) ritual, Broner's contemporary women reply to the traditions of Judaism with new mythic models of spirituality and new opportunities for ritual reenactment. A new Shabbat prayer, for example, reenforces the metaphor of Shabbat as bride, linking her with God and so promoting her to divinity: "Lady of the flame . . . of the spirit and the smoke . . . We are ready to light candles in honor of the Shabbat. Oh, my Lady, Bride, thus it is written that You have called the Sabbath a delight. . . . Melting, changing lady of the candles, meet among us, dwell among us."[9] The mythic association of Jewish women with divine Sabbath and the consequent possibilities of *imitatio Dei* is made explicit by the speaker who declares after her celebration, "I am the bride. . . . I am Shabbat."[10] The mythic imagination here plays the role of the theological imagination, and women-created "divine" fictions provide the new ritual modes.

Nessa Rapoport's "The Woman Who Lost Her Names" both chronicles the frustration Jewish women have felt because of their exclusion, and points to the ultimate healing ritual offered by Jewish feminist writers—the "ritual" of writing itself. Specifically, the story delineates one Jewish ritual that reflects the intermingled social and spiritual exclusion of the Jewish woman and suggests the double solution characteristically offered by Jewish feminist fiction.[11] The story tells of a young girl who loses control over her life as her husband systematically strips away her names. Sarah Josephine Levi, the young girl's original names, confer both individual and communal existence. Her fiancé, however, insists that she discard "Sarah," a name his mother bears. Searching for a new acceptable name, he transforms the woman into "Yosepha Peniel," a female Joseph whose last name (her husband's) recalls the place where Jacob wrestled with the angel for a new name and the new identity of Israel—an irony implicitly pointing to the parallel with the Jewish and feminist search for identity and self-definition. Yosepha's husband, a poet, tells her he transplants her phrases into his work, but when she peers "through the foreign marks for herself, not finding resemblance," her language appears lost.[12] When the couple has a child, the husband insists on naming her "Dina" despite his wife's objections. Utterly defeated, the woman is seen at story's end waiting to hear her daughter's name, knowing she has betrayed herself whatever the case: "Sarale," her mother would say to her, "remember who you are and you'll always have yourself. No matter what else you lose—"[13] Yet Sarah has lost not only her name but her right to name and, with it, her right to individual identity and a place in the tradition to which she was born.

Sarah here typifies the traditional state of the American Jewish woman—both are effectively in exile. Though she shares this state with the American Jewish man, who, like herself, is subject to Bellow's "dangling man" syndrome, the Jewish man has had far more power to control his world than has the Jewish woman. The key to this ritual and historical power is linguistic, and, specifically, literary. Within Jewish tradition, men alone have controlled biblical and liturgical texts. They created the literature in *man's* image, with powerful men and a powerful male God-figure for Jewish men to emulate. Women were powerless to alter the situation as they were denied the means—language—of controlling their world, for women had no voice in the Jewish community. How could one with no name, no claim to communal identity, claim communal leadership or determination? Too, a sense of namelessness leads further to feelings of indeterminacy, of being without existence—a recognized characteristic of the modern Jewish literary tradition since Franz Kafka.

Yet more than the loss of a name of one's own, lack of the very power to name is the most terrifying aspect of the Jewish woman's status until now, and the one Jewish feminist fiction eminently seeks to counteract. The ritual act of naming entails more than bestowing names on children; it includes the acts of creating images and symbols, interpreting perceived reality, telling personal and communal stories and rituals. In other words, one who controls names controls language. And if history is the product of its recordings, and tradition the accumulation of its tellings, language controls reality, for it is the means by which we conceive and perceive the world.

Because women have been denied control of language, they have been denied access to the necessarily linguistic reality that male authors have created—a reality past and present, religious and secular, which excludes women. As in the religious tradition, women have no voice and so no social or spiritual force in the American Jewish literary tradition. Though there are numerous strong women characters, these women, too, are nameless; they play significant roles only in terms of the men with whom they enter into relation and whose nature they exist to define. The men are men, Jews, but the women are mothers, sisters, wives, or lovers. As a corollary, Jewish women have been left with no sense of a usable past for creating new realities.

Esther Broner's *Her Mothers* underscores this lack by pointing out the inefficacy of the matriarchs, women's only traditional role models. Defined by men in the context of male-dominated values, Jewish foremothers are portrayed here as petty, unheroic characters: "What do I learn from my mothers?" asks Beatrix, the narrator. "Sister against sister, woman betrays woman. The man is the seed and the woman the gourd, filled with seed and rattling or dried and to be discarded."[14] A jealous Sara commands Abraham, "Kill Hagar. Kill her child," writes Broner,[15] while Rivka "would make her son her lover,"[16] create enmity among brothers, and disenfranchise the wives of her other son. Asking, "Mothers, what have you taught me?" the narrator answers, "Mothers! Sara! Rivka! Lea! Rahel! You have taught your daughters that women fight for the penis of a man. The winner will be honored with burial in the Cave of Machpelah or under a standing marker on the road to Bethlehem. Who named *you* my mothers? Who named *this* a matriarchy?"[17] Judaism provides no viable models on whom women can base their lives, no mythic heroines whose acts they can imitate and so reclaim themselves, no images of powerful creators/artists in whose image women readers can find their own in either history or the literary tradition. According to *midrash,* Adam gave life to the animals by naming them; what is left to women?

What is left, for one thing, is the redistribution of roles, the wresting of linguistic control from men and a literary re-visioning of Jewish reality. Judaism itself as a text-centered religion provides a model for the activity of these writers, for the central theme of Jewish feminist fiction is the notion of the text. What unifies the books and stories of Broner, Greenberg, Lerman, Ozick, and Rapoport is their insistence upon fiction and its power to create meaning for individuals and a people. These works are, then, self-reflexive fictions, fictions that investigate the power of the word and the artist to establish and revitalize the world. As the term "self-reflexive" suggests, implying both reflection on and a turning back on and self-conscious perceiving of itself, such fiction calls attention to the novel or story as process, as object, and as "fiction."[18]

Jewish feminist fiction differs from male-dominated American Jewish literature, which is largely realistic: Bellow and Roth have been called the eye and ear, respectively, of Jewish America. However, the quality and theme of self-reflexivity are not unique to Jewish feminists, although the aims are unique. Many critics claim that this concern with the potential of language characterizes the canon of American fiction beginning with Melville.[19] The contemporary impetus for self-reflexive literature is an awareness of the insufficiency of the "real" world, given women's shadowy existence in this world. The "real" world's traditional forms and institutions (including traditional religion and art) no longer provide meaning or coherence for feminists and so no longer offer themselves as testing ground for the development of personal and communal identity. Consequently, if art simply imitates life, as in characteristically realistic fiction, it offers nothing of value, especially to feminists. Contemporary secular male authors such as John Barth, Donald Barthelme, Robert Coover, and William Gass, and Jewish feminist writers all shift the idea of the "real" from the external, already existing world to that of fiction and the fictive world: fictions become the "real." Life now imitates art—or, in the case of the feminists, should imitate it. The "world" whose boundaries are the covers of Broner's *A Weave of Women,* for example, the rituals that the work recreates or creates for the first time—these establish the real or valid or imitable world, replacing the untenable world of nonfictitious reality.

Writing itself, for feminists, is a form of rebellion, usurpation, or re-visioning; it also marks the beginning of a new ritualization and a new myth-making, for language is intimately bound up with religious ritual. More than the vehicle for performing rituals, language establishes the reality of myth. As sacred *stories,* myths are verbal incarnations. Ritual repetition of the myth relies on verbal performance as the sphere of the verbal codes for meaning: the words, not the actions, recall and so imitate the archetype, and actions without words are meaningless.

This newly emerged canon, then, seeks to make fiction a ritual form, a primary concern not shared by most contemporary American writers. These Jewish feminists, deliberately locating themselves within the framework of Jewish rituals, wrest spiritual control from men, as Broner's characters show us. In this context, Jewish feminist fiction participates in the general Jewish feminist movement toward the formation of women's rituals such as the hymenotomy or baby-naming ceremonies and the feminist recontextualization of rituals such as the seder (producing a "woman's Haggadah") or the ceremony for the new moon.[20] But this fiction does more than present accounts of these new woman-oriented and -controlled ceremonies. The extreme self-consciousness of the literary form, the constant references to language and literature make clear that these authors are offering an alternative to an inadequate reality which is much more than just another woman's ritual. Even while these texts provide the necessary framework for understanding the significance of the new ritual forms, they do not just depict the forms; they embody them.

Herein lies the power of the works' contribution to Jewish feminism. Literary works often seem to present alternative worlds, but, in fact, the alternatives merely replicate a picture of a world already past. Jewish feminist texts, in contrast, are actual agents of change in an uncompleted society, that of contemporary Judaism. They effect the changes they portray, not merely redistributing roles, but realigning and revaluing the realms of ritual and history.

The women narrators and characters presented in these feminist works become social and spiritual models for women readers to emulate, with the text functioning simultaneously on the historical and mythic levels. On the one hand, the stories present vivid portraits of women characters who succeed as women in the various self-appointed tasks the books outline. Significantly, all of the women in every work are recognizably women, rather than unrealistic "superbeings." These women share the fears and aspirations of the readers whose lives theirs deliberately resemble: they worry about growing old, losing husbands, enhancing sexuality, alienating children. Through the inevitable process of identification, the characters provide readers with a sense of their own creative power and control. On the other hand, the authors and their narrators and characters are also new archetypal "ancestors," with all that implies. If women create the new myths, they are the Creators as well, those whose Word bestows meaning and significance: reading offers the opportunity for reenactment as the reader relives the text, recreating it for herself. The self-consciousness of presentation in these works—the preoccupation with the power of words, the use of first person narrators and the presence of author-figures, the telling of stories within stories, the sense of linguistic newness that characterizes many of the rituals—indicates the unique nature of the texts. In each case, they emphasize that fictive works here fulfill the role of transcendentally "true" myths, indicating at once the breakdown between the supposedly discrete categories of "fiction" and "reality" and the merging of text and Text.

Not surprisingly, Jewish feminist fiction emphasizes discussions of the "miraculous" power of language. Cynthia Ozick's novella *Usurpation* offers one such example of a narrative examining the nature of narrative, coincidentally recalling the traditional fear of such a merging of literary categories. In it, a woman author discovers the magical powers of the storyteller. Though, in Ozick's words, the tale is "a story written against story-writing, against the Muse-goddess, against Apollo," both author and the author-figure are compelled by the powers offered by the literary imagination.[21] Lest the reader mistake the intent of the story and read it as pure condemnation of idolatry in the form of a book,

Ozick acknowledges both the anti-Mosaic magic of literature and its compelling fascination for her. Admitting that "storytelling, as every writer knows, is a magic art. Or Eucharist, wherein the common bread of language assumes the form of a god,"[22] she nonetheless frames her investigation of the confrontation between "the Name of names" and Apollo in that same magical form—a story. If the story warns of "the dread of fantasy and fancy," it casts fantasy and fancy as terms of the proof, reflexively examining its own nature and motives.

Joanne Greenberg similarly writes of the mystical power of the word in "The Jaws of the Dog."[23] The niece of two elderly women (again, a first-person female narrator) tells of her battle to end the aunts' superhuman fear of venturing from their home. Though deteriorating, the state of the neighborhood does not justify the degree and nature of their paranoia. As an antidote to powerlessness, the narrator engages the aunts in a series of ritualistic acts, each based on the power of the word. First, she places a mezuzah on their door, not in legalistic fulfillment of a *mitzvah,* but in totemic recognition of the power of the written amulet. Next, she has them eat their words by ceremoniously copying out psalms, burning the paper on which they are written, and baking the ashes into a cake for the aunts to eat.

Finally, after a demand for yet more power over their lives, the woman gives the aunts a silver *yad* [Torah pointer], but the *yad* itself does not provide the power: the *yad* is no more than a "lovely artifact," "not magic, but Jewish house-wifely art work," until the women ritualistically repeat the "formula." The nature of the *yad,* used so that the Torah reader will not profane or obliterate the letters, indicates the source of the magic—the realm of the verbal, the ordered text. Not the *yad* as artifact but the *yad* in context of the verbal protects the women from their significantly *nameless* fears. As antidote, the formula requires that the women recite "Psalm 22, full of terror of things that are images for what cannot be named—the dog, the bull, the lion"[24] while facing in four directions, symbolically naming their fears, and so obliterating them, by pointing to them. The very articulation of the ritual determines its effectiveness as the narrator demands that "they read with Sephardic pronunciation, the one used now in Israel. I did not want an eastern-European sound to the Hebrew, one that recalled ghettos and persecution."[25] By the conclusion of the story, the aunts control their own lives once more and, with their newfound "magical" power, have begun to control and change their families and their immediate world. The possibilities of power through language appear infinite.

With the ability to control present reality comes the power to reshape past as depicted in the quest-motif of *Her Mothers* and in episodes such as that following the hymenotomy in *A Weave of Women.* Both offer more than accounts of increased ritual possibility, for the books themselves are ritual forms in a new historical myth. Although the wounds inflicted on women cause spiritual damage, they are historically inflicted through the force of religious and literary traditions. To annul the effects of time and cure the diseased image of women, a verbal ritual is necessary, one that returns the performer to the beginning of history. This process requires a meticulous and exhaustive recollecting of personal and historical events in a manner much like that of psychoanalysis. The rationale of the two is identical: to know is to control.

Beatrix, in *Her Mothers,* is ostensibly searching for her runaway daughter, but the very form of the novel implies that she is searching for much more. The book is divided into sections ranging from "Looking for Friends" to "Historical Mothers" and "Foremothers" with only one small chapter explicitly devoted to "Looking for Daughters." The bulk of the novel is a response to the opening refrain, the first lines of which are repeated throughout as a chorus:

A.
"I'm pregnant, mother."
"Have a girl."
"Why?"
"A girl should have a girl."

B.
"Mother, I'm pregnant with a baby girl."
"How old is she?"
"Seventeen years old."
"Then you're pregnant with me."[26]

Both mother and daughter in this book, Beatrix gives birth to herself as she gives birth to new images, new children, by first recalling her personal history as an oppressed girl-child and then the abuse of secular and religious mothers, literary women such as Margaret Fuller, Louisa May Alcott, and Charlotte Fortes, and the biblical figures Sarah, Rivkah, Rahel, and Leah. Essentially, Beatrix returns to the beginning of recorded history to look for *her* mother/role model; finding none, she writes of her spiritually orphaned state. The self-conscious journey through personal and communal history annuls the power of time through the power of the word. In the ironic phrase of one male acquaintance, incapable of understanding Beatrix's needs or journey but disapproving nevertheless, "Beatrix destroyed the present, but, much worse, the past."[27] In control of her history as a result of her verbal journey, Beatrix is no longer a victim of that history, for she is creating a new one. The lines of the final refrain exemplify her self-conscious knowledge of control of past and present:

> *"Mother, I'm pregnant with a baby girl."*
> *"What is she doing?"*
> *"She is singing."*
> *"Why is she singing?"*
> *"Because she's unafraid."*[28]

Ultimately, if Beatrix the mother gives birth to Beatrix the daughter, the book, no less than the baby, is offspring. The purpose of the story, then, is to produce a story.

Readers of *Her Mothers* benefit on both social and ritual levels in a manner characteristic of the genre of Jewish feminist fiction. The narrator deliberately offers herself as an alternative "foremother" to the debased images of the secular and religious ones she depicts: the "Her" in the title here refers both to Beatrix and the woman reader. However, the nontraditional narrative form of the novel, common to many Jewish feminist texts, requires—and provides—much more than simple identification with the narrator. The novel is a nonchronological, noncontinuous narrative with no apparent connections between chapters or even episodes. The reader is given pieces of information about events, random thoughts about the past, but the author does not provide a completed work. There are gaps in the text which the reader must bridge to read the novel, and by continually providing a context for the plot, a time scheme and rationale for the story's events, the reader completes the text, authoring and creating as she reads.[29] As a result, the reader travels with Beatrix on her journey through the book. Her fragmented history becomes the reader's own, and the reader's successful integration of the book's fragmented sections parallels Beatrix's successful creation of a new life through her own successful integration of a fragmented history. Knowledge and the control it implies is not limited to the fictional character; the reader, too, has a new history, which she has created by producing her own story and becoming her own ancestor.

The ceremony in *A Weave of Women* is much more intimate and concrete. The "weave" of women communally recall their "piercings"; physically, their initiations into sex at the hands of uncaring men, and spiritually, their psychic and emotional rape by these and other men. As time-honored tradition, condoned and even encouraged by men, such piercings—the violating of women in one way or another—are a communal experience. The ceremonial results are, consequently, the desired ones even though the experiences and recallings are individual and specific rather than collective and across time. The women are made whole by their recitations: "They are all virgins again," ends the chapter.[30] The act of *telling* a story or *naming* an event ritually deprives a violation of its power. Much like a consciousness-raising group, the book heals all participants/readers and not just the single teller.

But where is the new image of God and Judaism in these books? A creator is not necessarily the Creator, and an equalized degree of ritual involvement does not necessarily insure women's spiritual equality. Ritual performances and fictive creations place women in the realm of the mythic, but these alone are inadequate, for even in the most conservative version of the tradition women performed some ritual functions—lighting candles, keeping the kitchen kosher, visiting the *mikvah*. The problem with this traditional mode is that myth and its rituals do not necessarily imply spirituality: women were not considered spiritual beings. Stories and storytelling alone, though ritualized, do not bestow spirituality on writers, tellers, or readers—remember the existence all along of a nonfeminist Jewish literary tradition with its old wives' tales and *mayse bukhs,* collections of morality tales.

The truly sacred nature of the woman artist, and the key to the mythic power of her work, is demonstrated by that which makes Jewish feminist fiction not just another literary occurrence, but an attempt at new Jewish culture-making. By extension, it is this same quality that makes these works religious rituals rather than just secular ceremonies.[31] Literature, like ceremony, is a formalized mode of presentation and behavior, and we interpret each as "a cultural statement about cultural order as against cultural void." In other words, both literature and ceremony offer a solution to (and declaration against) indeterminacy through their formulative nature, which "celebrates the man-made meaning, the culturally determinate, the regulated, the named, and the explained."[32] Ritual is unique, however, in having *dis*order as its essential quality. Deliberate destruction of the social order as presently constituted and reconstruction, transformation culminating in reordering—this is the significance of ritual. Within a traditional Jewish context, ritual must disorder and reconstruct both the social and spiritual divisions of the universe, realigning the realms of sacred and profane, *gashmiut* and *ruhniut,* male and female, fiction and myth. The role of Jewish feminist fiction is not to reject the physical world—to become men in the pejorative sense—but to reconcile it with the spiritual in a manner that will result in the transformation and revaluation of the customary realm of women. These works suggest that the only sure way to prevent the separation of the historical and the ritual is to ritualize the quotidian, the physical everyday world of food and sex and housewifely art that has proven so threatening to the Jewish man's sense of sanctity and sacredness.

In other words, the goal of Jewish feminist writers is not limited to opening traditionally male rituals to women as well, although such a change is, in itself, a disordering. However, merely including women in an otherwise unchanged ritual context would not fundamentally alter the perception of women as "mere" physical beings—would not imbue spirituality—since these changes do not address the issue of women's daily activities, which may remain largely physical/profane. Therefore, Jewish feminist writers seek out the activities that women perform as part of their everyday routine because they are women *and* because they are Jews. These writers seek to make such activities as spiritual and as divinely imitative as the acts that Jewish men have routinely performed for centuries. The preparation of food, sexual functions—all aspects of a woman's life that designate her as physical in the traditional ordering of the universe will be transformed into spiritually significant acts and revalued as such. The work of Jewish feminist texts is to effect this reordering, ritually redefining the way we divide the universe.

The resulting synthesis of the physical/historical and the mythic/spiritual produces a new art form, one which offers the newest and most creative means of coping with that state of spiritual exile represented by the "dangling" man or woman. Only women could produce such a synthesis, given the male insistence on strict separation of sexuality—the epitome of the physical, the everyday—and spirituality. Men, not women, mandated ritual "purification" after ejaculation or menstruation, signifying the unclean state of such sex-related bodily functions. Even within the Jewish-American literary tradition, and historicized, postreligious tradition, men have been unable to synthesize secular modernity and the traditional ritual spirituality. Themselves victims of the separation, characters such as Philip Roth's Portnoy and Saul Bellow's Herzog can only accept their status, accommodating themselves to the situation rather than seizing control of it or changing it. The very nature of their symptoms indicates the irreconcilable split that men perceive between the physical and the spiritual: Portnoy indulges in wild sexual forays with *shiksas* in America, yet he is impotent with a Jewish woman in Israel.

A Weave of Women and Rhoda Lerman's *Call Me Ishtar* characterize the fruits of this new culture-making by their very form, that which indicates their synthetic nature. Each work provides new myths, created by women authors and narrators for women readers to reenact, cast in fictive form. *Call Me Ishtar* presents woman as author and woman as Creator, and so the work corrects the inequities in Judaism with a new myth even as it insists on the Jewishness of its characters. Despite the title and the narrator's assertion that she *is* Ishtar, Queen of Heaven, deposed by Moses and now returned to demand homage, the novel does not urge the creation of a pagan mythology or Ishtar cult. Instead, it combines the necessary prototype of feminine divine power concealed in Jewish mythology with the historical account of a Jewish woman in upstate New York. Her husband, Robert Moses, would like to limit her to housecleaning and sexual favors. The goddess-narrator, in her opening address to the readers, recognizes her role in ritual transformation and the production of synthesis. "If your philosophers insist that the world is a dichotomy, tell them that two plus two don't make four unless something brings them back together. The connection has been lost. But I'm back. Don't worry."[33] The *woman*-figure keys and codes the ritual action.

Ishtar is a particularly appropriate figure inasmuch as biblical accounts see her as the incarnation of all goddesses. ("Ashtoreth," an alternative name for her, is the generic term for goddesses.)[34] Her attributes reveal the reasons why: Ishtar was traditionally the goddess of fertility and *eros,* and her divine principles included that of compassionate motherhood. These attributes hardly qualify her for Jewish patriarchal spirituality. However, the same qualities and the ritual practice of baking as offering to and as imitation of the goddess produces a modern goddess/Creator whose parables are cast in simultaneously spiritual and domestic terms. The book's epigraph, written in biblical language, establishes these terms:

> And She spread it before me and it was written
> Within and without this roll of a book.
> A roll of a book was therein, and there was written lamentations, mourning, and woe.
> "Moreover," She said unto me, "Son of Man, eat that thou findest; eat this roll and go speak onto the House of Israel."
> So I opened my mouth and She caused me to eat that roll.
> And she said unto me, "Son of Man, cause thy belly to eat.
> Fill thy bowels with this roll that I give thee."
> Then did I eat it; and it was in my mouth as honey for sweetness.[35]

The book, itself a "lowly" domestic creation, presents and is presented as myth, a notably feminized one. Moreover, according to Ishtar, the book is also a sexual product, again recasting everyday activities as spiritually powerful. As part of her education as the new Ishtar, the narrator receives the historical wisdom of the goddess in words that remind us that feminized, eroticized language is the key to all meaning as it ritualizes the everyday, transforming the profane into the sacred in new syntheses:

> "*Cunt,*" she began, "is from the Sumerian *cunnus* and means burden. *Fuck,*" she continued, "is from the Sumerian *furca* and means cross, indicating a point of meaning. All cookies," she went on patiently into the night, "are cognate, as are bread, bagels, and language." The lessons continued until sunrise. They included the terribly important recipes for balancing sexuality, for preparing mandragora juice for ecstasy and general comments on the state of the world, which was, of course, degenerate.[36]

The sanctification of the physical/sexual characterizes *A Weave of Women* also as the narrator recounts new myths. Although there is no Ishtar figure, the narrator retells the story of one foremother, Esther, promoting Esther to quasi-mythic status as a descendent of Ishtar. As one character relates during a Purim celebration, "The source of Esther is Ishtar, born of sea foam, the goddess who nightly rides the heavens in a chariot pulled by a tiger. . . . Esther's ancestor was the goddess of night and love. Her ritual was pleasure."[37]

Broner explicitly addresses the issue of Ishtar's attributes, especially the area of sanctified sexuality, opposing the traditional Orthodox condemnation of the physical to the new ritual powers of the body. A traditionally religious father commands his daughter, "Don't draw attention to your physical attributes. . . . Each reference to the body erases a reference to the spirit."[38] To countermand the effects of this command, the weave of women conducts an exorcism to rid itself of the "demons" of false self-images and observes a "Holy Body Day" to counter man's degradation of women's "impure" bodies. On that day "the women pray that they be restored to their own Temple, that they no longer be captive, for there is no God of women, there has been no reaping of the sheaves in the land of women and no bringing in of tribute of dry measure."[39]

The ending of *A Weave of Women* signifies the victory won by Jewish feminists: 'How goodly are thy tents, thy reclaimed ruins, O Sara, O our mothers of the desert."[40] Women have ended their sojourn in the desert with new role models, new rituals, a new access to Judaism, and, above all, a new language and a new literature. Women now control both literary forms and their consequence—communal identity as Jewish feminists. They have reconstituted themselves as Jews by establishing a claim to Judaism on uniquely feminist terms by appropriating, redistributing, and revaluing Jewish rituals, Jewish communal life, and the Jewish reverence for the written text. Moreover, women have appropriated the American Jewish literary tradition as well, again with the goal of reclaiming identity.

From this perspective, the new (post-1973) Jewish feminist fiction leads a trend in contemporary Jewish-American fiction, away from the mainstream of the Bellow-Roth-Malamud tradition toward what Cynthia Ozick has termed "liturgical fiction," a program she outlines for Jewish self-preservation in America. In her call for a new *midrash,* a new culture-making, Ozick proclaims that "in our age," [this] takes on the urgent form of imaginative literature." She compares the task to that of Yochanan ben Zakkai, who "plunged into the elaboration of Aggadah and preserved Torah by augmenting it."[41] The very phrasing of her essay (notably entitled "America: Toward Yavneh") suggests the necessarily ritualistic tenor of this vital literature. In their presentation of new myth and *midrash*—and the very fact that they can "augment the texts"—Jewish women are recasting tradition and pronouncing a previously unspoken word.

The importance of the books here discussed, however, extends beyond the presentation of new ritual options offered (and shaped) by a new literary synthesis. As embodiments of new mythic forms, fictions such as these offer the possibility of ritual reenactment by the very fact of their literary nature. Through reading, an act which is viewed as *real*izing the text, readers participate in and perform that text, reenacting its myths and so reconstituting themselves through the proffered new beginnings. Reading time—historical, profane time—flows into sacred time, the domain of the ritual, once more underscoring the liturgical nature of these fictions, and the "housewifely" art of storytelling self-consciously transforms itself into a new Jewish reality. In this sense, these works are like biblical altars, once the symbols of ritual rededication and the physical sites of the ritual acts. But we, authors and readers, are not so much making a sacrifice, with its connotations of loss, as we are designating sacred offerings to reaffirm the communal link with the tradition. Jewish feminist fictions are like the altars of Joshua, which our biblical ancestors used not for actual sacrifice but as continual reminders of the potential inherent in that ritual act: "Let us now build an altar, not for burnt offering, nor for sacrifice; but to be a witness between us and you and between the generations after us." So it is with these fictions: they bear witness to the ritual possibilities offered by Jewish feminism and, especially, by Jewish feminist writers. Yet these authors can only give us the words of the gods/goddesses, the form of the new *midrash,* the stones of the altar. It is left to us to read and heed and imitate and so renew the life of Jewish literature and community.

NOTES

1. Anzia Yezierska, *Bread Givers* (1925; reprint ed., New York: Persea Books, 1975), p. 13.
2. Yezierska, p. 24.
3. Yezierska, pp. 137–38.
4. While there are a number of additional feminist writers who are Jewish, including women such as Diane Levenberg, Tillie Olsen, Grace Paley, and Muriel Rukeyser, most of these are not self-conscious Jewish feminists participating in a specifically Jewish feminist movement. At the same time, all the writers I do discuss may not specifically label themselves "Jewish feminist writers." Nonetheless, their work clearly fits into the scheme I have outlined.
5. E. M. Broner, *A Weave of Women* (New York: Holt, Rinehart, and Winston, 1978), p. 26.
6. Broner, p. 25.
7. Mircea Eliade, *Cosmos and History: The Myth of the Eternal*

Return, trans. Willard R. Trask (New York: Harper and Brothers, 1959), pp. 34–35.

8. See Victor Turner's comment on this recognition by Arnold van Gennep (*The Rites of Passage*) in Turner, "Social Dramas and Stories about Them," *Critical Inquiry* 7 (Autumn 1980), p. 160.

9. Broner, *A Weave of Women,* p. 58.

10. Broner, p. 65.

11. Nessa Rapoport, "The Woman Who Lost Her Names," *Lilith,* 1979, reprinted in *The Woman Who Lost Her Names: Selected Writings of American Jewish Women,* ed. Julia Wolf Mazow (New York: Harper and Row, 1980), pp. 135–42.

12. Rapoport, p. 139.

13. Rapoport, p. 136.

14. E. M. Broner, *Her Mothers* (New York: Holt, Rinehart, and Winston, 1975), p. 164.

15. Broner, *Her Mothers,* p. 153.

16. Broner, *Her Mothers,* p. 159.

17. Broner, *Her Mothers,* p. 168.

18. For one of the fullest discussions of self-reflexivity (to which I am indebted for this short explanation), see Barbara Babcock's dissertation, "Mirrors, Masks, and Metafiction: Studies in Narrative Reflexivity" (University of Chicago, 1975), pp. 2–13.

19. See, for example, Tony Tanner, *City of Words: American Fiction, 1950–1970* (New York: Harper and Row, 1971).

20. Rituals and ceremonies such as these are discussed in a number of Jewish (and non-Jewish) feminist articles. The ritual of hymenotomy is first suggested by Mary Gendler in "Sarah's Seed: A New Ritual for Women," *Response* 24 (1974), pp. 65–78. For a collection of articles on women's rituals, see *The Jewish Woman: New Perspectives,* ed. Elizabeth Koltun (New York: Schocken Books, 1976), which includes Daniel I Leifer and Myra Leifer, "On the Birth of a Daughter"; Arlene Agus, "This Month Is for You: Observing Rosh Hodesh as a Woman's Holiday"; and Aviva Cantor Zuckoff, "Jewish Women's Hagadah."

21. Cynthia Ozick, Preface to *Bloodshed and Three Novellas* (New York: Alfred A. Knopf, Inc., 1976), p. 10.

22. Ozick, p. 11.

23. Joanne Greenberg, "The Jaws of the Dog," in *High Crimes and Misdemeanors* (Holt, Rinehart, and Winston, 1979), pp. 66–97.

24. Greenberg, p. 74.

25. Greenberg, p. 93.

26. Broner, *Her Mothers,* p. 3.

27. Broner, *Her Mothers,* p. 240.

28. Broner, *Her Mothers,* p. 241.

29. For a full discussion of this theory of narrative and reading, see Wolfgang Iser, *The Implied Reader: Patterns of Communication in Prose Fiction from Bunyan to Beckett* (Baltimore: The Johns Hopkins University Press, 1974).

30. Broner, *A Weave of Women,* p. 31.

31. The distinction is made by Victor Turner in "Social Dramas and Stories about Them" (cited in note 8, above). See especially pp. 158–164.

32. Sally Falk Moore and Barbara Myerhoff, eds., *Secular Ritual,* quoted in Turner, pp. 162–163.

33. Rhoda Lerman, *Call Me Ishtar* (New York: Holt, Rinehart, and Winston, 1973), p. xii.

34. See, for example, Jer. 44:17–19; Jer. 7:18.

35. Lerman, *Call Me Ishtar,* p. xiii.

36. Lerman, p. 36.

37. Broner, *A Weave of Women,* p. 125.

38. Broner, *Weave,* p. 72.

39. Broner, *Weave,* p. 258.

40. Broner, *Weave,* p. 294.

41. Cynthia Ozick, "America: Toward Yavneh," *Judaism* 19 (1979), p. 276.

And Deborah Made Ten

Deborah E. Lipstadt

EVERY year when the day of my father's *yahrzeit* arrives I am faced with the same dilemma. The *minyan* with whom I *daven* on Shabbat does not meet during the week. The local Orthodox synagogue, which has numerous daily *minyans* to accommodate all schedules, makes no provision for women in their chapel. When I do go there the men who occupy the back benches are asked to move up front so that a *mehitzah* can be set up between the men and women—in this case me—and I can take my place. The process generally elicits grumbles and glares. Neither I nor they are particularly happy with the arrangement. This year I decided to go to the storefront shul around the corner from my home. It consists of a group of old men who attend in a devoted fashion. It is a nondenominational mutation of Orthodox and Conservative: a traditional service with mixed seating; women are not counted in the *minyan* or given *aliyot.* Though the sign in front of the shul proclaims "BAR/BAS *Mitzvahs,*" once a woman reaches adulthood she does not count.

On the night of the third of *Nisan* I took my place among the eleven men gathered for *Ma'ariv*. The rabbi, an elderly retired gentleman with a thick European accent, invited me to sit near him so that he could show me the place. Within a few moments he realized that I was quite familiar with the prayer book and the service. At the conclusion of *Ma'ariv* I asked when *Shaharit,* the morning prayers, would be said. One gentleman answered: "At

8:00 A.M. Another corrected him: "No, at 7:45." The first man said: "*She* can come at 8:00."

Promptly at 7:45 the next morning I entered the shul, took a prayer book from the shelf and opened it to *Birhot HaShahar,* the morning blessings. Somewhere in the middle of *Pesukei d'Zimra* the gentleman who had decided *I* could come at 8:00 walked over, took the Hebrew/English prayer book I had in my hands and gave me a *Tikkun Mayer,* a prayer book with neither English translations nor instructions. The assumption is that someone who uses this prayer book needs neither. I smiled at him and knew that with that simple act he had just welcomed me into the club. When services ended he looked at me and simply said: "5:45."

At 5:45 that evening I arrived for *Minhah,* the afternoon prayers, feeling good that the day had gone so smoothly. I anticipated being greeted by the strains of *Ashrei,* the psalm which introduces *Minhah,* because the sun was already beginning to set. Instead the room was unnaturally still as the men sat talking quietly. When I walked in they all turned their eyes toward me. The expectant look on their faces and a quick head-count revealed that they were waiting for the ninth and tenth men. I heard the rabbi on the phone trying to find them. "I understand, Mrs. Cohen. No, he shouldn't come out if the doctor told him to stay home. At our age one must be careful." After a few more calls the rabbi announced, "Schwartz is coming." Schwartz would be number nine. We all watched the door, hoping number ten would materialize. I berated myself for not having gone to the Orthodox synagogue, where I would have been guaranteed a *minyan,* even if I had to endure some discomfort.

As they waited for Schwartz to arrive the president of the shul announced, to no one in particular, "In some shuls they now count women." A number of men nodded silently. The sun was disappearing and the time for *Minhah* rapidly passing. Finally the door opened and in walked Schwartz. The rabbi glanced at the president and said, "Well, if we are going to say *Minhah* we better start right now." I counted heads to make sure I was right. There was a *minyan:* nine men and one woman.

As *Minhah* ended, I glanced at the clock, knowing that a friend was waiting to take me out for dinner to celebrate my birthday. (Even as we remember our losses we go on living and celebrating. And where is it written that you can't laugh and cry on the same day?) Reservations had been made for 6:30, and I had solemnly promised that *this* time, unlike previous dinner dates, I would not be late. I knew I could leave right after *Minhah,* for with that service the *yahrzeit* ended. As *Ma'ariv* began I was about to leave when I suddenly realized that I had to stay. When I finally arrived at the restaurant I breathlessly explained to my somewhat perturbed friend: "I'm sorry I'm late, but I couldn't leave. I had to stay for *Ma'ariv.*" Then I felt a wonderful wash of warmth and fulfillment fill my body and I smiled a very big smile: "You see, they *needed* me for the *minyan.*"

Yes, they needed me.

Reactions to a Woman Rabbi

Laura Geller

AT the conclusion of High Holiday services during my first year as an ordained rabbi, two congregants rushed up to talk to me. The first, a middle-aged woman, blurted out, "Rabbi, I can't tell you how different I felt about services because you are a woman. I found myself feeling that if you can be a rabbi, then maybe I could be a rabbi too. For the first time in my life I felt as though I could learn those prayers, I could study Torah, I could lead this service, I could do anything you could do. Knowing that made me feel much more involved in the service—much more involved with Judaism! Also, the service made me think about God in a different way. I'm not sure why." The second congregant had something very similar to tell me, but with a slightly different emphasis. He was a man, in his late twenties. "Rabbi, I realized that if you could be a rabbi, then certainly I could be a rabbi. Knowing that made the service somehow more accessible for me. I didn't need you to "do it" for me. I could "do it," be involved with Jewish tradition, without depending on you."

It has taken me five years to begin to understand the significance of what these people told me.

Throughout most of Jewish history the synagogue has primarily been the domain of men. It has also been a very important communal institution. Was the synagogue so important because it was the domain of men, or was it the domain of men because it was so important? Perhaps the question becomes more relevant if we ask it in another way. If women become leaders in the synagogue, will the synagogue become less important? This concern was clearly expressed in 1955 by Sanders Tofield of the Conservative Movement's Rabbinical Assembly, when he acknowledged that one reason women are encouraged to remain within the private sphere of religious life is the fear that if women were to be completely integrated into all aspects of Jewish ritual, then men might relegate religious life to women and cease being active in the synagogue.[1] The fear connected with the "feminization" of Judaism is, largely, that once women achieve positions of power within the synagogue, men will feel that the synagogue is no longer sufficiently important to occupy their attention. The other side of the question is also being asked. Is the fact that women are becoming leaders in synagogues a sign that the synagogue is no longer an important institution?

The fact that these questions are posed increasingly suggests to me that the synagogue is not very healthy. Are synagogues so marginal in the life of American Jews that men really would limit their involvement because women are active participants?

The participation of women as leaders and especially as rabbis raises another concern for synagogues. Those two congregants on Rosh Hashanah expressed a feeling that has been echoed many times since then. When women function as clergy, the traditional American division between clergy and lay people begins to break down. Let me give an example from another religious tradition. A woman who is an Episcopal priest told me that when she offers the Eucharist people take it from her differently from the way they would take it from a male priest, even though she follows the identical ritual. People experience her as less foreign, and so the experience is more natural, less mysterious.

People don't attribute to women the power and prestige that they often attribute to men. Therefore, when women become rabbis or priests, there is often less social distance between the congregant and the clergy. The lessening of social distance and the reduction of the attribution of power and status leads to the breakdown of hierarchy within a religious institution. "If you can be a rabbi, then certainly I can be a rabbi!"

Clearly some would argue that the breakdown of traditional religious hierarchy is bad. However, in my view this change could bring about a profound and welcome change in American Judaism. It could lead to synagogues that see their rabbi not as "priest" but as teacher, and that see the congregations not as passive consumers of the rabbi's wisdom but as active participants in their own Jewish lives.

The ordination of women will lead to change in another important area of Judaism: the way Jews think about God. On a basic, perhaps subconscious, level, many Jews project the image of their rabbi onto their image of God. As Dr. Mortimer Ostow has pointed out, "While it is true that no officiant in the service actually represents God, to the average congregant God is psychologically represented by the rabbi, since he is the leader and the teacher and preacher of God's word."[2]

Most adult Jews know that it is inappropriate to envisage God as a male. But given the constant references in Jewish prayer to God as "Father" and "King," and given our childhood memories of imaging God as an old man with a long white beard, it is no surprise that to the extent Jews do conceptualize God in human terms, they often think of God as male or masculine.

Jewish tradition recognizes that God is not male. To limit God in this or any way is idolatrous; God is understood by tradition to encompass both masculinity and femininity and to transcend masculinity and femininity. Unfortunately, many Jews have never incorporated this complex image of God into their theology.

As long as the rabbi is a man, a Jew can project the image of the rabbi onto God. But when Jews encounter a rabbi who is a woman, it forces them to think about God as more than male or female. It provokes them to raise questions that most Jews don't like to confront: What or who is God? What do I believe about God? That primary religious question leads to others. How can we speak about God? What are the appropriate words, images and symbols to describe our relationship to God? Does the English rendering of Hebrew prayers convey the complexity of God? How can we change language, images, and symbols so they can convey this complexity?

All of these questions could lead to a more authentic relationship to Jewish tradition and to God. Once Jews begin to explore their image of God, they will also reevaluate their image of themselves. Because all of us are created in God's image, how we think about God shapes how we think about ourselves. That thinking leads to a reevaluation of men's and women's roles within our tradition and our world.

The ordination of women has brought Judaism to the edge of an important religious revolution. I pray we have the faith to push it over the edge.

NOTES

1. Sanders Tofield, Proceedings of the Rabbinical Assembly 19 (1955), p. 190 as cited in Ellen M. Umansky, "Women and Rabbinical Ordination: A Viable Option? *Ohio Journal of Religious Studies,* vol. 4, Number 1 (March 1976), p. 63.

2. Dr. Mortimer Ostow, "Women and Change in Jewish Law," *Conservative Judaism* (Fall 1974), p. 7.

Part Three

CREATING A FEMINIST THEOLOGY OF JUDAISM

Introduction

THEOLOGY functions in two ways: by critically examining a particular religious tradition, and by creating new interpretations of its meaning. On the one hand, feminist theology traces the exclusion of women from the heart of Judaism throughout the course of history, from its basic texts, observances, liturgy, and language. On the other hand, feminist theology tries to develop new understandings of Judaism that will support feminist values and allow Jewish women a full range of religious expression.

Theology brings the problems and questions of our human experiences to its reading of specific religious traditions, which themselves constitute the questions and responses of earlier generations. Neither theology nor the most sacred texts can claim to be the unmediated word or will of God; rather, theological interpretation presents the understandings of that word and will by a particular generation, transmitted, often not without distortion, to later generations.

Many of the particular questions and demands now being raised by feminists did not arise earlier in Jewish history, at least as far as we know; even today there is often silence or rejection when women's problems are brought to bear upon Jewish tradition. Yet insisting upon a response encourages exploration of little-known aspects of Jewish tradition that sometimes do resonate strongly to feminism. For example, interest in female images of God is leading to greater exploration of the Jewish mystical tradition, generally neglected or even denigrated by modern Judaism's rationalist bias. For women, such recovered images become voices within the tradition to express their own, personal religious experiences.

Judaism is centered around both texts and observances. Most Jewish theology is expressed through interpretations of biblical and rabbinic texts, including commentaries on the prescribed commandments. Such interpretations are rarely systematic, but they do carry implicit theological messages regarding God, revelation, redemption, and human life. At the same time, critical treatises systematically examine many of the same theological problems in more explicit form, often from a philosophical perspective. Much of the feminist theology composed during the past decade is comparable, consisting of critical analysis of key issues in Judaism, as well as poetry, liturgy, and *midrash* based on sacred texts and observances.

These two approaches mirror two trends within Jewish thought, one that seeks to define positions on particular issues, and another that attempts to articulate the religious experience of the Jew. Clearly, Judaism has no single, normative tradition, but contains a diversity of often conflicting and even contradictory tenets. Similarly, Jewish experience leaves room for manifold and diverse expression. Yet all these teachings are homogeneous inasmuch as they have been formulated only by Jewish men. The fact that women have not participated in the writing of Jewish theology is far more than an accident. It reflects and supports the long unquestioned patriarchal basis of Western culture: to identify human experience as male experience.

Questions of method become crucial as women begin to engage in the enterprise of Jewish theology. How can we uncover the source of women's exclusion from Judaism? How can women's spirituality be expressed in Jewish religious language? How can Jewish tradition be interpreted and even transformed by the feminist perspective? The essays in this section address these questions by delineating the central issues for a feminist theology of Judaism.

Judith Plaskow's essay sets forth the heart of the feminist critique of Judaism's exclusion of women. Examining the key elements of Jewish theology—God, liturgy, community, and *halakhah*—she finds a pervasive and consistent view of woman as Other. Changes in *halakhah* to improve women's status will not be fruitful, she argues, because the problem is far more deeply rooted, inherent in Judaism's language and conceptualization of God. Jewish understanding of God affects far more than liturgy or scriptural interpretation: "If God is male, and we are in God's image, how can maleness not be the norm of Jewish humanity? If maleness is normative, how can women not be Other? And if women are Other, how can we not speak of God in language drawn from the male norm?"

Students of religion have long recognized that religious symbols function as both models *of* and *for* the life of the community. Incorporating female language and imagery of God would both reflect and impel women's inclusion as shapers and leaders of the Jewish community. Moreover, such language will strengthen Judaism's insistence that God is beyond anthropomorphic designations and should not be identified with maleness. Plaskow writes: "Acknowledging the many aspects of the Goddess among the names of God becomes a measure of our ability to incorporate the feminine and women into a monotheistic religious framework. At the same time, naming women's experience as part of the nature of the deity brings the suppressed experience of women into the Jewish fold."

Making such changes is no simple task, since they cannot follow any established mechanism: "Since language is not a halakhic issue, we cannot change this situation through halakhic repair." Focusing attention on *halakhah* will not fundamentally alter women's situation, since *halakhah* itself is not the problem, but a symptom of it: "To settle on *halakhah* as the source of justice for women is to foreclose the question of women's experience when it has scarcely begun to be raised."

If the way we conceive God is central to feminist theology, how can such conceptions be brought into a Jewish context? Rita Gross, in her essay, "Feminine Imagery of Deity," explores the impact upon women of Judaism's exclusively male language. What if, she suggests, the situation were reversed, and exclusively female language were employed? To demonstrate just how foreign our present, exclusively male language is, she composes an imaginary scenario in which women try to explain why men are excluded from Jewish observance, prayer, and community.

Her goal is not to eliminate gender, but to add female language to our prayers, and then develop that language into images. After we say, *"ha-kedoshah berukhah hee,"* the language must "blossom into full-blown images . . . whether the images are female versions of traditional male images of God or whether they have little precedent in Jewish tradition."

A key question Gross raises is the source of these images. She rejects the feminine imagery found in Judaism, particularly in the mystical tradition, because those images are limited to "some sort of attachment to or appendage of the more familiar male images." Just employing feminine imagery is not enough, she argues: it is the *type* of imagery that counts. She urges women to project their own images, from motherhood to physical strength to sexuality into Jewish values and activities: "Goddess completes the image of God and brings wholeness. . . . God, as well as woman, has been imprisoned in patriarchal imagery."

Gross draws mainly from personal, inner symbols and experiences in her description of female imagery of deity, and urges that these sources be brought into a Jewish context. The transition to that context comes through Arthur Green's essay, "Bride, Spouse, Daughter." According to Green, feminine imagery has never been altogether absent in Judaism. In fact, he argues, men are as much in need of female religious language as are women: "Might one not argue that men need the feminine, as women would need the masculine, if religious life involves something like what the depth psychologists call a search for polarities?"

But although feminine imagery is not entirely absent from Jewish literature, "all the images we find are those of women as imagined by or created by men," Green points out. In seeking to describe their spirituality, the male rabbis who have composed and transmitted Jewish tradition have drawn from their personal lives: "There is no way, without turning to images of the feminine, or without thinking of the relationships between men and women, that most men can express the degree of love, passion, and warmth that the spiritual life may arouse in them."

The very fact that Jewish spirituality incorporates so many female images makes it imperative that women become involved in the creativity of Jewish expression, Green argues. The female images that are employed in the tradition need interpretation by women: “Being the King’s daughter is different than being His son; there is a relationship being spoken of here that a male can never fully understand, and that the tradition itself has not been able to fully appreciate until now, because there has never been a commentator on any of this material who was herself a daughter and knew what the relationship between father and daughter was about.”

In becoming part of the heritage of interpretation and commentary on such texts, women will restore a missing dimension to Jewish spirituality. But, as Green acknowledges, women’s commentary on literature composed by men is not sufficient. Women will be continuing Jewish tradition only when they, like the male authors of Jewish tradition, introduce their own images and language.

Religious language can never simply remain on the printed page; if it possesses energy it will clamor for expression through observance and reinterpretation of tradition. Arthur Waskow views feminism as a source for the restoration of important elements of Judaism that have long been buried by misinterpretation. Feminism, he says, calls not only for equality of women and men, but also for new approaches to prayer, religious observance, relations with others, and definitions of our humanity: “To some extent, it is the struggle of modern feminists to raise some profound questions that has brought to the level of audibility some yet-unheard proto-feminist concerns that lay beneath the surface of Torah. It is as if the voice of modern feminism woke a Sleeping Beauty in the Torah, a wisdom that recognized her daughter’s voice.”

For Waskow, bringing women and the feminine fully into Judaism means eliminating projection and dualism from our thinking, developing androgyny within ourselves, caring more for others, and renewing political commitments to equality and justice. Feminism is not only a movement to liberate women, but to redeem much within Judaism, he argues, since many old Jewish traditions speak of redemption in terms of restoring the feminine: “When that ‘someday’ comes, women will not simply take a numerically equal place in the traditional forms of Jewish religious practice; the forms of practice will themselves be transformed as women’s spiritual experience is discovered, uncovered.”

Clearly, Waskow considers feminism to be a movement of great importance for the renewal of Judaism. Yet he also contends that Judaism is important for feminists, because "there is powerful truth in the tradition's resistance to power, in the multilevel poetry of its rituals, in its sardonic view of the transitory idols of convention, in its commitment to the creation of counter-institutions reaching toward equality and community."

Underlying Lynn Gottlieb's prose-poems are several arguments central to a feminist theology of Judaism. She looks both to the spoken and unspoken voices of Jewish women of the past, recovering forgotten traditions and trying to articulate what they could not: "How would they have spoken of their own religious experiences if they had been given a space to record their stories?" she asks. Next, she borrows from known traditions of Jewish history, giving them new meaning based on the experiences of contemporary Jewish women. The Marranos, Jews of medieval Spain and Portugal who hid behind the pretense of being Christian, identified with the predicament of Queen Esther, who was also forced to keep her Jewish identity a secret. While Esther was eventually able to reveal her Jewish identity, the Marranos kept their secret to themselves. Women of the current generation, like those of generations past, also have been forced to conceal their religious strivings behind rigid roles that exclude them from full expression of their religiosity. But women today, Gottlieb suggests, "by transmitting the hidden voices of the past, pray with messianic fervor for that time when we can unite the oral and written tradition of our mothers with the oral and written tradition of our fathers."

Her second poem draws from the cleaning labors in preparation for Passover that have devolved primarily upon women during the centuries. This cleaning, which is traditionally understood as a symbolic spiritual cleansing, includes the search for and setting aside of *hametz,* any food or vessel not kosher for Passover. Here, Gottlieb interprets this removal of *hametz* in terms of feminists' inner struggles. The bitterness of Egyptian enslavement must be rooted out. Liberation requires cleansing not only of the house of Judaism, but of each Jew, "for the last crumbs grown stale inside us, for the last darkness still in our hearts."

The Right Question Is Theological

by Judith Plaskow

IN an article on the situation of Jewish women, Cynthia Ozick offers fourteen "meditations" pointing to the sociological status of the woman question in Judaism.[1] The subordination of women, she argues, is not deeply rooted in Torah but is the result of historical custom and practice, which can be halakhically repaired. Only in her last meditation does she raise the great "what if?": what if the Otherness of women is not simply a matter of Jewish incorporation of surrounding social attitudes but is in part created and sustained by Torah itself? What if the subordination of women in Judaism is rooted in theology, in the very foundations of the Jewish tradition?

The fact that Ozick postpones this question to the end of her paper, that she is reluctant to explore the theological underpinnings of women's status, places her in the mainstream of Jewish feminism. The Jewish women's movement of the past decade has been and remains a civil-rights movement rather than a movement for "women's liberation."[2] It has been a movement concerned with the images and status of women in Jewish religious and communal life, and with halakhic and institutional change. It has been less concerned with analysis of the origins and bases of women's oppression that render change necessary. It has focused on getting women a piece of the Jewish pie; it has not wanted to bake a new one!

There are undoubtedly many reasons for Jewish feminism's practical bent; absence of a strong Jewish theological tradition;

the minority status of Jews in American culture; the existence of laws (e.g., divorce) that have the power to destroy women's lives and thus require immediate remedy. But such emphasis is no less dangerous for being comprehensible. If the Jewish women's movement addresses itself only to the fruits but not the bases of discrimination, it is apt to settle for too little in the way of change. It may find that the full participation of women in Jewish life—should it come—will only bring to light deeper contradictions in Jewish imagery and symbolism. And most likely, far-reaching change will not come until these contradictions are examined and exorcised. It is time, therefore, to confront the full extent of our disablement as Jewish women in order that we may understand the full implications of our struggle.

Of the issues that present themselves for our attention, *halakhah* has been at the center of feminist agitation for religious change, and it is to *halakhah* that Ozick turns in the hope of altering women's situation. But while this issue has been considered and debated frequently in the last ten years, it is specific *halakhot* that have been questioned and not the fundamental presuppositions of the legal system. The fact that women are not counted in a *minyan,* that we are not called to the Torah, that we are silent in the marriage ceremony and shackled when it comes to divorce—these disabilities have been recognized, deplored, and in non-Orthodox Judaism, somewhat alleviated. The *implications* of such laws, their essentially nonarbitrary character, has received less attention, however. Underlying specific *halakhot,* and *outlasting their amelioration or rejection,* is an assumption of women's Otherness far more basic than the laws in which it finds expression. If women are not part of the congregation, if we stand passively under the *huppah,* if, even in the Reform movement, we have become rabbis only in the last ten years, this is because men—and not women with them—define Jewish humanity. Men are the actors in religious and communal life because they are the normative Jews. Women are "other than" the norm; we are less than fully human.[3]

This Otherness of women as a presupposition of Jewish law in its most central formulations. In the last section of her article on Jewish women, finally turning to the sacral nature of women's status, Ozick points out that the biblical passion for justice does not extend to women. Women's position in biblical law as "part of the web of ownership" is taken as simply the way things are; it is not perceived as or named "injustice." One great "Thou shalt not"—"Thou shalt not lessen the humanity of women"—is absent from the Torah.[4] The Otherness of women basic to the written law also underlies the Mishnaic treatment of women. Jacob Neusner points out that the Mishnah's Division of Women deals with women in states of transition, whose uncertain status threatens the stasis of the community. The woman who is about to enter into a marriage or who has just left one requires close attention. The law must regularize her irregularity, facilitate her transition to the normal state of wife and motherhood, at which point she no longer poses a problem.[5] The concerns of the Division, and even the fact of its existence, assume a view of women as "abnormal" or "irregular" and therefore requiring special sanctification. While the mechanisms of sanctification are elaborated extensively, the need for it is never questioned. It is simply presupposed by the text.

That women have a "special" status, one that is taken for granted by the tradition, is underlined by another factor: all reasons given for women's legal disabilities—e.g., they are exempt from positive time-bound commandments because of household responsibilities; they are closer to God and therefore do not need as many commands—presuppose the sex-role division they seek to explain.[6] But while the origins of this division are thus hidden from us—they remain part of the broader historical question of the roots of female subordination—the division itself is imaged and elaborated in clear and specific terms. As in the Christian tradition, in which the Otherness of women is expressed in the language of mind/body dualism, Judaism tenders a similar distinction between *ruhniut* [spirituality] and *gashmiut* [physicality], men and women.[7] The need to regulate women is articulated not as a general problem but as the need to control their unruly female sexuality because of its threat to the spirituality of men.

This fear of women as sexual beings finds expression in both halakhic and aggadic sources. Neusner suggests that it lies just under the surface of the Mishnah's whole treatment of women.

Even where a text's explicit topic is the economics of property transfer, it is the anomaly of female sexuality, with its "dreadful threat of uncontrolled shifts in personal status and material possession," that is the motive of legislation.[8] But rabbinic concern with female sexuality need not always be deduced from discussion of other matters. The rabbinic laws concerning modesty, with their one-sided emphasis on the modesty of women, make clear that it is women who endanger public morality through their ability to tempt men. These careful regulations of dress and exposure lack any sense of reciprocity, any sense that men tempt women and may therefore also be defined as tempters. Woman may be a bag of filth; "it [may be] better to walk behind a lion than behind a woman,"[9] but apparently men are different since there is no danger in a woman's walking behind a man!

The concepts of woman as Other and as temptress are certainly not new to Jewish feminism. They were articulated by Rachel Adler in her classic essay on women and *halakhah,* elaborated by others, and recently reiterated by Ozick.[10] These writers seem not to have fully understood the implications of their own categories, however, for they tend to assume that the Otherness of women will disappear if only the community is flexible enough to rectify halakhic injustices.[11] Would this were true! But the issue is far deeper than is suggested by this assumption.[12]

Indeed, the situation of the Jewish woman might well be compared to the situation of the Jew in non-Jewish culture. The Gentile projection of the Jew as Other—the stranger, the demon, the human non-quite-human—[13]is repeated in—or should one say partly *modelled on*?—the Jewish understanding of the Jewish woman. She too is the stranger whose life is lived parallel to man's, the demoness who stirs him, the partner whose humanity is different from his own. And just as legal changes have ameliorated the situation of the Jews without ever lifting the suspicion of our humanity, so legal change will not restore the full humanity of the Jewish woman. Our legal disabilities are a *symptom* of a pattern of projection that lies deep in Jewish thinking. They express and reflect a fundamental stance toward women that must be confronted, addressed and rooted out at its core. While it is Jewish to hope that changes in *halakhah* might bring about changes in underlying attitudes, it is folly to think that justice for women can be achieved simply through halakhic mechanisms when women's plight is not primarily a product of *halakhah.*

But this is just one issue. The Otherness of women is also given dramatic expression in our language about God. Here, we confront a great scandal: the God who supposedly transcends sexuality, who is presumably one and whole, is known to us through language that is highly selective and partial. The images we use to describe God, the qualities we attribute to God, draw on male pronouns and male experience and convey a sense of power and authority that is clearly male in character. The God at the surface of Jewish consciousness is a God with a voice of thunder, a God who as Lord and King rules his people and leads them into battle, a God who forgives like a father when we turn to him. The female images that exist in the Bible and (particularly the mystical) tradition form an underground stream that reminds us of the inadequacy of our imagery without, however, transforming its overwhelmingly male nature. The hand that takes us out of Egypt is a male hand—both in the Bible and in our contemporary imaginations.

Perceiving the predominance of male language is not the same as understanding its importance, however. Ozick, for instance, begins her article with the question of God and dismisses it quickly. She does not deny the dominance of male imagery, but argues that reflection on the absence of female anthropomorphisms "can only take us to quibbles about the incompetence of pronouns."[14] If the Jewish-woman question is unrelated to theology, theological questions can only lead to dead ends. But as with Ozick's treatment of *halakhah,* this position seriously underestimates the depth of the issue. Religious symbols are significant and powerful communications. Since through them, a community expresses its sense and experience of the world, it cannot allow missing pronouns to determine its sense of reality.[15] The maleness of God is not arbitrary—nor is it simply a matter of pronouns. It leads us to the central question, the question of the Otherness of women, just as the Otherness of women leads to the maleness of God.

Anthropologist Clifford Geertz offers us important insights into the function of religious language. In an essay on "Religion as a Cultural System," Geertz argues that religious symbols express both the sensibility and moral character of a people and the way in which it understands and structures the world. Symbols are simultaneously *models of* a community's sense of ultimate reality and *models for* human behavior and the social order. The Sabbath, for example, as a model of God's action in creating the world, is also a model for the Jewish community which, like God, rests on the seventh day. The double reference of symbols, up and down, enforces a community's sense of its symbols' factuality and appropriateness.[16] If God rested on the seventh day, can we fail to do so, and how can our doing so not bring us closer to God?

If we apply Geertz's analysis to the issue of male God-language, it is clear that such language also functions as a model-of and model-for. This language both tells us about God's nature (it is, after all, the only way we know God) and justifies a human community which reserves power and authority to men. When Mortimer Ostow used the maleness of God as an argument against the ordination of women rabbis, he made the connection between language and authority painfully clear.[17] But we do not need Ostow's honesty to grasp the implications of our language; language speaks for itself. If God is male, and we are in God's image, how can maleness *not* be the norm of Jewish humanity? If maleness is normative, how can women not be Other? And if women are Other, how can we not speak of God in language drawn from the male norm?

One consequence of the nature of male God-imagery as a model for community is that the prayer book becomes testimony against the participation of women in Jewish religious life. Women's greater access to Jewish learning, our increased leadership in synagogue ritual only bring to the surface deep contradictions between equality for women and the tradition's fundamental symbols and images for God. While the active presence of women in congregations should bespeak our full membership in the Jewish community, the language of the service conveys a different message. It impugns the humanity of women and ignores our experience, rendering that experience invisible, even in the face of our presence. But since language is not a halakhic issue, we cannot change this situation through halakhic repair. It is not "simply" that *halakhah* presupposes the Otherness of women but that this Otherness reflects and is reflected in our speech about God. The equality of women in the Jewish community requires the radical transformation of our religious language in the form of recognition of the feminine aspects of God.

Here we encounter a problem; for it is impossible to mention the subject of female language without the specter of paganism being raised. For critics of (this aspect of) Jewish feminism, introducing female God-language means reintroducing polytheism into the tradition and abdicating all that made Judaism distinctive in the ancient world.[18] While, on the one hand, cries of "paganism" couch the question of language in dishonest and hysterical terms, they also make clear that the issue evokes deep emotional resonances. Rationally, it seems contradictory to argue that the Jewish God transcends sexuality, that anthropomorphism—while necessitated by the limits of our thought—is not to be taken literally; and at the same time to insist that a broadening of anthropomorphic language will destroy the tradition. As Rita Gross asks in her article on Jewish God-language: "If we do not mean that God is male when we use masculine pronouns and imagery, then why should there be any objections to using female imagery and pronouns as well?"[19] Use of sexually dimorphic images may be the best way to acknowledge the limits of language and God's fullness, so that the inclusion of women becomes, at the same time, an enrichment of our concept of God.

But the issue of female God-language touches chords that are not reached or responded to by rational discussion, and so such arguments do not do. The exclusive worship of Jahweh was the result of a long, drawn-out struggle, not simply with the people of the land, but with the many within Israel who wanted to maintain Goddess-worship alongside the worship of God. The victory of Jahwehism entailed suppression of the female side of divinity (and of women as members of the cult), almost as if any recognition the feminine was accorded might overwhelm the precarious ascendency of God. The gods could seemingly be superseded, their qualities included in the many-named God and recognized as aspects of himself. But the goddesses were apparently too real and too vital for their attributes to be incorporated in this way.[20]

It might seem we are now distant enough from paganism to understand the historical context of suppression of the Goddess without feeling the need to refight this struggle. But if Ba'al is impotent and voiceless, an object of purely theoretical condemnation, the Goddess still evokes resistance which is vehement and deeply felt. Albeit through the lens of our monotheistic tradition, she seems to speak to us as powerfully as ever. Yet this is itself a strong argument for the incorporation of female language into the tradition. It is precisely because she is not distant that the Goddess must be recognized as a part of God. For the God who does not include her is an idol made in man's image, a God over against a female Other—not the Creator, source of maleness and femaleness, not the relativizer of all gods and goddesses who nonetheless includes them as part of God's self. Acknowledging the many aspects of the Goddess among the names of God becomes a measure of our ability to incorporate the feminine and women into a monotheistic religious framework. At the same time, naming women's experience as part of the nature of the deity brings the suppressed experience of women into the Jewish fold.

This brings us to our last issue, one that is closely related to the other two. As Ozick points out in a particularly eloquent meditation, the Jewish tradition is not the product of the entire Jewish people, but of Jewish men alone.[21] Of course women have lived Jewish history and carried its burdens, shaped our experience to history and history to ourselves. But ours is not the history passed down and recorded; the texts committed to memory or the documents studied; the arguments fought, refought, and finely honed. Women have not contributed to the formation of the written tradition, and thus tradition does not reflect the specific realities of women's lives.

This fact, which marks so great a loss to tradition and to women, is cause and reflection both of the Otherness of women and the maleness of God. Women are not educated as creators of tradition because we are Other, but of course we remain Other when we are seen through the filter of male experience without ever speaking for ourselves. The maleness of God calls for the silence of women as shapers of the holy, but our silence in turn enforces our Otherness and a communal sense of the "rightness" of the male image of God. There is a "fit" in other words, a tragic coherence between the role of women in the community, and its symbolism, law, and teaching. The Otherness of women is part of the fabric of Jewish life.

Once again, and now most clearly, we are brought up against the impotence of halakhic change. For *halakhah* is part of the system that women have not had a hand in creating, neither in its foundations, nor as it was developed and refined. Not only is this absence reflected in the content of *halakhah,* it may also be reflected in its very form. How can we presume that if women add their voices to the tradition, *halakhah* will be our medium of expression and repair? How can we determine in advance the channels through which the tradition will become wholly Jewish, i.e., a product of the whole Jewish people, when women are only beginning consciously to explore the particularities of our own Jewishness? To settle on *halakhah* as the source of justice for women is to foreclose the question of women's experience when it has scarcely begun to be raised.

Clearly, the implications of Jewish feminism, while they include halakhic restructuring, reach beyond *halakhah* to transform the bases of Jewish life. Feminism demands a new understanding of Torah, God, and Israel: an understanding of Torah that begins with acknowledgment of the profound injustice of Torah itself. The assumption of the lesser humanity of women has poisoned the content and structure of the law, undergirding women's legal disabilities and our subordination in the broader tradition. This assumption is not amenable to piecemeal change. It must be utterly eradicated by the withdrawal of projection from women—the discovery that the negative traits attributed to women are also in the men who attribute them, while the positive qualities reserved for men are also in women. Feminism demands a new understanding of God that reflects and supports the redefinition of Jewish humanity. The long-suppressed femaleness of God, acknowledged in the mystical tradition, but even here shaped and articulated by men, must be recovered and reexplored and reintegrated into the Godhead. Last, feminism assumes that these changes will be possible only when we come to a new understanding of the community of Israel which includes the whole of Israel and which therefore allows women to speak and name our experience for ourselves. The outcome of these new understandings is difficult to see in advance of our turning. It is clear, however, that the courage, concern, and creativity necessary for a feminist transformation of Judaism will not be mustered by evading the magnitude of the required change.

NOTES

1. Cynthia Ozick, "Notes toward Finding the Right Question," *Lilith* 6, (1979), pp. 19–29 [pp. 120–151 in this volume].

2. Judith Hole and Ellen Levine, *Rebirth of Feminism* (New York: Quadrangle Books, 1971), pp. ix–x.

3. Simone de Beauvoir describes woman as the Other in *The Second Sex* (New York: Bantam Books, 1961), pp. xvi–xxix and *passim*. Rachel Adler ("The Jew Who Wasn't There: *Halakhah* and the Jewish Woman," *Response,* 18, Summer 1973, pp. 77–82; pp. 12–18 in this volume) and Ozick (p. 21; pp. 123–124 in this volume) make use of this basic concept but without understanding its implications for halakhic change. See below.

4. Ozick, pp. 27, 29 [pp. 144, 149 in this vol.].

5. Jacob Neusner, "Mishnah on Women: Thematic or Systemic Description," *Marxist Perspectives* (Spring 1980), pp. 94–95.

6. See Moshe Meiselman, *Jewish Woman in Jewish Law* (New York: Ktav Publishing House and Yeshivah University Press, 1978), p. 43f.

7. There are, of course, important differences between Judaism and Christianity on this issue. Dualism did not receive the same theological expression in Judaism as it did in Christianity, nor in Judaism did dualism find expression in asceticism.

8. Neusner, p. 96.

9. Ber. 152a; Louis Epstein, *Sex Laws and Customs in Judaism* (New York: Ktav, 1967), p. 114.

10. See note 3, above. See also Paula Hyman, "The Other Half: Women in the Jewish Tradition," *Response* 18 (Summer 1973), pp. 67–75.

11. This applies to Adler and Ozick. Hyman calls for changes in "attitude" as well as law.

12. The absence of full equality for women within Reform Judaism is one clear indicator that *halakhah* is not the real issue.

13. The specific phrase is Dorothy Sayers', "The Human-Not-Quite-Human," *Are Women Human?* (Grand Rapids, Michigan: William B. Eerdmans Publishing Company, 1971), pp. 37–47. Rosemary Ruether has dealt extensively with the issue of projection as it affects women, Jews, blacks and other oppressed groups. See, e.g., her *New Woman/New Earth* (New York: Seabury Press, 1975), especially pp. 89–114.

14. Ozick, p. 20 [p. 122 in this volume].

15. In saying this, I am not denying that language shapes our sense of reality—quite the contrary. It is just that there are simply ways around male pronouns for any community that wants to find them: e.g., male pronouns but male and female imagery.

16. In *Reader in Comparative Religion: An Anthropological Approach,* William Lessa and Evon Vogt, eds. (New York: Harper and Row, 1965), pp. 205, 207, 213. See also *Womanspirit Rising: A Feminist Reader in Religion,* Carol P. Christ and Judith Plaskow, eds., pp. 2–3.

17. "Women and Change in Jewish Law," *Conservative Judaism,* vol. 29, no. 1 (Fall 1974), pp. 5–12.

18. E.g., Ozick, p. 20 [pp. 120–21 in this volume] (Ozick is obviously not a general critic of Jewish feminism). Ostow gives the impression that women are intrinsically pagan and that justice for women necessarily means the paganization of Judaism—but that raises other questions, which we cannot consider here.

19. "Female God-language in a Jewish Context," *Womanspirit Rising,* pp. 170–171.

20. Raphael Patai documents both the persistence of Goddess worship in Israel and the fact that suppression of the Goddess was never complete. *The Hebrew Goddess* (N.p.: Ktav Publishing House, 1967).

21. Ozick, p. 24f [pp. 136–38 in this volume].

Steps toward Feminine Imagery of Deity in Jewish Theology

Rita M. Gross

THE most profound, intriguing, and inviting of all Jewish theologies—the *Kabbalah*—teaches us that *galut*—exile—is the fundamental reality and pain of present existence. It teaches that one of the causes of *galut* is the alienation of the masculine from the feminine in God, the alienation of God and the *Shekhinah*. But it also teaches, especially in its Lurianic phases, that each of us can effect the turning of *galut* by dedicating all our efforts to the reunification of God and the *Shekhinah*. Now that the masculine and feminine has been torn asunder and the feminine dismembered and banished, both from the discourse about divinity and from the human community, such a *tikkun* [reparation] is obligatory, is a *mitzvah*. When the masculine and feminine aspect of God have been reunited and the female half of humanity has been returned from exile, we will begin to have our *tikkun*. The world will be repaired.

I can no longer remember the first time I imagined a *berakhah* in the female grammatical form. I do remember the first time I heard it voiced aloud communally, years after having first experienced participation in my own right in the Jewish ritual covenant community. It was as appropriate and natural as any Jewish expression—and less problematic and alienating than many. In fact, the potential for meaning and identification experienced by saying "God-She" convinced me that it must be so. Since then, I have been using female pronouns of God relatively frequently in various contexts—teaching, reflection, private religious expressions. As the linguistic forms and the sound of the words become less exotic, it no longer seems daring or unconventional to speak of God in such a manner. Instead, it seems appropriate, natural, what one would expect, the way things would be except for a massive skewing and programming of religious consciousness. It also frees from alienation, anger, pain, and sorrow over the exclusion of women from the religious and spiritual dimensions of being Jewish in a way that is unsurpassed.

It is time, therefore, to move beyond the image of God the Father to a more complete set of images of God. To do so requires some clarity about what is at stake in the use of the image of "God the Father." The most crucial points, I believe, are thorough awareness of the inherent limitations of any theological or religious language, combined with some awareness of the inevitability of anthropomorphic images in the Jewish religious enterprise.

Before anything else can be properly discussed, one must understand the inevitable limitations of all religious language. *All* expressions used in the religious enterprise are, in the long run, analogous and metaphorical. Every statement contains a bracketed "as if" or "as it were." Statements about God should not be taken literally. They do not exhaust the possibilities at all. Rather, they are the most adequate expressions available within current idioms—linguistic conventions that function as tools, used to point to that which transcends language.

Therefore they contain no inherent finality or unalterable relevance, and convey no ultimate truth. To ignore this limitation by fixating on one set of ideas and thinking that a real correspondence exists between these images of God and God is to be unrealistic, self-aggrandizing, and fundamentally idolatrous. Nevertheless, because expression and communication are inevitable, images and concepts of the Ultimate are also inevitable. Therefore, the limitations of language present no problem—if one is willing to remember those limits whenever one is tempted to literalize and absolutize one's language.[1] The only problem is that temptation.

It is clear that the tendency to absolutize some manners of speaking about God has been very strong throughout the history of the Jewish tradition. Specifically, masculine pronouns are always used for God by traditionalists and even by atheists and philosophical critics of anthropomorphism. Closely linked to the masculine pronouns, especially in the imagination of traditionalists, is a whole array of masculine images—father, king, judge, warrior. At the same time, an automatic and very strong prejudice against using feminine pronouns and images exists, not only in the minds of traditionalists, but also in those of atheists and philosophical critics of anthropomorphism, who usually justify that response by appealing to the inherent limitations of language. They contend that their automatic use of male pronouns and images as well as their out of hand rejection of female images and pronouns doesn't mean anything; certainly it does not mean, they contend, that they think of God as male. "That God is exalted above all sexuality is part of *His* transcendence," one commonly hears. However, if one insists that one must use the pronoun "His" in the preceding sentence and that the pronoun "Her" is improper, the claim that gender-specific images are not part of one's image of God becomes self-contradictory and a bit ridiculous. Likewise, the claim that one is not absolutizing one's image of God becomes untenable. What *is* going on?

I suspect that those who become entangled in such absolutizing of masculine pronouns and imagery genuinely do believe in and are trying to express the concept of a God who transcends sexuality. At the same time, however, they wish to retain the concept of a personal God—a theistic rather than a nontheistic Ultimate—because the concept of a personal Ultimate is at the living heart of the Jewish symbol system. The whole *siddur,* most of *halakhah* and *aggadah,* in short, almost everything that makes the Jewish religious enterprise distinctively *Jewish* becomes non-sensical without the metaphor of a divine Person in a covenant relationship of mutual responsibility and love with human persons.

However, the metaphor of a gender-free person is impossible. Persons are male or female. A person without gender defies the imagination; few people can imagine a concrete specific person without also imagining some female or male characteristics.

Equally, no set of religious images has ever talked of a personal Ultimate without the use of masculine and/or feminine imagery as a tool. Theistic religions, including Judaism, have always had to make peace with anthropomorphism, which necessarily includes making peace with genderized language about deity. Unless Jewish theology *and practice* take a 180-degree turn from the metaphor of relationship with a personal deity to the metaphor of a nonpersonal Ultimate, to which one could scarcely *daven* and which would be unlikely to give *mitzvot,* they too will have to continue to utilize anthropomorphisms, all of which are always problematic and inaccurate nonliteral manners of speaking.

Why then the knee-jerk refusal to speak to God-She? To answer this question, we must move from the level of abstract theological analysis to the level of more empirical study of religion. Historical and cross-cultural studies of religion demonstrate a great deal about how religious metaphors function in religious communities. Though language about God cannot really tell us about God, because of the limitations of language and the nature of God, it can tell us a great deal about those who create and use the God-language. The metaphors and concepts used to communicate about the inherently translinguistic Ultimate must come from somewhere; furthermore, it is impossible to avoid the recognition that they bear strong resemblance to basic human experience, especially valued aspects of human experience and aspiration.

What then of the common Jewish usage of "God-He" and shock at the idea that Jews might *daven* to God-She? I contend that it mirrors and legitimizes the profoundly androcentric character of Jewish society, especially "spiritual Judaism" or the religious dimensions of being Jewish. It expresses a profound and long-standing alienation between women or femaleness and the central values of Jewish religious tradition—an alienation that I believe stretches to the origins of our tradition. That usage and the alienation it reflects is also the most basic explanation for the traditional exclusion of women from almost all the most meaningful and most normative dimensions of Judaism—its covenanted, "religious" and "spiritual" aspects.[2]

Courageous honesty is required to acknowledge the exclusion of women from the most meaningful and important aspects of

Jewish living. Perhaps it is more difficult yet to realize the extent to which that painful exclusion is bound up with traditional Jewish ways of speaking about the Ultimate as a male person but not as a female person. Role-reversal fantasy[3] may be the most potent way of driving home both points, since in role-reversal fantasies what is normally done to females becomes intolerable, simply because it is being done to males instead. Therefore, I ask you to imagine the following situation:

The male Jew grows up securely knowing his place in the community. Some day he will be a father in Israel, enabling his wife to fulfill her *mitzvah* of reproduction, making himself available for her sexually by maintaining the laws of purity, surrounding his body and its strange, periodic, regular secretions and no less scrupulously maintaining the ritual purity of the food eaten in his home. Most important of all, he will pass on the faith of the mothers, at least until his daughters are five or six and start religious school. What more could any man want? Especially when he knows that God Herself intended this role for him, this special role which wins him a weekly moment's notice and praise: "A virile husband, who can find him? He is far more precious than wealth, for he busies himself making wealth for his wife. She is praised in councils of the leaders for such a husband."

He does not envy the world of women, the world of synagogue and school, for he has never really been taught about it. "It is better for Torah to be burned than to be entrusted to a man," he has been told; and "She who teaches her son Torah teaches him lewdness." Besides, "men are lightheaded." So only the women learn. Every morning they wrap themselves in those mysterious wonderful prayer shawls. They look so comforting and so private, as if one could sense more strongly the love and warmth of God-Mother. But they are feminine garments, he has been told, even though there are no laws actually prohibiting men from wearing them. He would lose his masculinity and women would be defeminized if he started davening in a *tallit,* assuming he davens at all, which no one has ever seemed that concerned about. As for *tefillin* . . . don't even think of that. The synagogue, with its beautiful haunting rituals and melodies, further justifies this division of labor between women and men, spiritual and physical. The preciousness of being Jewish is especially clear to him when he watches the Torah scrolls being taken out and seven women being called to read Torah. Perhaps the highest moment comes as he watches the women undressing and dressing the Torah scroll, that supreme masculine symbol that contains the essence of the Jewish faith. From behind the high curtains you can almost see what's going on in most synagogues, even though it's very far from the reader's stand and often very difficult to hear the reader above the din of gossiping men's voices. But it *must* be that way. Think how disruptive it would be if men ritually took part in the synagogue davening. Why, the women might even be distracted by the presence of sex objects erupting into their world of spirituality. To protect the women's concentration at prayer, it is necessary to separate the men and put them out of the way.

If there are vague feelings of discontent, the very words of Torah hasten to quench them. After all, God is always referred to as "She"—even though everyone says that doesn't mean we should think of God in a sexual sense, since God is beyond all human qualities. But language is limited and we use the most honorific terms for God, despite their obvious limitations. All the prophets were women—except for a few that nobody talks about much; and God *chose* Sarah, our Mother, and the promise descended through the line of her daughters. The covenant is addressed to the *b'not Rahel v'Leah,* which means the *daughters,* not the *children,* of Rahel and Leah. And finally, God will send Her *goelet,* and She will end the suffering of the daughters of Rahel and Leah—we pray in those terms all the time—*Berukhah at ha-shem, elohenu malkat ha-olam elohai Sarah, elohai Rivkah, elohai Rahel v'Leah ha-elah ha-gedolah, ha-giborah, v'ha-norah. Elah elyonah, gomelet hasidim tovim, v'konah et ha-kol, v'zoheret hasdei imahot u'meve'ah goelet livnot bnotehen l'ma'an shema b'ahavah.* When God gave Her Torah to Her daughters through Miriam, She said to the women, Do not go near a man," before the theophany . . . just as men shouldn't intrude into the women's spiritual universe today.

Besides, the outside world also reinforces this natural division of labor. All important positions in education and business are filled by women. Rarely, one sees a male professor, and then his voice sounds funny—too low. Recently they hired a male to be a newscaster, and a lot of people thought that was noteworthy and strange. There has never been a male president of the United States either, though the last president got a lot of publicity by appointing two men—an unheard-of number—to her cabinet.

When we try to explain all this, it is obvious. Whether or not people believe in God-Mother anymore, it is clear that this division of labor is grounded in nature itself, and we religious Jews know that God Herself intended things this way. Why, any discontented male is denying his true vocation bestowed on him by the Creator Herself. No one is wise enough to know why God made female reproductive organs compact and internal so that woman is physically free to move about unencumbered and take her natural place of leadership in the world of womankind. Or why She made male organs external and exposed so that man would demand sheltering and protection from the outside, in order that he may be kept for reproducing the race. The very vulnerability of the penis is a paradigm of all vulnerable things in need of protection, and explains why men are naturally more nurturing than women. Surely this is why God Herself made men that way. And if men, dismissed from the time-bound *mitzvot* because of their heavy involvement in nurturing roles that come to them naturally, ever feel deprived, they should only remember that God is already close to men and that they, naturally, without benefit of the covenant, do God's will and are close to God. That is why She gave the covenant through women instead.

Furthermore, men don't need those *mitzvot,* which seem to be the core of Judaism, because what they do is create for women a sense of rhythms and cycles and flow. Women can't do that without ritual, but men already experience that in the periodic, mysterious risings and fallings of their bodies, imitated by the tides and many other natural phenomena . . . Surely we don't want to disrupt all these harmonies and balances created by God Herself in Her Wisdom.

Theological analysis of the nature of God-language, combined with some understanding of the social origins and ramifications of specific images of deity, are my major arguments for abandoning forthwith traditional modes of religious expression that utilize masculine imagery of deity while refusing to use feminine imagery of deity. The social destructiveness of the exclusively masculine style of religious expression, so evident in the role-reversal fantasy, is of more concern to me than are its theological inadequacies. It would seem that the Jewish sense of justice would demand that such inhumane practices be transformed.

Frequently those who realize the inappropriateness of the exclusively masculine language and imagery of traditional Jewish religious expressions want to opt for a style of language that speaks of the Ultimate as "neither male nor female." At a certain level of philosophic analysis that is, of course, a viable and perhaps even a more adequate concept than the theistic and therefore inherently anthropomorphic imagery of a personal God in covenanted relationships. I will concede to them the use of female pronouns and imagery of deity, but obviously, only in return for an equal ban on all masculine pronouns and images of deity—since their case is that God should be imaged as *neither male* nor female. I await their *siddur* in English, let alone in Hebrew.

It seems much more feasible *and traditional* to take some steps toward feminine imagery of deity in Jewish theology. The first step is theologically relatively simple and unproblematic, though emotionally profound. It requires only that female language, especially pronouns, be used of deity in *all* the familiar contexts. It seems to me that for every assertion one wishes to make of God, one must be willing to say that it characterizes God-She as well as God-He. In other words, the familiar *ha-kadosh barukh hu* is also *ha-kedoshah berukhah hee* and *always has been.* Only the poverty of our religious imagination and the repressiveness of our social forms prevented that realization. Everything that has ever been said or that we still want to say of *ha-kadosh barukh hu* can also be said of *ha-kedoshah berukhah hee* and, conversely, "God-She" is appropriately used in every context in which any reference to God occurs. That is to say, wherever the symbol or metaphor "God" is still relevant in any way, we must imagine "God-She" and speak to Her.

That first step must be experienced to understand its subtle but overwhelming and profound effect. However, the pronouns begin to blossom into full-blown images, which is another and much more revolutionary step, whether the images are female versions of traditional male images of God or whether they have little precedent in Jewish tradition. That development of full-blown female imagery of deity is difficult and revolutionary because it goes beyond traditional Jewish sources, both in expression and for inspiration. Immediately, the problem of locating appropriate resources for developing feminine imagery of deity is more pressing than the problem of expressing those images in Jewish modes. Psalms, prayers, *midrashim,* etc., will follow once the imagery really takes hold in the imagination.

Two major reservoirs for developing feminine imagery of God exist. First, it is important to highlight the rather considerable amount of feminine imagery of deity that has already developed throughout the history of Jewish tradition. Few Jews really take the time to put all the scattered feminine imagery together and thus to acknowledge that this combined resource has already made inroads on the assumption that "God-He" is proper while "God-She" is improper.

Nevertheless, that resource by itself is probably not enough. It is too imbedded in patriarchal contexts. Almost without exception, traditional Jewish usage speaks of some variant of "God and *his Shekhinah.*" Seeing feminine imagery of God as some sort of attachment to or appendage of the more familiar male images of God would only compound the current inadequacies. Something like the coequal balance of the attributes of justice and mercy is a much better model for the relationship between the attributes of femininity and masculinity in deity.

Because both the coequal balance of maleness and femaleness in metaphors about God and a full-blown feminine imagery of God go beyond Jewish resources, these developments, though desirable, are difficult. When I first began to think about these necessary outgrowths of saying "*ha-kedoshah berukhah hee,*" my mind simply stopped as if it had encountered an impenetrable veil. Fortunately, however, I am by training and conviction a student of the cross-cultural comparative study of religion, and my exposure to feminine imagery of deity in other religious contexts proved to be a godsend, so to speak. Religious-symbol systems that have not been so wary of feminine imagery of deity are the second great source of inspiration in developing feminine imagery of deity.

People often seem more upset by my suggestion that religious insights and images important for Jews can be found outside Jewish tradition than they are by the clear imperative to develop female imagery of God. That attitude seems very strange to me, since it would require some sort of antiseptic barrier between what Jews think and what other people are thinking. Such conditions have never prevailed, and many elements of the world view of most contemporary religious Jews depend significantly on the thought of non-Jews. Furthermore, I am not advocating mindless borrowing or wholesale syncretism. I have in mind something more like the creation of a Jewish version of insights gleaned from relevant religious-symbol systems.

Years of living with both the lack of Jewish female imagery of God and with knowledge about non-Jewish Goddesses have led me to envision five basic images that need translation into Jewish media.[4] I am sure that they are not the only relevant images and that the resources I have drawn upon are not the only relevant resources. However, they are offered as a starting point. It is especially important to note both their continuity with traditional Jewish concepts about God and the subtle ways in which they go beyond and enrich traditional Jewish theology.

The most significant of these five images involves a combination of symbols that is usually called "the coincidence of opposites" or "ambiguity symbolism." This image of the Goddess is very close to many Jewish insights about God Who creates both light and darkness, Who has both the attribute of justice and the attribute of mercy; but it also develops these Jewish insights in significant ways. The images of the divine feminine who contains all opposites and manifests the coincidence of those opposites have more ability to communicate acceptance of limits and finitude than anything in Jewish resources. The basic message is the coincidence and relativity of "positive" and "negative," "good" and "bad," "creation" and "destruction." The Goddess gives and She takes away, not out of transcendent power but because that is the way things are. She patronizes both birth and death, and neither is desired or undesirable. Both are part of the order of existence. Birth without death would be a monstrosity—a cancer. What is born must die, and what dies nourishes life in some form or other. Two things should be especially noted. In this symbolism, the deity does not stand outside and above this round but rather *is* the round. Secondly, limits, end points, and death are not punishments dealt by an external, transcendent deity but simply part of reality and thus neither positive nor negative. The deity who is the eternal round of growth and decay, birth and death, increase and decrease, encourages in the worshiper an attitude of receptivity to the given rather than willful attempts to remake the given.

Within this matrix, four additional images of the Goddess find expression in my vision. Some of them are most significant for their power to break stereotypes of the feminine; others are significant for the insights about deity they contain.

It is important to discuss the need for images of Goddess as an extremely capable and strong figure—one worthy of trust and able to aid. This kind of image, which runs counter to popular expectations, is found in every example of imagery of the divine feminine in world religions. It undercuts the objection I sometimes hear that the deity can only be imaged as male because God must be strong and trustworthy and female imagery cannot invoke those responses. Goddess can be fully as strong, even as omnipotent, as God. Thus the image of Goddess breaks the stereotype of feminine weakness, which is important for women. Secondly, there is no hint that this strength and capability is at the expense of the femaleness of Goddess. In fact, if anything, the images and stories of the hero Goddess exaggerate her female characteristics and her beauty; thus another stereotype is broken—that strength and femininity or beauty are incompatible, especially in women.

The next two images of Goddess that I envision as part of feminine imagery of the divine within Jewish theology are somewhat interdependent and need to be discussed together since, in combination, they also break many stereotypes. Images of God the Mother are inevitable and to be expected. It is important immediately to join that image with the image of Goddess equally involved with culture in all its aspects.

One of the strangest and most inexplicable features of Judaism to me is that while images of parenting are so central, "God the Mother" brings a shudder to people who daily use metaphors of God the Father. How can it be? How can God be a parent but not a Mother? How can the Creator and Caretaker of the world be devoid of femaleness? Nothing seems more obvious than the fact that our current imagery of the Father without the Mother is a bit one-sided and unbalanced, to say the least.

On the other hand, it is equally important to point out that God the Mother is not just a mother and nothing else. The fact that when most people do image a female deity, they talk only of some sort of "fertility Goddess" and nothing else—this fact reflects the way we think of women today: they are mothers and nothing else. Goddess as patron of culture breaks the stereotype that the feminine and women are involved mainly with nature and reproduction, while culture and the spirit are male and masculine pursuits. Instead, we would find Goddess involved in the broad range of valued Jewish traits and activities, from defense, study, and livelihood to nurturance and housekeeping, without regard for whether men or women are expected to perform these tasks in society. Especially noteworthy would be images of Goddess as giver of wisdom and patron of scholarship and learning, as teacher and meditator. These are already found to some extent in traditional Judaism but are in need of much more emphasis.

The last image that I will discuss is as significant as the first image, and often even more disturbing. Once we begin to speak of deity in both female and male terms, sexuality reemerges as a significant metaphor for imaging both intradivine relating and the divine-human relationship. This is sometimes disturbing because people imagine that the traditional images of deity, God the Father, the God of our fathers, is a nonsexual symbol. We have already seen how possible it is to have a concept of a theistic Ultimate that is also exalted above all sexuality. In fact, God has been exalted above female sexuality only. This results in the destruction of the personhood of those who do not accept what is generally taken to be Divine Personhood, as opposed to a gender-free image of God.

Using sexuality as a religious metaphor will add a great deal to the texture of Jewish religious expression. To see part of its enriching effect, it is necessary to ask why there has been some reluctance to use sexuality as a religious symbol in Jewish tradition, though that reluctance is not omnipresent, as we can see in segments of Kabbalistic imagery. The rejection of sexuality as an acceptable religious symbol is, I believe, closely connected with fear and rejection of our embodied condition, particularly the female body. Because we are embarrassed by our own sexuality, we reject it as a suitable symbol for the diety, while those aspects of ourselves that are not embarrassing to us—honor, fidelity, justice, military prowess, the ability to arrange our societies hierarchically, with rulers and ruled—become symbols of deity. But why should sexuality be so problematic?

The answer brings us back to the first image I discussed, the coincidence of opposites, and indeed, there is a strong correlation between the occurrence of a coincidence of opposites and the use of sexual symbolism in world religions. Sexuality is strongly connected with the experience of limits and with the kind of transcendence that the coincidence-of-opposites symbolism teaches us. Sexuality limits us to being one sex or the other, and sexuality is closely connected with the limitations of our birth and death. If we did not die, we would not need to be sexed. Rebellion against the closed round of our natural existence and our attempts to identify with a nontemporal principle transcending that closed round necessarily deny any ultimate significance to the primary method of continuity within that round—sexuality. When sexuality loses its significance as a sign of the Ways Things Are, one can pretend that women/Goddess don't exist significantly (or that men/God don't exist significantly, I suppose—though it didn't happen that way). Thus one has lost, all at once, the symbolism of the coincidence of opposites in the great round of birth and death; the realism of sexuality as a primary metaphor for expressing of our deepest insights about reality; and Goddess Herself. Yet I think they all return together. This combination also brings with it a different kind of transcendence, the kind of transcendence that comes with discovering the meaning available *within* the circle of existence. Reconciliation—with ourselves, our bodies, our limits—is the gift of Goddess.

My remarks on the imagery of Goddess, which I think takes us far beyond the simple insertion of female pronouns into familiar contexts, seem to have stressed two points over and over. One is that we need Goddess because She breaks stereotypes of the feminine and thus frees women from the limitations of that stereotype. Women can be strong *and* beautiful, feminine *and* wise teachers, mothers *and* participants in culture. If Goddess provided that much it would have been enough. But it seems that She brings much more. Dimensions of deity that have been lost or severely attenuated during the long centuries when we spoke of God as if S/He were only a male are restored. They seem to have to do with acceptance and immanence, with nature and the cyclic round. Metaphors of enclosure, inner spaces, and curved lines seem to predominate. What a relief from the partial truth of intervention and transcendence; of history and linear time; of going forth, exposure and straight lines! For insights that are true but incomplete, when elevated into the totality of truth, become false and dangerous. Goddess completes the image of God and brings wholeness. One begins to sense that God, as well as women, has been imprisoned in patriarchal imagery.[5] That discovery is at once scary, painful, and exhilarating.

NOTES

1. For a longer, more detailed statement of this argument, see Rita M. Gross, "Female God-Language in the Jewish Context," *Womanspirit Rising,* ed. Carol P. Christ and Judith Plaskow (New York: Harper and Row, 1979).

2. For more detailed discussion, see Rachel Adler, "The Jew Who Wasn't There: *Halakhah* and the Jewish Woman," *Response: A Contemporary Jewish Review,* vol. 7, no. 2 (Summer 1973), pp. 77–89; and Rita M. Gross, "On Being a Religious Jewish Woman," *Ancient Roots and Modern Meanings: A Contemporary Reader in Jewish Identity,* ed. Jerry Diller (New York: Bloch Pub. Co.).

3. I am indebted to Nelle Morton's Christian role-reversal fantasy in *Sexist Religion and Women in the Church: No More Silence* (Association Press, 1976), pp. 29–31, for inspiration for this role-reversal fantasy. Several sentences have been quoted directly.

4. For a fuller discussion of these images as well as all the issues involved in rediscovering female imagery of deity and utilizing non-Western resources as a tool, see Rita M. Gross, "Hindu Female Deities as a Resource in the Contemporary Rediscovery of the Goddess," *Journal of the American Academy of Religion,* September 1978, pp. 269–291.

5. For a brilliant demonstration of this point, see Carol Christ, "The Liberation of Women and the Liberation of God," *The Jewish Woman,* ed. Elizabeth Koltun (New York: Schocken Books, 1976), pp. 11–17.

Bride, Spouse, Daughter

IMAGES OF THE FEMININE IN CLASSICAL JEWISH SOURCES[1]

Arthur Green

FOR the first time in Jewish history, women are taking a full and equal role in the search for religious meaning in Jewish tradition. This coincides with their admission to positions of religious leadership in the community and with their full involvement in the life, on all levels, of the Jewish people. It seems entirely appropriate, at such a moment in history, that we comb our sources for images of the feminine in Jewish religious literature as they might be of use to such a generation of women. On the face of it, all of this is both obvious and entirely legitimate. As we probe a bit more deeply, however, two questions emerge that must be treated at least briefly as we begin to engage in such a search.

Is it really women who alone are in need of feminine imagery? Do images of the divine feminine belong only to women? Might they not belong to, and respond to the needs of, men as well as women? Or, as a friend posed the question a long time ago, with reference to Catholic spiritual literature, does Theresa of Ávila need to be the bride of God more than does John of the Cross? Does John need God the Father more than God the Mother? Indeed, is it Mother whom the passionate Theresa seeks so boldly? Might one not argue that men need the feminine, as women would need the masculine, if religious life involves something like what the depth psychologists call a search for polarities? In the course of our intense longing for the divine Other, a longing long depicted as having a strong erotic component, might it not be opposite rather than like that needs first to be sought out? This brings us, automatically, to a second important question in the anomalous situation in which we find ourselves.

As we turn to the tradition to seek out images of the feminine, we will have to admit that all the images we find are those of women as imagined by or created by men. We are not looking at the spiritual life of Glückel of Hameln or the pitifully few other women who have left us anything at all by way of written record, in the annals of Jewish history prior to modern times. Rail against this fact as we may, we simply cannot create historical sources that do not exist. Women as created by men, women in the fantasies of men, albeit sacred fantasies, are what we have.[2] Are these the kinds of texts women will need? Will the fact that such images of the feminine are male creations in itself somehow negate their usefulness? Might there emerge a feminist and female-created commentary or literature of commentary on the old male-created series of feminine images? Or need the old be negated altogether in the quest of women of our times?

Both of these questions, the question of who needs feminine imagery (in the truly spiritual sense, and not in the political appropriation of religious symbols) and the question of the usability of feminine imagery as created by a male religious community, will plague us throughout any such search.

The Jewish religious community, insofar as it existed as a public and corporate body in pre-modern times, was a male community. Women surely had a place in that community, indeed they had a vital role in Jewish life throughout history, one that need not be defended here. But insofar as that community saw itself as an assembled group, insofar as it came before God in the house of prayer or the house of study, it existed, it wrote for itself, it thought of itself, by and large, as a community of men. What does it mean then to note that this community regularly spoke of itself in the feminine, as *knesset Yisrael*? What does it mean that this primarily male community saw itself as the bride in its commentary on the Song of Songs? What does it mean that this male community saw itself as the female spouse, as it were, of the masculine God? There are some who would turn to the sense of powerlessness and castration in Jewish history in order to answer such a question. It would be argued that it was because the Jewish people had no political independence, because we were not masters of our own lives and of our own historical situation, that we saw ourselves as "mere" powerless women rather than as real men. That works until one notices that the linguistic tradition is much the same in the Church. The Church, too, the allpowerful Church of the Middle Ages, saw itself as the *Ecclesia,* as the bride of God. While women had a more active role in the Church than in the synagogue, surely those images there too reflect the self-description of a male-dominated community.[3]

Why is it that men, in talking about their relationship with God, turned to images of the feminine in order to describe themselves? This seems to be a major issue in understanding the psychology of a religious community. What I want to propose is simply this: in the search for the kind of intimacy, tenderness, and warmth that such people wanted to express in talking about the relationship between God and Israel, they could not remain in the domain of the all-male universe where they lived their public lives. There is no way, without turning to images of the feminine, or without thinking of the relationships between men and women, that most men can express the degree of love, passion, and warmth that the spiritual life may arouse in them.

All this imagery of the feminine still assumes the basic masculinity of God. If we talk about the female community of Israel, or Israel as the bride, in such word pictures we are talking about God, of course, as "man." When the sages spoke of the relationship between God and Israel in "man-to-man" terms, they found themselves limited primarily to two images: Israel (or the individual) as son and Israel as servant. The son, as is said so clearly in the Rosh Hashanah liturgy, may duly expect to be the object of divine loving kindness, while the servant may but turn to his Master in supplication for His pity (or His justice?). There is, of course, a depth of love between Father and son depicted in Jewish sources that is not to be underestimated. Much of the love literature, particularly within the context of liturgy, speaks about

Israel as the son of the King. *'Eved,* the servant, brings out more clearly the aspect of *yir'ah,* [the fear of God] and of a sense of complete dependency, while at the same time perhaps pointing to mutual responsibilities in a relationship of fealty.

Neither of these images, however, exhausts the full measure of our capacity for love, surrender, or passion. In a touchingly understated article published some years ago,[4] Judah Goldin indicated that Rabbi Akiva's emphasis on love as the center of the religious life—it was Akiva who said that "all of Scripture is holy, but the Song of Songs is the holy of holies"—had to do with his attitude toward his own marriage, and that his marriage was somehow a model for him of the relationship between God and Israel.

The rabbis say that the handmaiden at the crossing of the Red Sea saw more than Ezekiel the prophet. Ezekiel, it will be recalled, was the prophet who spoke in the most bold, open way of what he had seen in a visionary state. Here the handmaiden—not the servant, but the handmaiden—is said to have seen more than Ezekiel. Why the handmaiden? Only in the context of the rabbis' reading of the Song of Songs does the passage make sense. God is Israel's great lover, liberator, bringing her out from Egypt and across the sea. At that moment, the moment when she greets her lover, she sees more than the male Israel, Israel the son or servant, might. This is consistent with the imagery that runs through the entire Midrash on the Song of Songs. Despite a highly conservative and, from our point of view, at times prudish attitude toward the erotic in a religious context—an attitude in part inherited from the old biblical struggle against cultic sexuality—we find in early rabbinic sources a significant strand that recognizes the inevitability of this theme's reappearance as one discusses "matters that touch the human heart."[5]

The imagery of Israel as the bride of God shares its place in this search for feminine metaphors with another interesting and perhaps surprising image, that of Israel as the daughter of God. For this we turn to a text, quoting the Midrash on the Song of Songs (3:7):

"King Solomon made a palanquin for himself" (Cant. 3:9). Rabbi Azariah in the name of Rabbi Judah the son of Simon interpreted this verse as speaking of the Tabernacle.[6] The Palanquin is the Tabernacle. Said Rabbi Judah the son of Ilai, This may be compared to a king who had a young daughter. Before she grew up and the signs of puberty were found in her, the King would see her in the market place and speak to her openly, in the courtyard or in the alleyway. When she grew up, however, and she reached puberty, the king said: "It will not be proper for my daughter that I speak to her in public. Rather make her a pavillion, and when I need to speak to her I will speak to her in the pavillion." Thus, Scripture says, "When Israel was a lad I loved him" (Hos. 11:1). In Egypt they saw Him in public, as Scripture says, "The Lord passed by to smite the Egyptians" (Ex. 12:23). At the sea they saw Him in public, as Scripture says, "Israel saw the great hand" (Ex. 14:31). And then the young children pointed to him with their fingers and said, "This is my God and I will glorify Him" (Ex. 15:2). At Sinai they saw Him face to face, as Scripture says, "The Lord comes from Sinai" (Deut. 33:2). But once Israel had stood at Mt. Sinai and received the Torah, saying, "All that the Lord has said we shall do and obey" (Ex. 24:7) they became a mature people. Then the Holy One, blessed be He, said: "It is not proper for my children that I speak with them in public, rather let them make a Tabernacle for Me; when I need to speak with them I'll speak to them from within the Tabernacle." Thus Scripture says, "When Moses came into the Tent of Meeting to speak with Him" (Ex. 34:34). This palanquin was made by King Solomon; "Solomon" here refers to the King of Peace.

What we see in this text is surely a reflection of proper royal-class behavior in Mishnaic times. The daughter has a right to the protection of her modesty, and a casual approach to her on the streets, even by her own father, would demean her. This image is then applied to the relationship of God and Israel, superimposed on the classical period of Israel's sacred history. The truth is that there is something distinctive here in the relationship between father and daughter which is not present in the relationship between father and son. Father and daughter develop a certain shyness with one another as the daughter reaches puberty, a shyness which is not the same between fathers and sons. The daughter now has a right to privacy; the father accepts her as a mature woman and respects, indeed helps to set, the bounds of her contacts with men, including himself. Being the King's daughter is different from being His son; there is a relationship being spoken of here that a male can never fully understand, and that the tradition itself has not been able to fully appreciate until now, because there has never been a commentator on any of this material who was herself a daughter and knew what the relationship between father and daughter was about.

But it is not only Israel who is described as being the king's daughter. We find quite a few sources describing *Torah* as daughter of God. In this example the reference is again to the building of the Tabernacle:

> "Moses has commanded the Torah to us, an inheritance for the house of Israel", read not "inheritance" [*MoRaSaH*] but rather "betrothal" [*Me'oRaSaH*]. The bridegroom, so long as he has not actually married his bride, becomes a regular visitor in the house of his future father-in-law. From the time they are married, however, her father must come to visit her. Similarly, so long as the Torah had not been given to Israel, Scripture tells us, "Moses went up to God" (Ex. 19:3). Once the Torah was there with Israel, God said to Moses, "Make Me a Tabernacle and I will dwell in their midst" (Ex. 25:8).[7]

The image of Torah as feminine is, of course, related to ancient traditions of wisdom, *hokhmah* or *sofia,* which in biblical literature and elsewhere is frequently described in feminine terms. Such description has a long history, first in ancient Wisdom-literature, later in both Gnostic and Neo-Platonic sources. A latterday mystical transformation of that symbol lies behind the well-known passage of the *Zohar* that describes the Torah as a beautiful and stately maiden, hidden away in a castle, who reveals bits of herself only to her lover as he walks by her gate each day to seek her out. It is a passage filled with the imagery of medieval courtly love.[8] These passages demand that we consider seriously the notion that the Torah is woman. This becomes particularly interesting in the context of the current controversy over the ordination of women as rabbis. The rabbi in Judaism, unlike the Christian priest, is in no way the personification of God in the liturgy. If anything, the rabbi is the embodiment of Torah, the one who represents Torah in the midst of the Jewish community. But if the Torah, in a significant part of ancient rabbinic imagery, is described in feminine terms, what inadequacy can one find in its being represented by a woman?

Still, let us not rush to politicize our study of symbols. The question is meant in the first place as a devotional one: What does it feel like to be the King's daughter? What particular devotional content might a woman find in that metaphor of relationship? Might it offer some new/old enrichment to *all* of us who seek, both male and female? What does it feel like for a man to be wedded to the daughter of a king? Have we fully understood both the joy and the awesome responsibility of that self-description?[9] What does it feel like to be an embodiment of Torah, Torah as a feminine presence, perhaps a female wisdom on a deeper, more hidden, or more subtle level than the conventionally "masculine" wisdom of cumulative law and tradition.

There is in the tradition of the rabbis a great love of feminine imagery. Again and again the most poignant passages to be found in rabbinic literature will involve a female voice or image. One need think perhaps only of one of the most famous of rabbinic homilies on the destruction of Jerusalem, in which, after the Patriarchs, Moses, Jeremiah, and the Prophets all stand up to accuse God of His unfaithfulness in allowing His Temple to be destroyed, it is only mother Rachel, in talking about how she set aside her jealousy of Leah, who can shame God into setting aside his jealousy of the petty and foolish idols that Israel had taken to worship.

There is little question that even this wealth of traditional imagery will not suffice for our own day. Many will rightly claim that new kinds of female images are needed, and that the multiplicity or variety of female models sought today are not all there in the early sources. There is, however, a body of material to work with, and it is considerably greater than many would first assume when looking at what is frequently dismissed as a male-dominated religious tradition. This material might form the basis of a contemporary commentary—though surely such commentary must go beyond anything found in the prior literature.

All of the above has to do with the situation in which the masculinity of God is still assumed, while that which stands in relation to God may be seen as feminine. We turn now to a new sort of literature, that of the Kabbalah, in which a female component of divinity itself is given place. Here, of course, the roster of sources is somewhat shorter, and we must beware of exaggerated and ahistorical claims that are sometimes made for this material. A new myth of Judaism emerged in the twelfth and thirteenth centuries, hiding behind the word *kabbalah,* which means tradition itself. Here is presented a Judaism of mythic complexity that had been previously unknown, one in which the single, static, and essentially masculine God of biblical-rabbinic monotheism is replaced by a dynamic, multifaceted, ever-flowing, separating and uniting, new kind of ten-in-one monotheistic deity. In that paradigm of the inner life of God, described through so many rich and varied images in the kabbalistic literature, the *Shekhinah* took a major role.

Using an ancient term for the indwelling or presence of God, the Kabbalists now employed *Shekhinah* to symbolize a particular realm within the divine world. Described as daughter, bride, mother, moon, sea, faith, wisdom, speech, and a myriad of other figures, usually but not always feminine by fact or association, the *Shekhinah* is the chief object of both the divine and human search for wholeness and perfection. She is the bride of God within God, mother of the world and feminine side of the divine self, in no way fully separable from the male self of God. Indeed, the root of all evil, both cosmic and human, is the attempt to bring about such a separation. The picture of that feminine aspect of divinity is a complicated one. As the tenth of the *sefirot,* or manifestations of divine selfhood, she is, when facing those above, passive and receptive. She takes all the upper powers into herself; "All the rivers flow into the sea," as the Kabbalists love to quote from the Book of Ecclesiastes (1:7). But as the sea transforms all the rivers, gives them new life as a dynamic power all her own, and reaches her destined shores as a new being, so is the *Shekhinah,* when facing the lower worlds, described as giver, provider, ruler, and judge. In a way that cannot be fully understood, she is represented as the mystical embodiment of the Community of Israel: the Kabbalist has transferred the locus of mystical marriage from the relationship of God and the earthly Israel to an entirely divine plane. Rather than seeing himself and his people as the bride of God, he now joins with God above in rejoicing at a sacred marriage that has taken place, as it were, within God. Perhaps most interestingly, *Shekhinah* is the only aspect of divinity that most Kabbalists ever claim really to experience. The *Shekhinah,* the outermost gate to the divine mysteries, is all the Kabbalist dares to say that he has attained. It is through the union of *Shekhinah* with God above that the Kabbalist, too, is bound to those higher forces. He serves as "attendant of the bride," knowing secretly at the same time that his soul is born of this union that he has helped to bring about.

We read now of the *Shekhinah* from the earliest text we have in all of Kabbalistic literature, the *Sefer HaBahir,* that appeared in southern France in the latter decades of the twelfth century. The *Bahir* is written in an intentionally mystifying and yet defiantly simple tone, one that does much to set the stage for the later symbolic development within Kabbalah. Here the *Bahir* is commenting on the biblical verse "Blessed be the Glory of God from His place" (Ezek. 3:12). *Glory,* in Hebrew *kavod,* is the Biblical term which the Kabbalists (following the *Targum*) usually took as a code word for the *Shekhinah.*

> This may be compared to a king who had a matron in his chamber. All his hosts took pleasure in her. She had children, and those children came each day to see the king and greet him. They would say to him, "Where is our mother?" And he would answer, "You cannot see her now." To this they would reply, "Blessed be she, in whatever place she is."

Immediately the *Bahir* adds a second parable:

> This may be compared to a princess who came from a faraway place. Nobody knew where she came from. Then they saw that she was an upstanding woman, good and proper in all her deeds. They said of her, "This one surely is taken from the place of light, for by her deeds the world is enlightened." They asked her, " Where are you from?" She said, "From my place." They said, "In that case, great are the people of your place. Blessed are you; blessed is she and blessed is her place."[10]

The *Shekhinah,* the mysterious woman, queen or princess, hidden or coming from a place beyond, is the only one we see, the only one we greet. What is her place, what is her origin? These are hidden somewhere in the mysteries of God beyond. All we can say of the God we know, of that feminine God we encounter is "Blessed is she and blessed is her place." The glory of God is apparent to us, the glory of God lies within the realm of human experience. The *Shekhinah* is the God we know. Surely, that *Shekhinah* stands in relation to a transcendent deity, whether described in male terms or in terms of more pure abstraction, but our knowledge of that is only through her. Blessed is she and blessed is her place.

While the *Shekhinah* plays a central role in all of Kabbalistic literature, it is especially in the *Zohar* that its feminine character is highlighted. The author of the *Zohar* was possessed of a seemingly boundless mythic imagination, a great deal of it centering on female figures, both sacred and demonic, as well as on deeply ambivalent fantasies concerning human women in this world.[11] In what is surely one of its most strikingly impassioned passages, the *Zohar* speaks of the love of God through the symbol of the kisses that Jacob gives to Rachel. From the passage it becomes clear that the experience of the mystic is that of being aroused, drawn into, and kissed by God. As the passage develops, Rachel, the recipient of the kisses, is really related to an entirely hidden and abstract God beyond, a God so abstract and hidden, however, that He cannot be described as one who kisses. How, indeed, can one be loved by a God who is hidden beyond all being? Jacob is the personified manifestation of this hidden God, personified only, as it were, in order that the great mystery be enabled to kiss the bride. The passage reads as follows:

> When it (the spirit of love) enters the palace of love, the love of supernal kisses is aroused, those of which Scripture says: "Jacob kissed Rachel" (Gen. 29:11). This arousal brings about the kisses of supernal love, as needs to be. These kisses are the beginning of all love, attachment, and binding above. That is why the Canticle opens its praises with: "Let Him kiss me." Who is to "kiss me"? The one hidden in sublime hiding. but should you ask: "Do kisses apply to the most hidden One? Does that one kiss below?"—come and see: that most hidden of hiddens, no one knows it. It reveals of itself but a slim ray of hidden light, revealed only through a narrow path that proceeds from it. But this is the light that gives light to all. This is the arousal of all the sublime secrets, yet it remains hidden. Sometimes hidden, sometimes revealed. But even when it is not revealed at all, it remains the source of arousal for those ascending kisses. And since it is hidden, the Canticle begins its praises in a hidden (i.e., third-person) way.[12]

> But if kisses are from there, what need have we of Jacob here? Do not the kisses proceed from Him? The matter is thus: "Let Him kiss me—the One who is hidden above. But how? Through that plane in which all the colors are reflected and joined together, and that is Jacob.[13]

So here we are, Israel, male and female, personified together as Rachel, receiving the kisses of God as Jacob. No, we receive the kisses of the God beyond, the God who is neither male nor female, neither here nor there, not this way or that way, the God who is utterly beyond all such duality and polarization. Here it seems that it is only the reality of human life and the gender-defined nature of our passions that cause the mystic to speak, for those of us who cannot follow him utterly into abstraction, in the language of male and female.

This all-too-brief selection from the Kabbalistic sources on *Shekhinah* might best be concluded with a line from another thirteenth-century work, the *Gates of Light* by Joseph Gikatillia. We have seen the *Shekhinah* as locus of the classic symbols of the feminine and as the mystical Community of Israel. Here we see her represented by *individual* women, an aspect seldom found in the early sources. Gikatillia writes:

"In the time of Abraham our father, of blessed memory, the *Shekhinah* was called Sarah. In the time of Isaac our father, she was called Rebecca. In the time of Jacob our father, she was called Rachel."[14]

The point is clear. The names of the *Shekhinah* change with the generations, as do the names of every other aspect, male and female, of divinity. God is identified with all of the patriarchs, with all of the heroes, *Shekhinah* is identified with all of the mothers, the heroines of the Bible.

Are we the bride of God, the people whom He weds on that Sabbath of revelation? Are we related to God as female to male, seemingly an image so clear in commentary on the Song of Songs? Or are we, as some other imagery seems to say, God's son-in-law, wedded to his daughter the Torah or his daughter the Sabbath? Try to sort out the imagery of *lekhah dodi,* "Come, my dear friend to greet the bride." Whose bride is it that we are greeting? Sabbath, *Shekhinah,* the bride of God? Ourselves, collectively Israel, the bride of God? Or Sabbath, the bride of Israel? Or can no such clear or clean distinctions be made? Must we not rather say that we are at once male and female in relating to God, who is Him/Herself at once male and female; both of them inadequate metaphors to describe the mysterious self beyond all gender, indeed, beyond all distinction, but lacking none of the passion we know in our fragile human attempt to unify the polarities?

None of this will probably suffice for a new generation of women, those who are for the first time becoming fully involved in the creative spiritual life of the Jewish people. The foundation for such creativity, however, is here. The situation of women fully entering participation in the Jewish community is entirely anomalous. The new generation should rejoice in that, seeing its holy duty as one of creating an element in our shared myth that has been developed in only a fragmentary way. It will be a tragedy—one of the great Jewish tragedies of our age—if those women who enter roles of leadership in Jewish life become "sons of the King." That will do none of us any good. They will remain awkward in that role, and the Jewish people will remain unenriched. A truly feminine, and truly Jewish, spirituality is one of the urgent tasks of our age. A proper point of origin for it would be the encounter of contemporary Jewish women with those symbols of the sacred feminine given us by our tradition.

NOTES

1. Adapted from an address given to the Women's Rabbinical Alliance, 1979.

2. A possible exception is provided by some of the literature of *tehinot:* prayers and supplications written specifically for women. Quite a number of these were published in various collections, especially in Yiddish, over the past three hundred years. In most cases it is unknown, however, whether the authors themselves were women.

3. Of course the marital motif for the relationship of God and Israel goes back to the Bible; the prophet Hosea makes especially strong use of it in describing Israel's infidelity. Given their early histories of persecution as well as their later competitive claims, it is not hard to see why both the rabbinic and the ecclesiastic authors chose to highlight the faithfulness of God's spouse and the undying affection He has for her.

4. "Toward a Profile of the Tanna, Aqiba ben Joseph," *Journal of the American Oriental Society* 96, 1976, p. 1.

5. I have discussed these sources more fully in an article published in *Judaism* 24 (1975), p. 4.

6. The portable sanctuary, in the form of a tent, that was used during the forty years of wandering.

7. *Exodus Rabbah* 33:7.

8. *Zohar* 2:99a–b.

9. They are most fully drawn out in the fantasy-creations of Rabbi Nahman of Bratslav. See the first two in his collection of *Tales,* now available in the faithful English rendition of Arnold Band, published in the *Classics of Western Spirituality* series of the Paulist Press.

10. *Bahir* (Margoliat edition, 131–2; Scholem edition 90).

11. The reader of Hebrew or German will have access to Gershom Scholem's study of *Shekhinah,* either in its original form in *Von der mystischen Gestalt der Gottheit* (Zürich, 1962) or as translated in *Pirkei Yesod be-Havanat ha-Kabbalah u-Semaleha* (Jerusalem, 1976). Isaiah Tishby's lengthy introduction to the notion of *Shekhinah* in his *Mishnat ha-Zohar* is also a basic source for the Hebrew reader. A study of the *Zohar*'s author with emphasis on psychosexual attitudes, if possible, would be a major contribution to Jewish scholarship.

12. Rachel does not say to Jacob: "Kiss me!" as the Canticle opens, but rather "Let Him kiss me." The hidden God beyond cannot be addressed in the second person of prayer, but can only be hinted at in the more secretive third person manner.

13. *Zohar* 2:146b.

14. *Sha'arey Orah,* ed. Ben-Shlomo, ch. five, p. 230.

Feminist Judaism
RESTORATION OF THE MOON

Arthur I. Waskow

THERE is a strand of Jewish tradition that has some curious things to say about the moon. Says the Prophet Isaiah (30:26), "The light of the moon shall become like the light of the sun." And the Babylonian Talmud expands on this unsettling notion:

> [When God created the sun and moon, the two great lights], the moon said to the Holy One, "Sovereign of the Universe! Can two rulers wear one crown?" He answered, "Go then and make yourself smaller!" . . . R. Simeon ben Lakish declared, "Why is it that the he-goat offered on the New Moon [for a sin-offering] is distinctive in that there is written concerning it, 'unto the Lord'?" Because the Holy One said, "Let this he-goat be an atonement for Me [for My sin] in making the moon smaller." (*Hullin* 60a)

> R. Akha said to R. Ashi: In the West, they pronounce the following blessing: "Blessed be the One Who renews the moons." Whereupon he retorted: "Such a blessing even our women folk pronounce." [Let there be added] . . . "The moon He ordered that she should renew herself as a crown of beauty for those whom He sustains from the womb, and who will someday, like her, be renewed and magnify their Maker in the name of the glory of His Kingdom." (*Sanhedrin* 42a)

These texts express an ancient tradition that when Creation began, the moon was equal to the sun; that God reduced its brightness just as the *Shekhinah*—God's Presence in the world, a brooding, nurturing female aspect of God—went into mourning exile; and that the moon will again become equal to the sun when the Messianic redemption comes and the *Shekhinah* returns to Her full glory in the days of love and justice. Arlene Agus has suggested that we read this strand of the tradition as a veiled comment on the possibility of a profound change in the relationships of women and men in Jewish religious life—with the moon symbolizing women and the sun, men.

The Talmud promises that the moon will be made bright again in Heaven when those who are like her on earth are restored to their rightful place: those whom God has sustained "from the womb" but whose splendor God has dimmed. Who are these? According to rabbinic and mystical tradition, these are the people of Israel—who almost disappear from history and then return in unexpected glory; disappear and return, over and over. We can accept this tradition that the redemption of Israel is one meaning of the passage, and believe as well that the passage should be read to include the female half of humankind—who also, like Israel and the moon, have been pushed to the shadowy side of history.

For it would not be surprising for the moon to be a symbol of women. The "moonthly" and menstrual cycles have in many religious traditions been seen as echoes of each other. And the imagery of God as Midwife and Mother who sustains "from the womb" would fit well with God's concern for those people whose womb moves and changes with the moon.

What else in the tradition might suggest this outlook?

The tradition teaches that for the sake of their refusal to give their jewelry to the making of the Golden Bull-calf at Sinai, the women of Israel were given by God an exemption from work on Rosh Hodesh—the renewing of the moon at the beginning of the Jewish lunar month. This, it seems to me, can be understood as a kind of anthropological field-observation with a religious dimension: that men, remembering the cults of Egypt, cast the male-fertility idol of the Golden Bull-calf; that women refused to join in its worship; and that God confirmed their right and affirmed their desire to continue celebrating (not worshiping) the moon, which symbolized female spirituality because her ebb and flow seemed akin to the menstrual cycle.

The Jewish Patriarchs Isaac and Jacob, according to tradition, married into a family of strong women—the family of Rivkah, Rahel, and Leah. It was, by the way, the family of Lavan—a name for the pale-white moon, as in *kiddush levana,* the ceremony of hallowing the moon. These women had strong associations with a well—and of Rivkah there is a traditional *midrash* that when she met Abraham's servant Eliezer at the well, the water rose to meet her.[1] When would water do this? When it is attracted by the moon. Is it possible that the household *terafim* that Rahel took from Lavan's household when she left with Jacob were sacred moon-symbols, and it was no mere accident or trick that led her to conceal them from Lavan by explaining she was in the time of her menstrual flow? (Genesis 31:19, 31:30–35) Was it necessary for those women to become the mothers of Israel precisely because they carried a strong "feminist," moon-centered religious tradition, but were not moon worshipers?

The first four chapters of Exodus lay out a female-male rhythm of the first stage of the liberation from *Mitzrayim* in which women are crucial. It is they who take the initiative and teach men the process of freedom, because they know the mysteries of birth. (The birth of a new person is the biological archetype of freedom in the historical-political arena. Every birth brings newness, uncontrollability, into the world.) Thus the midwives save the baby boys; Miriam and Pharoah's daughter save Moses; Moses must flee to seven women and a well, marry Zipporah, and *have a child* before he can experience the Burning Bush; and Zipporah must complete the birth by teaching him to circumcise his son before he can reenter Egypt to become the liberator. Zipporah was not Jewish. Was she a celebrator of the moon? (Note her association, like that of Rivkah and Rahel, with a well.)

The Book of Ruth goes out of its way to assert that Lot's nameless daughter, Tamar, and Ruth—all women who invoked something like the levirate law, the right of a childless widow to marry a close kinsman of her dead husband, in order to transcend the normal law-code and claim their husbands—were crucial elements in the genealogy of King David (and therefore the Messiah). All these women were also non-Jewish. Were they celebrators of the moon?

The Song of Songs, which Akiba called "the holy of holies" among the Holy Writings, affirms and celebrates not only an assertive woman, but a mode of spirituality that flows from the life-experience of women.

Thus at a number of moments of great mythic power—crucial points in the earliest stages of Jewish peoplehood and in the progenitoring of David—women and symbols of women (such as the moon and wells) were absolutely crucial.

To read the tradition this way would mean that these texts preserve both a dim memory of the past and a shadowy prophecy of the future: A dim memory of a time in the early history of the people of Israel—perhaps even before it viewed itself as Israel—when women and the symbols of their spiritual experience (e.g., the moon) were equal to men and their symbols, in the religious life of the people; and a prophecy that someday, in Jewish practice, not only women but also the symbols of women's spiritual experience will be restored to equality with men and their symbols.

When that "someday" comes, women will not simply take a numerically equal place in the traditional forms of Jewish religious practice; the forms of practice will themselves be transformed as women's spiritual experience is discovered, uncovered.

I think "someday" is now, if we will make it so.

I am suggesting that in the fragments of mystical thought quoted above and in some other fragments of the Tradition are hints toward a feminist transformation of Torah—expected and invited by Torah herself, as part of the unfolding of the oral tradition.

What would it mean for God and the Jewish people now to restore the former brightness of women and their spiritual experience?

It would mean that women and men come to understand the Jewish feminist movement as a process in which there must be several levels of change. One necessary level is the demand that women must count in the *minyan,* be called for *aliyot* to read the Torah, become rabbis—and that men must rear children, care for households, feed the hungry. In short, the demand that *all* the *mitzvot,* all the commandments, apply fully to *all* adult Jews.

It is true this demand has not yet been accepted even in theory in some areas of Jewish life. It has not yet been carried out in practice even in most of the areas where it is accepted in theory. So Jewish feminists must continue to press this demand. Yet there are other levels of change that Jewish feminists need to pursue as well—the changes involved in the brightening of "the moon"—that is, the forms by which women can more richly express their spiritual experience.

These deeper levels of change are necessary because the Jewish people—women and men—need more than the inclusion of women in the same kind of Jewish life the rabbis knew. We need the *renewal* of Jewish life—its becoming as fresh, creative, and new in its response to Torah after the earthquakes of the last generation as it was after Sinai, in the wilderness; as it was after the First Destruction, when it gave us "the Prophets"; as it was after the Second Destruction, when it gave us the Talmud.

And in our generation we need this renewal to include the lessons of the life-experience of women. Some aspects of the special life-experience of women may be biologically rooted. Most are culturally rooted. This matters, but it does not matter as much as our being open to the lessons women might teach—whether these lessons are rooted in biology or culture. It is true that some men experience in some degree the elements of a life that we often think of as especially part of women's experience. That is, men experience the moon, water, life cycles, feeding, giving birth, rearing children, caring for households, nurturing families and communities, even *nekevah* [feminine] sexuality—open, pierced, and receptive. But all these are, for biological and cultural reasons, *more* fully experienced by *more* women.

Now we need to reclaim and renew this "women's element" in Judaism.

Some feminists have been concerned that focusing on the "womanliness" of the aspects of life may encourage old stereotypes of women's roles, and thereby assist in the resubjugation of women into these roles. My own view is that women can draw on these elements of their own past special experience without fear, if two conditions are met: if women and men are clear that both men and women can draw on the whole spectrum of life-experience, even if perhaps to different degrees; and—most important—if women hold enough power in our culture to control the use of these symbols and roles—enough power to make sure that they are used in the service of a broader "feminization/humanization" rather than resubjugation. That is why the demand for equality for women in Jewish institutions cannot be separated from the demand for a feminist transformation of those institutions.

Why do we need to pursue these intertwined issues at this moment of Jewish history? We need to do this for the sake of those women who have been excluded and whose life-experience has been ignored—and for the sake of justice toward them. We also need to do this for the sake of giving health to a Judaism that is now suffering from the exclusion of much else in life. In this sense we may see the restoration of the moon more broadly still—meaning the messianic liberation and redemption, not only of women and of the Jewish people, not only of the poor, the weak, of all who have been excluded, diminished, demeaned, but also the liberation, the reemergence of all that is valuable *within* each human being, but that has been repressed.

For Isaiah and the Talmud to see even the moon as a diminished equal who will return in splendor to her place, as the weeping *Shekhinah* will return to hers, can be seen as a metaphor for all *tikkun:* all repair of the world.

In this way there would emerge as part of the Jewish feminist process what might be called a "feminist Judaism"—a Judaism informed and transformed throughout its fabric by the feminist consciousness. Such a feminist Judaism would mean not only the restoration of women to their almost forgotten equal place in life, but also the "return of the repressed" in other spheres—for example, the reawakening of the repressed sense of sexuality that is celebrated in the Song of Songs, and that was pushed underground by tradition even when it elevated the Song of Songs. For example, the reawakening of music and dance, the celebration of our bones and muscles that was repressed when the Temple was destroyed. For example, the celebration of the earth through the cycles of *shmitah* and Jubilee (a kind of body-cycle writ large, a kind of menstrual cycle of the *Shekhinah,* expressed in the land

and the society). For example: the celebration of equality that is expressed in a circle dance (where everyone must sooner or later stand in the footsteps of everyone else) and the circle of recycling the wealth from the rich to every newly equal family. For example, the repressed sense of God not as a separate Other, "out there," but "in here," in process.

What specific actions could we undertake in order to effect a feminist transformation of Judaism?

First, we can strengthen moon- and water-symbolism in our liturgies. This has already begun as women and men have developed various kinds of liturgies for Rosh Hodesh, the Renewing of the Moon. As these spread, and especially as groups of women develop more and more expressive ceremonials, they need to be shared with and taught to the Jewish people as a whole. So do rituals of water, old and new—wells, rivers, seas, *mikvah, tashlikh,* the bitter water/sweet water ceremony of reconciliation developed for *Slichot* by the *Menorah* journal, perhaps a reworking of the water-pouring that was celebrated at the Temple for Sukkot.

Second, we can encourage circles in planning space. The fluid and circular seating arrangements of the *havurot* seem to owe something to the (unconscious?) influence of women who fully participated in forming *havurah* practice. For the biology of women's inner life-space, as contrasted with men's outward life-projection, seems to be congruent with the circular seating where God feels present in the center, not far out along one dimension. These *havurah* circles have taught us that when we look for God, what we see is not the Ark or the rabbi—but one another's faces. And the circles have encouraged a sense of equality, participation, and community that may also stem partly from the life-experience and needs of women. What would happen if all Jewish meetings, for prayer and for discussion, were held in circles small enough for us to talk with each other, instead of in rows where we see only the back of each other's heads, plus the face of one Grand Master? If we *talked* in circles, we could stop *going* in circles. If we do not live out the circle, the circle lives us: Zero.

Third, we can look for circles and spirals in time. We need to strengthen our sense of the cycles in our bodies and in society.

For example, we need to see the holy days as not simply individual events but parts of the spiritual cycles of the month and year. The social-political cycles of *Shabbos,* the *shmitah,* and Jubilee need to be renewed, accentuated, made much more real. These cycles alternate hard work toward economic development, with contemplative rest; the swift piling-up of wealth and power, with an equal sharing of all wealth and power; doing, with being.

Fourth, we can celebrate, honor, and materially support the life-moments of sexuality, sexual intercourse, menstruation, giving birth, nursing, parenting, and grandparenting, much more richly and thoroughly than we do now. For example, in an era when the overwhelming proportion of Jewish women ignore *niddah* and abhor the *mikvah* as a demeaning of menstruation, what if there were *one* or *two* days of sexual separation around menstruation, precisely to celebrate it without treating it as a time of "impurity"? For example, what if there were ceremonies around first menstruation and menopause? Around beginning to nurse and weaning? Could such ceremonies include men, even at some remove, as *brit milah* did women? Could we create ceremonies to mark the shift that occurs when children leave home—away from parenting toward the provision of wisdom to a wider world? Ceremonies to honor the link with an older culture that is represented by those who are grandparents—either through their own bodies or in a cultural, generational sense? And what if we honored all these processes in the "workaday" world by making time (and money) available for child care, for menstruating, grandparenting, and so forth? How would our bureaucracies and our volunteer organizations change?

Fifth, as we have suggested in the previous chapter, we can enrich the Jewish sense that the spirit *is* the body, that the spiritual and the physical fuse, by encouraging dance, mime, body movement, breathing, the arts and artisanship, and theatrical "acting" as part of prayer, Torah study, and midrashic storytelling. Already this process is being renewed by many women and some men.

Sixth, we can develop that element of Jewish theology, already present in Kabbalah and Hassidus, that focuses on God *within* us and the world, the "still small voice," the *Shekhinah.*

These six will be enough to begin with. For on the seventh day Queen Shabbos, the Bride, will teach us how to continue.

To this point what I have said is midrashic. It uses an ancient process to draw on the ancient texts, in order to make new solutions grow for our new life-problems. By coming to the old texts with new questions, we newly discover—dis-cover—meaning that was always there within them, waiting till we needed it. This is the authentically and perhaps uniquely Jewish process, which the "modern" Jews of every generation from the wilderness of Sinai to the *Lehrhaus* in Frankfurt have used to create new meaning for their lives.

But why should modern feminists desire to use this method? Why should women who seek an equal share of power in all the institutions that control their lives not simply shrug off the sexist institutions of conventional Judaism and refuse to let these institutions any longer control their lives? Why should women and men who share a feminist vision of a transformed society bother to transform the one minor subculture in which, it has been argued, the vision and practice of patriarchy may have been born, and may have been most forcefully transmitted across the millennia from civilization to civilization? Why take the trouble?

The reasons are partly personal, partly public or political.

The personal reasons are that for some Jewish families, specific strands of Jewish memory, ceremonial, community, and practice still have a powerful appeal. Whether it is identification with the oldest, longest-lived resistance movement against oppression that is known to human history; or the sense of fulfillment that arises from participation in such a ceremony as the Passover seder, or a strong rush of feeling about one's foggy mental picture of pioneer kibbutzniks in the Land of Israel—for *some* Jewish feminists (although by no means for all) this appeal is there. If the tug is real, and if "the personal is political," as feminists have reminded us, then the turf of Judaism must be struggled for.

In itself, this tug might or might not be enough to "go with," might or might not be enough to spark a growing fire of interest in Jewish renewal. But these personal responses are not casual or accidental—they do not in fact simply exist "in themselves." The personal response is a symptom, a sign, of the powerful truths within Jewish tradition.

It is *because* there is powerful truth in the tradition's resistance to power, in the multilevel poetry of its ritual, in its sardonic view of the transitory idols of convention, in its commitment to the creation of counterinstitutions reaching toward equality and community—that feminists feel pulled toward the kibbutz, the seder. The truths of the tradition have retained their power to work toward justice, community, holiness in the world, even when women and their deepest truths were kept on its margins. But all this is not enough. There is good reason for feminists, both men and women, to struggle for a major forward step in the tradition.

Some of the truths-toward-change that already are fermenting in the tradition not only accord with feminist perceptions of the world, but might even—at the very moment when patriarchal power was defeating the ancient matriarchies—have been smuggled into Torah through the insights of certain ancient matriarchs, the moon-celebrators of whom we have spoken. Many of these insights have been smuggled into, around, and underneath the patriarchal surface of the Torah. And some of these are insights that modern secularists, even feminists, need to hear about—insights that secular liberal, socialist, and feminist thought may not supply.

To some extent, it is the struggle of modern feminists to raise some profound questions that has brought to the level of audibility some yet-unheard proto-feminist concerns that lay beneath the surface of Torah. It is as if the voice of modern feminism woke a Sleeping Beauty in the Torah, a wisdom that recognized her daughter's voice.

What are these truths of Torah that our world-on-the-brink-of-dissolution needs to hear? Here we will sketch two of them, which we will explore in detail afterward.

First: the necessity of rhythm, of making *Shabbos,* of pausing to take a breath, to rest, to meditate, to contemplate. Especially the necessity of pausing from incessant, explosive economic development—not to *end* development, but to pause long enough to sense again its limitations, its purpose, its Owner. In the last decade or so we have come to see that 300 years of life without a

Shabbos has brought us to the edge of killing the human race and poisoning the biosphere. The world is teaching us that if we will not stop ourselves in accord with Torah, by making *Shabbos,* we will stop ourselves by catastrophic force. The sense of biological and social rhythms—the week, month, year, Jubilee—may very well have come into our tradition out of some matriarch's close sensing of her body and of Mother Earth. We need to hear that Teaching.

Second: the necessity to act consciously in order to keep ourselves from murdering the next generation. Over and over, from the Binding of Isaac to the *bris* of circumcision, to the biblical horror at the offering up of children through fire to Moloch to the rigorous restrictions in Deuteronomy against the old sending the young to kill and die for their wars—over and over, the Torah teaches that there is a serious danger: that the older generation will want to kill the younger; that especially fathers will want to kill their sons; and, most important, that we must create law-codes, rituals, and stories that train ourselves to struggle against this danger. Elijah will come, says the last passage of the last Prophet, before the great and terrible day of the Lord—to turn the hearts of the fathers to the sons and the hearts of the sons to the fathers. This too is a feminist teaching. One commentator on the Torah, David Bakan,[2] has even said that the Torah comes precisely to "motherize" men—to teach men to love and care for the community, as mothers have to act if their children are to live. And in our time, when the human race stands poised on the brink of destroying not a son here or there or even one whole people, but the entire next generation—this teaching stands between us and the danger.

But it is now also clear that the Teaching as we have so far understood it is not yet strong enough to keep us safe from the over-arching dangers of destruction. If Torah once bore within herself a secret feminist guerrilla victory smuggled into an obvious public patriarchal triumph, then the victory has oozed away. The feminism must be made explicit and public. Torah must be transformed and the feminist element in it strengthened. The modern feminist "daughter" must revitalize the sleeping feminist "mother."

If we do this for the sake of human survival, we will also be aiding in the struggle for Jewish survival. For the Jewishness of the Jewish people will last only so long as most Jews find in Jewishness some sustenance for their lives. Not just sustenance for their "Jewish lives" seen as only holidays and life-cycle turning points, but for their whole lives, "all the days of their lives." So I am arguing that a feminist transformation of Judaism is now necessary for the sake of Jewish women who have been marginalized in Jewish life; for the sake of Jewish men who have had to repress those aspects of their selves that the tradition viewed as female; for the sake of the human race, which needs a renewal of Torah in order to solve the problems that it must solve to save its life; and for the sake of the Jewish people. For "the Jewish people" is neither an abstract entity nor the mere census-count of all the Jewish men and women on the earth. The "Jewish people" is made up of countless everyday acts of making a consciously Jewish life—the ongoing process of Jewish focusing by those flesh-and-blood Jewish men and women who will live or die according to how effectively they can draw on Jewish sources in order to live.

NOTES

1. *Midrash Rabbah,* ed. and trans. by H. Freedman and Maurice Simon (London: Soncino Press, 1939), vol. 2, p. 529. Citation is to *Genesis Rabbah* LX:5. This *midrash* was called to my attention by Ruth Sohn.
2. *The Duality of Human Existence* (Boston: Beacon, 1971).

The Secret Jew
AN ORAL TRADITION OF WOMEN

Lynn Gottlieb

NEARLY three thousand years have passed since Sinai, three thousand years since our ancestors received Torah as a way of life. From the beginning there were words. We know that our fathers of the past decided to transmit revelation and all subsequent events by word of mouth: first came the oral tradition, only later to be recorded as the written law. And so we moved through history, remembering and transmitting the past in the experience of our own lives.

And yet some of us remain at the beginning, the word still to be formed, waiting patiently to be revealed, to rise out of the white spaces between the letters in the Torah and be received. I am speaking of the tradition of our mothers, our sister-wives, the secret women of the past. How would they have spoken of their own religious experiences if they had been given a space to record their stories? How would they have transmitted the written word? Would their ceremonies, rituals, and customs have been the same?

In order for Jewish women truly to be present in Jewish history and everyday life we must find the female voices of the past and receive them into our present. Recently I rediscovered the voice of Esther, whose experience was received and made living by the Marrano communities during the Inquisition. The women of the Marrano communities thought of themselves as Queen Esther, living a secret existence very different from the reality perceived by the outside world. Living as Christians, they knew themselves as Jews. But what I find more intriguing are the roles they took on during this period: because of their lack of knowledge about the Jewish tradition, women did assume major leadership roles in the community. They led communal prayers, performed marriage ceremonies, and developed rituals around the Fast of Esther, which became a major *conversos* holiday (see Cecil Roth, *The Marranos;* Martin Cohen, *The Martyr*). *The Apocrypha of Esther* was used liturgically by these women (and men) as they prayed for a time when their lives would no longer be secret and the internal and external world could be united—when they could be Jews. And so a time of struggle for our people became a time of intense participation for Jewish women.

Each generation must find its own voice. *The Secret Jew* was written to give a voice of the past a present meaning. Esther was forced into hiding, living a deeply-felt inner life that found little expression in the outside world because that world could not receive her message. Yet the Marrano women and men received Esther's experience. Her voice helped them survive that time of split realities, of both inner and outer exile. Esther, through the voice of the Marrano women, speaks to me, a woman living today, trying to find a voice in the present, trying to transmit the oral traditions—the secret traditions of my mothers, trying to unite my desire to participate in the life of a whole people without hiding my real Jewish self. Esther finally declared herself a Jew, the Marrano women shared their Jewish secret among themselves. And we of the present, by transmitting the hidden voices of the past, pray with messianic fervor for that time when we can unite the oral and written tradition of our mothers with the oral and written tradition of our fathers.

The Secret Jew

In the Royal Palace of the Inquisition of Barcelona the Inquisitor begins his morning audience:

Confess your offenses to the cross
without concealing anything
relating to yourself or any other person,
but without uttering false testimony against anyone.

The Holy Office shows mercy to all who confess freely.
Otherwise Justice will be executed.[1]

Every day for six hundred years
people hid their faith
from the Inquisition.

And the seasons pass
saintly Esther
my soul stays hidden
speaking softly
words praising Adonai
time forgetting time
eyes forgetting light
we hide in order to survive
living in brief moments
whispering the truth to shadows
I am a woman and a Jew
Saintly Esther
how did you endure those long months
of living what you were not
of embracing what you loved not.
As I enter this house of wood and stone
give me
your poor handmaiden
strength enough to pass through
this night of fear.

Into this house I go O Lord
forced by the sword into this house.
My soul moans
but God can see I don't believe
in images of wood and stone.[2]
Years pass
winter to spring
brown hills to waiting green
but we live in an endless winter
covering our lives with a stillborn spring
hoping for the restoration of our souls.
Esther our queen
in the passing of the generations
we have inherited your suffering
we have come to possess your woe
for in the house of a strange king
you hid your race and birth.

Like you queen Esther
we fast for three days and nights
to remember our private lives
to purify our souls.
Esther, the women of this household pray with your words:

And Esther prayed to the Lord God of Israel saying:
My Lord Adonai help me for I am alone
give me courage, Master of all powers
put clever words into my mouth
as I face the lion.
You know Lord
I hate the symbol of my high position
the crown I wear upon my head in court
I loathe
and do not wear it when I am alone
I have found no pleasure in this house.
O God whose strength prevails over all
listen to the voice of the victim
save us from the hand of the wicked
and free me from my fear.

Seasons pass
saintly Esther
and yet
this time
of dark burning fires
has given me a place
to praise the name of the Lord Adonai.
Though I hide my true self from the outside world
my people learn
the passion of my faith
for I am needed to remember the past.
I lead my people Israel in prayers my mother taught me
as we lit the Sabbath candles in the cellar.

Blessed be the name of the Lord Adonai forever amen,
who brings the light of morning to the afternoon
and from afternoon carries it to evening
and from evening until dawn
and from dawn brings light to the morning.[3]

Every day
for six hundred years

people hid their faith
from the Inquisition.
But in the tradition of Esther
we survived the secret.

NOTES

1. From the records of the Inquisition.
2. Adapted from the prayer whispered by Marranos upon entering a church.
3. Marrano liturgy.

Spring Cleaning Ritual on the Eve of Full Moon Nisan

Lynn Gottlieb

HOUSECLEANING is a basic preparation for the spring celebration of Passover. This ceremony unites spring-cleaning with the traditional ritual for removing the final crumbs of winter (*hametz*) from one's physical and spiritual house.

REMOVING THE HAMETZ
In the month of nisan
with the death of winter
and the coming of spring
our ancient mothers
cleaned out their houses.

They gathered brooms, mops, brushes,
rags, stones, and lime
they washed down walls
swept floors
beat rugs
scoured pots
changed over all the dishes in the house.
They opened windows to the sun
hung lines for the airing out of blankets and covers
using fire
air
and water
in the cleaning.

In the month of nisan
before the parting seas

called them out of the old life
our ancient mothers
went down to the river
they went down to the river
to prepare their garments for the spring.

Hands pounded rock
voices drummed out song
there is new life inside us
Shekhinah
prepares for Her birth.

So we labor all women
cleaning and washing
now with our brothers
now with our sons
cleaning the inner house
through the moon of nisan.

On the eve of the full moon
we search our houses
by the light of a candle
for the last trace of winter
for the last crumbs grown stale inside us
for the last darkness still in our hearts.

Washing our hands
we say a blessing
over water . . .
We light a candle
and search in the listening silence
search the high places
and the low places
inside you
search the attic and the basement
the crevices and crannies
the corners of unused rooms.
Look in your pockets
and the pockets of those around you
for traces of Mitzrayim.

Some use a feather
some use a knife
to enter the hard places.

Some destroy Hametz with fire
others throw it to the wind
others toss it to the sea.

Look deep for the Hametz
which still gives you pleasure
and cast it to the burning.

When the looking is done
we say:

All that rises up bitter
All that rises up prideful
All that rises up in old ways no longer fruitful
All Hametz still in my possession
but unknown to me
which I have not seen
nor disposed of
may it find common grave
with the dust of the earth
amen amen
selah . . .

Contributors

Rachel Adler has published numerous articles on women and Judaism. She is a psychotherapist living in Minneapolis.

Batya Bauman is a cofounder of *Lilith* magazine and of Feminists Against Anti-Semitism, a group of women organized to raise feminist consciousness regarding anti-Semitism in its many forms. She is a freelance editor and lives in New York City.

Alice Bloch is the author of *Lifetime Guarantee* and of *The Law of Return.* She lives in Topanga, California.

Aviva Cantor is a founding member of the *Lilith* magazine editorial board, the Jewish Feminist Organization, and the Socialist Zionist Union. She lives in New York City.

Erika Duncan's first novel, *A Wreath of Pale White Roses,* was published in 1977, and she is currently working on her second. Her critical articles have appeared in *New Boston Review, Changes, Human Behavior Magazine,* and *Book Forum* (for which she is a contributing editor). She lives in New York City, where she directs The Women's Salon, a literary group.

Laura Geller was ordained rabbi at the Hebrew Union College and is director of the Hillel Foundation at the University of Southern California in Los Angeles.

Lynn Gottlieb is a rabbi and a professional storyteller. She lives in New York City.

Arthur Green is an Associate Professor in the Department of Religious Studies at the University of Pennsylvania. He is the author of *Tormented Master: A Life of Nachman of Bratslav.*

Rita Gross is Professor of Comparative Religion at the University of Wisconsin at Eau Claire. She has published numerous articles on women and religion in *Journal of the American Academy of Religion and Anima,* and is coeditor of *Beyond Androcentrism.*

Lesley Hazleton is a journalist living in Israel. She has published numerous articles and is a contributing editor of *Harper's* magazine. She is the author of *And Mountains Roared,* a study of Beduins in the Sinai, and *Israeli Women: The Reality Behind the Myths.*

Paula Hyman is an Associate Professor of History and Dean of the Jewish Theological Seminary College of Jewish Studies. She is the author of *From Dreyfus to Vichy* and coauthor of *The Jewish Woman in America,* with Charlotte Baum and Sonya Michel.

Rosa Felsenburg Kaplan is a social worker and a social work educator. She was Visiting Associate Professor at Hebrew Union College in Los Angeles from 1973 to 1980.

Thena Kendall is a radio producer with the British Broadcasting Company in London. She is a founding member of the Hampstead Jewish Reform Community, which was established in London in 1974.

Deborah Lipstadt is an Assistant Professor of Modern Jewish Studies in the Department of Near Eastern Languages at the University of California at Los Angeles. She is currently engaged in a research project on American public opinion during the Holocaust.

Cynthia Ozick is the author of several volumes of fiction, most recently *Levitations* and *The Cannibal Galaxy.* She lives in New York.

Judith Plaskow teaches in the Religious Studies Department at Manhattan College. She is coeditor of *Womanspirit Rising: A Feminist Reader in Religion* and author of *Sex, Sin, and Grace: Women's Experience and the Theologies of Reinhold Niebuhr and Paul Tillich.*

Sara Reguer is an Assistant Professor in the Department of Judaic Studies at Brooklyn College. She is the author of *The Politics of Water: The Case of the Jordan River.*

Claire Satlof is a doctoral candidate in the Department of English at the University of Pennsylvania.

Mimi Scarf received her master's degree from Hebrew Union College, Los Angeles, where she wrote her thesis on wife abuse in the Jewish community. She is the founder and director of a shelter and 24-hour hotline for battered Jewish women in Los Angeles.

Gail Shulman attended Harvard University where she was active in the Women's Caucus at the Divinity School. She lives in Cambridge, Massachusetts, where she is a voice teacher and a counselor.

Arleen Stern is a social worker who works with the elderly. She lives in New York City.

Arthur Waskow is the editor of *Menorah,* a monthly journal of Jewish renewal. He is the author of *Godwrestling* and *Seasons of Our Joy.* He lives in Philadelphia.

Glossary

aggadah, aggadot (pl.) lit. "narration." The sayings, homiletic interpretations, historical information, legends, anecdotes, and folklore of rabbinic literature. *Aggadah* is the non-legal portion of rabbinic literature, distinguished from *halakhah,* which refers to the legal material.

agunah lit. "bound." The term is usually used of a woman whose husband is missing and presumed dead, but whose death has not been definitively confirmed. A deserted wife, whose husband cannot be located, is also an *agunah,* as is a woman whose husband refuses to grant her a *get* (divorce). An *agunah* is not a divorcee nor a widow, and under rabbinic law she cannot remarry, but must remain bound to her husband until his death is confirmed or until he grants her a divorce.

aliyah, aliyot lit. "going up." *Aliyah* refers to the honor of being called up to the Torah to recite the blessings before and after each section is read at public, communal services; also refers to the act of immigrating to Israel.

Alphabet of Ben Sira Hebrew text probably written in the early Middle Ages containing proverbs, epigrams, and satiric stories. The text includes the story of Lilith's creation and demotion.

bar mitzvah (male), **bat mitzvah** (female) lit. "son/daughter of the commandment," referring both to a person who has attained religious and legal maturity (thirteen for boys, twelve or thirteen for girls) as well as to the occasion at which this status is formally assumed.

barukh (masc.), ***berukhah*** (fem.) blessed

berakhah, berakhot (pl.) A prayer expressing praise of and thanks to God beginning and often ending with the words, *Barukh atta Adonai* (Blessed are You, O Lord).

bimah The podium in the synagogue where the Torah is read and from which services are led, and sermons are preached.

birkat HaGomel A prayer expressing thanks to God after a recovery from illness or deliverance from mortal danger, recited out loud in the synagogue in connection with the reading from the Torah.

b'not Rahel v'Leah Daughters of Rachel and Leah.

brit Covenant

brit milah The circumcision ceremony by which an eight-day-old boy enters the Covenant of Abraham

'eved servant

ezrat nashim Term for the women's section in the Temple in Jerusalem, and women's section in synagogues. Also the name of a Jewish feminist group based in New York.

Galut lit. "Exile." The term *galut* is used in three ways: not living in the land of Israel; a condition of oppression and persecution; countries and lands outside of Israel, namely, the Diaspora.

Gashmiut physicality.

Haganah lit., "defense." The underground military organization of the settlers in Palestine during the British rule from 1920 to 1948. With the establishment of the State of Israel, the *Haganah* became the official army of the State.

ha-Kadosh barukh hu (masc.) ***ha-Kedusha Berukhah hee*** (fem.) lit., "the Holy One, Blessed be He/She"; God/Goddess.

hakafot Processions bearing Torah scrolls, part of the celebration of the holiday Simhat Torah.

halakhah lit., "the way." Jewish law, which encompasses both the written Torah and the oral tradition.

halitzah lit., "taking off, removing." A childless widow was originally to receive protection and perpetuation of her husband's name through marriage to his surviving brother. The biblical ceremony of *halitzah* was performed by the widow to release her brother-in-law from his obligation to her. In the presence of a Jewish court of five or more, the ceremony is enacted by exchanging prescribed statements and by the widow removing a shoe from the foot of her brother-in-law and spitting on the floor in front of him. Rabbinic law prohibits the surviving brother from marrying his sister-in-law, even if he is willing and single, making *halitzah* a requirement today rather than an option.

hallah special bread, usually braided, served on Sabbaths and festivals.

halutz lit., "pioneer." Usually used in reference to settlers in Palestine at the turn of the century who engaged in agricultural work.

hametz Food and utensils forbidden to be used on Passover because they contain or have been used to contain leavened products.

Hasid, Hasidim (pl.) Adherent of Hasidism

Hasidism (Hebrew, "*Hasidut,*" Yiddish, "*Hassidus*") The popular religious movement founded in the mid-eighteenth century in Southern Poland by Rabbi Israel Baal Shem Tov ("master of the Good Name"). An adherent of *Hasidism* is called a *Hasid.*

Haskalah Enlightenment; a movement to promote modern European culture among Jews during the eighteenth and nineteenth centuries. An adherent was called a *maskil.*

Havdalah lit., "separation." The ceremony which concludes the Sabbath, separating it from the weekdays that follow.

havurah lit., "company, society, group, fellowship." Also refers to the recent movement among American Jews to form small, informal groups for prayer, study, and celebration of Jewish holidays.

herem excommunication; expulsion from the Jewish community.

hevrah kadishah lit., "sacred society." Group of people who prepare the body for burial and perform the required rites of purification.

hokhmah wisdom.

Humash Five books of Moses; the Pentateuch.

huppah The portable canopy under which the bridegroom and bride stand during the wedding service.

Ishah Woman.

Kabbalah The texts comprising the Jewish mystical tradition.

Kaddish lit., "sanctification." The prayer recited for a deceased parent, spouse, or child for eleven months or one year from the date of burial and again each year on the anniversary of the death.

Kashrut Jewish dietary regulations

kavod Honor, respect.

ketubah the Jewish marriage contract.

Kiddush Ha-Levenah Prayers sanctifying the new moon, recited each month.

Knesset Yisrael The community of Israel; of the Jewish people.

kol ishah The voice of a woman. Following the rabbinic statement, '*Kol be-Ishah ervah,*' hearing the voice of a woman is sinful, certain orthodox Jews have discouraged or prohibited women from singing in the presence of a man.

kol Yisrael haverim "All Israel is united in one fellowship."

Ma'ariv Daily evening prayers.

Maskil, Maskilim (pl.) An adherent of the Haskalah movement.

Mayse bukhs Pamphlets of popular literature, usually sold by itinerant peddlers, which contain vernacular translations of Hebrew liturgy, stories of wonder-working rabbis, moralistic teachings, model forms of correspondence, or divination practices.

Megillah A scroll. Although there are five scrolls, or *megillot,* only the Book of Esther is known as *The Megillah.* It is read on Purim evening and morning.

mehitzah The partition separating women from men used in many synagogues.

melamed Teacher

menorah Candelabrum; seven-branched oil lamp used in the Tabernacle and Temple; also, eight-branched candelabrum used on Hanukkah.

mensch, menschen (pl.) Yiddish word for man, human being, person.

menschlichkeit Yiddish for humanity, humaneness.

mezuzah lit., "doorpost." The small parchment scroll enclosed in a case attached to doorposts of Jewish homes. On the scroll are written verses from the Bible which set forth the commandment.

Midrash lit., "inquiry or investigation." A genre of literature which interprets the Bible, usually homiletically, to extract its implicit meanings.

mikvah A pool of water designed for the rite of purification, primarily used by married women after menstruating and following childbirth.

Minhah The daily afternoon prayers.

minyan A quorum of ten required for communal prayer services.

mitzvah Commandment; good deed.

mohel, mohelim (pl.) One who performs the circumcision.

niddah A menstruating woman.

nigun, nigunim (pl.) Tunes, melodies, songs, chants.

nisan A month in the Hebrew calendar during which Passover is celebrated.

pasuk, pesukim (pl.) A verse from the Bible.

Pesach Passover.

pesachdik Adjective, referring to that which is appropriate for doing or using on Passover.

Pesak halakhah, piskei halakhah (pl.) Judgment or verdict regarding an aspect of Jewish law.

Pesukei d'Zimra Verses of song taken from the Bible, primarily Psalms, which are recited before the morning service.

piyyutim (pl.) Hebrew liturgical poems included in private and public worship.

Rosh Hashanah The beginning of the Jewish year. It is referred to as a High Holiday.

Rosh Hodesh The first day of the Hebrew month, or New Moon.

Ruhniut Spirituality, spiritual.

Sefer HaBahir One of the earliest books of Kabbalah, the Jewish mystical teachings that developed during the Middle Ages.

sefirah, sefirot (pl.) Fundamental term in Jewish mysticism referring to the ten aspects of God's manifestation.

seihel Intelligence.

seudah shlishit lit., "third meal." Name for the third meal of the Sabbath, eaten on the afternoon of the Sabbath day.

Shabbat (Hebrew), *Shabbos* (Yiddish) The Sabbath, the seventh day of the week, a day of rest.

Shaharit Morning prayers.

shalom bayit lit., "Peace in the home."

Shekhinah Term for the Divine Presence in the world; Jewish mystical literature describes the *Shekhinah* as the feminine principle of God immanent in the world.

Shema Refers to the biblical verse beginning with the word *Shema* ("hear"), Deuteronomy 6:4. The verse is part of a prayer that is recited twice every day, during the morning and evening services and proclaims "Hear O Israel the Lord our God the Lord is One."

shmitah Sabbatical (seventh) year described in the Bible, during which all land had to be fallow and debts were to be remitted.

Shonda (Yiddish) a scandal

shtetl (Yiddish) village

shul (Yiddish) synagogue

siddur Prayerbook

sidra lit., "arrangement." The portion from the Pentateuch read on Sabbath mornings in the synagogue.

Simhat Torah lit., "rejoicing in the Torah." The holiday celebrates the annual conclusion of the reading of the entire Pentateuch (Torah) in the synagogue during the course of the year. It is observed during the autumn, at the conclusion of Sukkot.

Sukkot Festival of Tabernacles. The holiday which commemorates the Jewish wandering in the desert following the exodus from Egypt.

tallit Prayer shawl

Talmud The literature containing the Mishnah and the Gemara, the discussion on the Mishnah, compiled during the first five centuries of the Common Era.

Targum lit., "translation, interpretation." Aramaic translations of the Pentateuch and portions of the rest of the Bible.

tefillin Phylacteries. Small black leather cases containing passages from the Bible which are affixed, by means of black leather straps, to the head and arms during weekday morning prayers.

tehinah, tehinot (pl.) Prayers of entreaty and supplication usually in the form of poems, included as supplements to the prayerbook.

Terafim idols; *cf.* Genesis 32:19

Tikkun Mayer A particular edition of the prayerbook.

Tsena Urena lit., "come and see." A Yiddish translation of the Pentateuch, *haftarot,* and the Five Megillot, including a homiletical commentary drawn from Midrashic and later traditional sources. Composed at the end of the 16th century by Jacob ben Isaac Ashkenazi, it came to be used primarily by women in the East European Jewish community, who were not taught to read the Torah and its commentaries in Hebrew.

Tzaddik, tzaddikim (pl.) Person of outstanding piety and righteousness.

tzidkanit, tzidkaniot (pl.) Pious, righteous woman.

tzni'ut Modesty

yahrzeit Memorial anniversary of the date of death.

Yavneh City dating back to biblical times located on the coastal plain of Israel, south of Jaffa. After the fall of Jerusalem, the Sanhedrin was reconstituted at Yavneh and rabbinic discussions were conducted there.

Between 70 and 132 C.E., Yavneh was considered the center of Jewish scholarship and of the rabbinate.

Yeshivah, yeshivot (pl.) Traditional Jewish academy devoted primarily to studying the Talmud, its commentaries, and related rabbinic literature.

Yiddishkeit Yiddish word for Judaism, Jewishness.

yihus lit., "genealogy," a common term for family records or prestige.

yir'ah Awe, fear.

Yom Kippur Day of Atonement, solemn day of fasting and repentance.

Zohar Major text of Kabbalah, Jewish mysticism, composed in thirteenth century Spain and written in Aramaic.